The Psychic Life of Racism in Gay Men's Communities

Critical Perspectives on Psychology of Sexuality, Gender, and Queer Studies

Series Editors

AJ Jones (Retired academic and psychologist)
Damien Riggs (Flinders University)
Rebecca Stringer (University of Otago)

Mission Statement

The series seeks to publish scholarship that engages critically with the social and political uses of psychological knowledge, and with transformative paradigms that address obstacles to change. The series is open to a wide range of approaches that may be classified as "psychological," including manuscript proposals that focus on well-being, subjectivities, clinical practice, discourse, and their intersections.

Advisory Board Members

Meg John Barker, Virginia Braun, Chris Brickell, Heather Brook, Victoria Clarke, Charlotte Patterson, Elizabeth Peel, Esther Rothblum, and Gareth Treharne

Books in Series

The Psychic Life of Racism in Gay Men's Communities, Edited by Damien Riggs

The Psychic Life of Racism in Gay Men's Communities

Edited by Damien W. Riggs

LEXINGTON BOOKS
Lanham • Boulder • New York • London

Published by Lexington Books
An imprint of The Rowman & Littlefield Publishing Group, Inc.
4501 Forbes Boulevard, Suite 200, Lanham, Maryland 20706
www.rowman.com

Unit A, Whitacre Mews, 26-34 Stannary Street, London SE11 4AB

British Library Cataloguing in Publication Information Available

Library of Congress Cataloging-in-Publication Data

Names: Riggs, Damien W., editor.
Title: The psychic life of racism in gay men's communities / edited by Damien W. Riggs.
Description: Lanham : Lexington Books, [2017] | Series: Critical perspectives on the psychology of sexuality, gender, and queer studies | Includes bibliographical references and index.
Identifiers: LCCN 2017050917 (print) | LCCN 2017043594 (ebook) | ISBN 9781498537155 (Electronic) | ISBN 9781498537148 (cloth : alk. paper) | ISBN 9781498537162 (pbk. : alk. paper)
Subjects: LCSH: Gay culture. | Racism.
Classification: LCC HQ76.96 (print) | LCC HQ76.96 .P79 2017 (ebook) | DDC 306.76/62089--dc23
LC record available at https://lccn.loc.gov/2017050917

∞™ The paper used in this publication meets the minimum requirements of American National Standard for Information Sciences Permanence of Paper for Printed Library Materials, ANSI/NISO Z39.48-1992.

Printed in the United States of America

Contents

Acknowledgments

As editor of this collection, I begin by acknowledging the sovereignty of the Kaurna people, the First Nations people upon whose land I live and work.

Thanks must go to Amy King at Rowman & Littlefield for providing initial support for this project, and more latterly to Kasey Beduhn for seeing the project through to completion. Thanks also to Rebecca Stringer and AL Jones, my series co-editors, for believing in and supporting this project. Finally, thanks must go to Claire Bartholomaeus, for so thoroughly proofing the chapters, for attending to referencing and style, and for constructing the index.

This book was the outcome of a decade of conversations with people about racism in gay men's communities. Specifically, Aileen Moreton-Robinson, Fiona Nicoll, Donna McCormack, Derek Hook, Nathaniel Adam Tobias Coleman, Brodie McGee, Joanna McIntyre, and Martha Augoustinos. Earlier versions of some of the ideas that informed this book were shared with audiences at the 2012 Australian Critical Race and Whiteness Studies Association conference, the 2006 Society of Australasian Social Psychologists Conference, the 2006 Global Queeries Conference, and the 2006 Historicising Whiteness Conference.

I owe a debt to all of the contributors who wrote chapters for this book, including those working to very tight deadlines. It was a pleasure to work with you all, and to be able to publish such exciting and stimulating ideas alongside you.

Introduction

Towards a Typology of Racisms in Gay Men's Communities

Damien W. Riggs

As an identity category, "sexuality" has the tendency to cluster together diverse groups of people under singular terms. In this book our focus is on the ways in which the term "gay" collapses differences, and in so doing excludes certain points of difference, specifically with regard to race. In terms of collapsing and thus excluding racial differences amongst gay men, Epstein's paper published in 1987 on the idea of gay as an ethnic identity is an early example of this trend that continues to exert an influence on how we think about gay men's communities. Epstein argued that gay people as a collective can be viewed as constituting an ethnic group, that the analogy of sexuality and ethnicity is tenable precisely because in both cases the group shares a similar set of experiences. Central to the shared experiences of gay men, Epstein suggests, are encounters with homophobia and heterosexism, thus suggesting that gay men should be united by the goal of resisting discrimination on this basis. One consequence of this type of logic, and as Haritaworn, Tauqir, and Erdem argue, is that "most white gays d[o] not identify as part of a subculture whose internal heterogeneity requires justification. Rather, they locate questions of power and justice firmly *outside* their community" (2008, 74, emphasis in original).

While homophobia and heterosexism are most certainly common experiences amongst gay men, the ways in which these forms of discrimination are experienced are differentiated according to other identity categories. Further, and as Haritaworn, Tauqir, and Erdem note, locating issues of power and justice solely *outside* of gay communities fails to acknowledge the ways in which power and justice operate *within* gay communities. Which brings us to the point about exclusion noted above with regard to the category "gay." In collapsing gay men under one presumed shared homogenous "ethnic identity," excluded from this identity are those whose experiences lie outside of the dominant racial group, whose experiences and values dominate the homogenized gay "ethnic identity." Ignoring or denying heterogeneity within gay men's communities thus functions to establish a norm against which a diverse range of men are measured, and through which they may be excluded. Moreover, issues of diversity are typically marginalized in favor of claims to a shared group identity, the claim being that a focus on internal heterogeneity distracts from what is seen by dominant group white men as the key issue of challenging sexuality-based discrimination, as Lenon and Dryden argue:

> Such discussions [of racialization, diaspora, settler colonialism, and empire] are often framed as extraneous to the authentic, "real" question of the insider-outsider status of "sexual minorities," where the privileged positioning of injury (re)articulates and further solidifies a heterosexual-homosexual binary. This perpetuates a form of homo-innocence that positions gay and lesbian bodies outside of systems of coercive power and within the confines of a minority-status victimhood that ultimately forecloses any interrogations into its "naturalization." (2015, 9)

Recourse to notions of "homo-innocence," particularly here with regard to white middle-class gay men, are perhaps most evident when such men make recourse to analogies between race and sexuality in order to make rights claims about the latter. In the context of the United States, for example, recourse to legislative changes with regards to miscegenation has often been used to make arguments about marriage equality for gay men, ignoring that the effects of racism and heterosexism are substantially different historically and in the present, and further that racism and heterosexism intersect in the lives of racially marginalized gay men (Coolidge 1997; Hutchinson 2000; Kendell 2005; Lenon 2005; Mumford 2005). A narrative of "homo-innocence" thus allows white middle-class gay men to ignore these complexities, instead privileging their own interests.

In contrast to accounts that ignore heterogeneity within gay men's communities or indeed actively exclude diversity within such communities, the chapters in this book seek to examine how "power and justice" operate amongst gay men, specifically with regard to racism and sexual desire. Importantly, the chapters consider not only instances where some gay men may be positioned as undesirable to other gay men on the basis of race, but also where some gay men may be seen as desirable solely on the basis of race (i.e., in the case of racial fetishization). Refuting notions of "homo-innocence," then, the chapters in this book firmly situate gay communities within networks of power that are as much internally as they are externally imposed. Importantly, however, as a whole the chapters don't simply make a call for inclusion. Rather, they call for the dismantling of racialized norms as they operate within gay men's communities.

In order to more fully elaborate on the claims above, the sections that follow first explore why it is so important to map racism within gay men's communities, before then turning to consider precisely how it is that race functions within the psychic life of gay men's communities. Theorizing racism—as all of the chapters in this book do—is an important part of thinking through how racism in gay men's communities is so routinely overlooked or denied by white gay men, and yet how it is so firmly located as a normative mode of understanding desire amongst gay men.

A MAPPING PROJECT

In their quantitative analysis of racism amongst gay and bisexual men, Callander, Newman, and Holt (2015) suggest, at least at a statistical level, that there is little to distinguish racism that occurs in a sexual context from racism more broadly. While acknowledging that the broader logics of racism might be relatively similar across populations and contexts (i.e., logics premised on hierarchies, power, control, and privilege), the chapters in this book suggest that given its reliance upon both literal and figurate mapping devices (Khanna 2003), it is useful to consider any project of mapping out differing forms of racism within gay men's communities as a form of cartography that seeks to identify differences. Similarly, given the role of categorization within the history of racism (Richards 2003), it is useful to approach this mapping project as aimed at developing an initial typology of some of the forms of racism that occur amongst gay men. In other words, the driving factors behind racism outlined above may be broadly similar, but the ways in which they are enacted display considerable diversity.

This point about a diversity of racisms highlights the absolute importance of context when it comes to understanding racism in gay men's communities. Some of the more obvious contexts are ongoing histories of colonization, nationalism, and patriotism, all of which differentially co-opt racially dominant group gay men into logics of privilege, the corollary of which is the differential co-option of racially marginalized gay men into logics of marginalization. Another important context signaled in the introduction of this chapter are the resistances mounted within gay men's communities to homophobia and heterosexism. Such resistances have often emphasized the rights of gay men to sexual freedom, and in the context of race, this type of context can all too easily slip into arguments about the rights of white middle-class gay men to freedom in terms of sexual partners, specifically with regard to actively excluding certain groups of men from their sexual purview. Importantly, claims to sexual freedom do not simply shape how white gay men view what are construed as eligible sexual partners. Interview research by Callander,

Holt, and Newman with racially marginalized gay men suggests that notions of sexual freedom can also serve to curtail resistance to racism:

> Although most of the men with whom we spoke recognised some problems in the racialisation of desire, all were uncomfortable with putting limits on the desires of others. In some cases, participants were hesitant about recommending that others should limit how they chose to express their desires. It may be useful to think about this conflict in terms of the politics of sexual freedom and desire. As other commentators have noted, hard won and strongly held values of sexual liberty and choice may stifle conversations about racism in gay and bisexual communities. The readiness with which our participants avoided statements of judgement or condemnation reflects this idea and seems to anticipate challenges about the sexual rights and freedoms of gay men. (2016, 10)

As will be discussed in the concluding chapter to this book, resistance to racism within gay men's communities is still possible and most certainly does occur; however, it occurs in the face of powerful narratives voiced by some white gay men that emphasize what Puar (2007) refers to as "homonationalism" and Duggan (2012) "homonormativity," but also in the face of narratives of sexual freedom which frame any limiting of the "choices" of white gay men as an imposition upon their freedom.

Importantly, the mapping project that this book represents focuses most specifically on the realms of intelligibility generated through racialized logics. This is not to deny that individual gay men enact racism, but instead to locate their actions within broader discursive contexts through which the racialization of desire is rendered intelligible. In order to further unpack this claim, the following section considers how racialization is rendered as a central lens through which desire is shaped in gay men's communities.

THE PSYCHIC LIFE OF RACISM

To date, much of the empirical research on racism in gay men's communities has focused on challenging the idea that racialized desires or non-desires are mere "preferences," free from racism (see Riggs 2013 for summary). Extending this empirical work are theorizations of how racialized desire functions as a form of racialized looking that serves to recenter white entitlement and privilege. For example, in his account of the "down low," Snorton suggests that "the use of I/eye suggests that images of 'unembraceable' black men designate a psychic and visual 'other' that simultaneously enables the constitution of white subjectivity and the maintenance of white order" (2014, 9).

The scopic register evoked by Snorton's use of the "I/eye" highlights both the vision-oriented and regulatory aspects of white gay desire, which do more than simply relegate black men to a position of "unembraceability," but rather in so doing serve to promote white gay men to the position of "embraceable," and as arbiters of what counts as embraceable. Snorton goes on to evoke the idea of a "glass closet," in which black gay men are fixed by the scopic register of gay racialized desire:

> The glass closet shares with its syntactical cousin the glass ceiling a sense of immobility; each term describes alternatively how the materiality of racial and sexual difference structures a restrictive parameter that precludes movement. . . . Glass, as modifier, points to the simultaneous fragility and durability of the closet metaphor as it also gestures toward the terrifying realities of black sexualities being fixed under glass. (2014, 17)

Similar to the point made in the introduction to this chapter, it is not simply that racialized modes of looking within gay men's communities serve to *exclude* certain groups of gay men; they may also serve to *include* other groups on very specific terms. Yet either way, and as Snorton suggests, there is a fixity at play, a fixity that accords to white gay men the assumed power to determine who will, and who will not, be included, and on what terms. Yet importantly, and as Morgensen has so cogently argued with regard to "Native"/"settler" relations in the United States, the power of white gay men to determine what counts is always limited by the fact that the terms upon which racialized desire is founded are always tenuous:

> In a multiracial, transational white settler society, the relation of "Native" to "settler" articulates distinctions of Native from non-Native but *these two comparisons are neither identical nor parallel.* The teleological binary Native/settler is perpetually complicated by the *nonbinary* relations of diverse non-Natives and Native peoples across commonalities and differences. (2014, 22, emphasis in original)

In terms of the project that is this book, a key argument certainly is that racialized modes of looking—as informed by racist stereotypes and hierarchies—most certainly serve to instruct both racially dominant and marginalized gay men to recognize certain desires as legitimate and others as illegitimate, indeed in some cases as abhorrent. Yet this does not account for all that can be said of desire. The psychic life of racism in gay men's communities is most certainly a scopic racism founded on ways of looking that serve to either liberate (white gay men) or entrap (racially marginalized gay men), yet as with racism more broadly, racialized desires within gay men's communities cannot ever fully encapsulate or regulate all forms of desire.

It is this point about what exceeds normalizing and marginalizing accounts of gay desire that perhaps explains the often ferocious persistence of some white gay men's racialized accounts of desire. As Morgensen (2011) notes above, the nonbinary relations between dominant group and racially marginalized gay men is always contingent on the repetition of racialized norms, norms that are never guaranteed or certain (Riggs and Augoustinos 2005). It is not as though an individual or a group of white gay men have once claimed the veracity of their racialized desires and that was the end of the story. Rather, such claims are made repeatedly, in an attempt at shoring up a particular racialized mode of looking, and indeed to naturalize such a mode of looking. The repetition of claims about racialized desires, however, highlights that they are never truly naturalized or fixed, just as racial stereotypes and hierarchies are never truly naturalized or fixed. Rather, their repetition accords them a *semblance* of naturalization and fixity, but one that is always at threat of being undone.

The chapters in this book thus explore the specific iterations of racialized modes of address as they circulate within gay men's communities, and highlight both their repeated iterations, but also their limitations. This is not to say that racialized desires do not have powerful effects, as the chapters in this book attest, rather it is to suggest that their persistence is a product of the fact that such desires are always founded upon a particular logic that is open to challenge, and which is based in a particular psychic life that is itself conditioned through repetition, rather than being a pre-ordained fact. Focusing on the repetitions of particular racialized ways of looking—as the chapters in this book do—thus allows specific ways of looking to be seen, rather than to be left unmarked, or to be treated as accepted facts about gay desire.

To focus on the psychic life of racism in gay men's communities, then, is to examine how racialized embodiment as a mode of intelligibility is enacted amongst gay men. In other words, the task of this book is to map out specific contexts and populations, and how the racialized I/eye of gay desire is formed both by wider historical and contemporary understandings of "race," but also how such understandings take specific forms in gay men's communities. That gay men internalize race as a salient category is not surprising, given that race functions as a superordinate category shaping how we make sense of ourselves and those around us. Nor is it surprising that white gay men specifically should be any more or less enmeshed in racialized ways of looking and desiring, despite claims to the "inclusivity" of gay communities.

CHAPTER SUMMARIES

Following a logic introduced by Lenon and Dryden (2015) in their book on Canadian homonationalisms, the chapters in this book are not organized into sections. Certainly, some chapters focus more on interpersonal contexts, and others focus more on political contexts. And certainly, the chapters in this book cohere around regions and populations. Yet dividing up the chapters on any of these bases would ignore the overlaps across all of the chapters in their examination of the psychic life of racism in gay men's communities.

The first chapter by Denton Callander, Martin Holt, and Christy Newman explores in greater detail some of the concerns raised above about how racism in gay men's communities differs from racism more broadly. The chapter situates racism within the context of gay rights activism, documenting how despite claims by community organizations to addressing racism amongst gay men, such organizations largely enshrine the values of white men. By exploring the whiteness of many gay community organizations, the chapter situates individual enactments of racism amongst gay men in broader institutional contexts.

The following chapter by Ibrahim Abraham documents Islamaphobia in the context of gay men's communities, linking it to broader anti-Muslim sentiment. Specifically, the chapter explores how gay Muslim men are often faced with what is framed as a dilemma, namely the presumption that being gay is irreconcilable with being Muslim. Situating this presumption, or what Abraham refers to as a "mis-interepellation," as a product of exclusionary practices within gay men's communities and anti-Muslim sentiment more broadly, allows the chapter to stake a claim to the possibility that gay Muslim men can indeed imagine and live other ways of reconciling their sexuality and their faith.

The next chapter by Jacks Cheng documents what he frames as gay Orientalism. The chapter deftly outlines how representations of people who have immigrated from Asian countries to the United States first positioned such people as the "Yellow Peril," and latterly as "Model Minorities," and how these both play out within gay men's communities. Specifically, the chapter demonstrates how Orientalist accounts of gay Asian men serve to legitimate white gay identities, by positioning gay Asian men as "there for the taking." As a counter to this, the chapter explores multiple resistances to such positionings, thus challenging accounts of gay Orientalism.

Taking up Puar's (2007) work on homonationalism, the following chapter by Sonny Dhoot explores how "queers of color" are positioned within countries that purport to be "queer friendly." Specifically, and adding an important dimension to this book, the chapter considers how a focus on queer men of color in terms of homonationalism can serve to further marginalize the experiences of queer women of color. Echoing some of the arguments made in the chapter by Abraham, Dhoot suggests that for queer Muslim women intelligible subject positions under homonationalism are largely limited to "good" or "bad," the former referring to women who act as "native informants" bolstering nationalistic opposition to Islam, and the latter referring to women who resist reductive accounts of Islam. Through his analysis Dhoot carefully demonstrates how an exclusive focus on men in the context of homonationalism serves only to warrant further exclusions, and in so doing he provides an account of alternate subject positions available to queer Muslim women.

Returning to the context of Asia and Orientalism, the following chapter by Emerich Daroya explores how differing groups of gay men accrue cultural capital in the context of the dating marketplace, one that is shaped by racialized desires and stereotypes. Focusing specifically on the dating app Grindr, the chapter considers how despite claims to inclusivity through opposing discrimination, the app makes possible a new mode through which old racisms play out. As will be also explored in the concluding chapter of this book, Daroya argues that such new modes allow for the repetition of racial stereotypes that keeps them in circulation, and in so doing functions to normalize and naturalize them.

The following chapter by Sulaimon Giwa considers how racism within gay men's communities enacts a form of trauma upon men from the African diaspora. In line with the assumption that countries located in the West offer forms of liberal inclusivity, the chapter argues that gay men from the African diaspora who migrate to the West are struck by a barrage of racism within gay communities in the West, racism that is often unexpected, and which compounds other marginalizations that they experience as migrants. In response to the racism they experienced, Giwa's participants developed multiple means through which to mitigate further marginalization, means that repeated the onus placed upon gay men from the African diaspora to support themselves, rather than being supported and welcomed within gay communities.

Building on the literature on denials of racism, in the next chapter Jesus Gregorio Smith explores how white gay men deny "sexual racism" in the context of responses to an article on the topic posted on Facebook. Specifically, the chapter considers how sexually racist talk is reframed by white commenters as not being racist, emphasizing a liberal account of the right to "personal preferences." Importantly, and similar to the chapter by Dhoot, Smith adds a further dimension to discussions and justifications of sexual racism amongst white gay men by exploring how both gay and heterosexual white commenters justify racism. The analysis in the chapter thus demonstrates how racism is something in which all white people are invested, regardless of their sexuality.

In the final substantive chapter Alexandra Rivera and Dale Maglalang return us to the topic of homonationalism, and explore its operations in the lives of gay Asian men. To do so, the chapter carefully maps out some of the histories of anti-Asian sentiment within the West, and from there explores how white gay men become implicated in these histories in their engagements with Asian gay men. Importantly, and as with all of the other chapters in this book, the chapter speaks to resistance in the face of racism and nationalism amongst marginalized communities, and calls for increased visibility of ways of living that resist dominant tropes within gay communities.

The book concludes by exploring some of the gaps and absences within the book, before then considering questions of ontology, the role of new medias, and points of resistance. Specifically with regard to ontology, the chapter challenges the hegemony of whiteness in accounts of gay men's communities, highlighting alternate accounts of sexuality that radically bring into question white ways of being. As indicated above, the focus on new medias explores practices of surveillance in gay communities, specifically as they play out on dating apps. In considering resistance, the chapter concludes by exploring what it means to speak back to racism in gay communities, including turning the focus away from agendas determined primarily by white gay men.

CONCLUSION

Taking up the point above with regard to the agendas of white gay men, it is of course important to question my role as editor of this collection, as author of the opening and concluding chapters, and as a white gay man. What does it mean that this collection is framed by me? This is a question I have continued to ponder since beginning this project, building on a longer history of working in the field of critical race and whiteness studies with a focus on white queer privilege (Riggs 2006). My sense in doing this work, and given the histories documented in this book—of the imposition of white epistemologies and ontologies onto a diverse range of populations—is that the work of challenging whiteness cannot fall solely or even primarily to people who are racialized as not white. In other words, the problems of whiteness are the true white man's burden, and should not be perpetually shouldered by others.

At the same time, however, we know all too well the politics of representation, and the problem of speaking for others. Hence while as editor and author of the opening and concluding chapters I seek to position the psychic life of racism within gay men's communities as serving a purpose for white gay men (myself included), I cannot speak for the experiences of people whose experiences are marginalized as a product of such racism. Hence the diversity of voices in this book is vitally important to a project that seeks to destabilize whiteness in gay men's communities, and to speak back to the prominence given to white gay men's worldviews. It is nonetheless unfortunate that this book does not contain the voices of white men speaking about their enactments of sexual racism, though in the concluding chapter I do explore one such voice as documented in a media article.

Despite the caveats outlined above, and as we shall see further in the concluding chapter, there are a multitude of ways of framing the question of racism, and a multitude of standpoints from which concepts such as "gender" and "sexuality" may be framed, a greater majority of which do not reflect white narratives. Hopefully, the chapters in this book contribute to an ongoing discussion about diversity in gay men's communities, what happens when such diversity is viewed solely as a stage for white gay men's desires, and some of the many key junctures where racialized desires may be resisted or rewritten.

REFERENCES

Callander, Denton, Martin Holt, and Christy E. Newman. 2005. "'Not Everyone's Gonna Like Me': Accounting for Race and Racism in Australian Sex and Dating Webservices for Gay and Bisexual Men." *Ethnicities* 16 (1): 3–21.

Callander, Denton, Christy E. Newman, and Martin Holt. 2015. "Is Sexual Racism *Really* Racism? Distinguishing Attitudes Toward Sexual Racism and Generic Racism Among Gay and Bisexual Men." *Archives of Sexual Behavior* 44 (7): 1991–2000.

Coolidge, David O. 1997. "Playing the *Loving* Card: Same-Sex Marriage and the Politics of Analogy." *Brigham Young University Journal of Public Law* 12 (2): 201–38.

Duggan, Lisa. 2012. *The Twilight of Equality?: Neoliberalism, Cultural Politics, and the Attack on Democracy*. Boston: Beacon Press.

Epstein, Steven G. 1987. "Gay Politics, Ethnic Identity: The Limits of Social Constructionism." *Socialist Review* 93: 9–54.

Haritaworn, Jin, Tamsila Tauqir, and Esra Erdem. 2008. "Gay Imperialism: Gender and Sexuality Discourse in the 'War on Terror.'" In *Out of Place: Interrogating Silences in Queerness/Raciality*, edited by Adi Kuntsman and Esperanza Miyake, 71–96. York: Raw Nerve Books.

Hutchinson, Darren L. 2000. "'Gay Rights' for 'Gay Whites'?: Race, Sexual Identity, and Equal Protection Discourse." *Cornell Law Review* 85: 1358–91.

Kendell, Kate. 2005. "Race, Same-Sex Marriage, and White Privilege: The Problem with Civil Rights Analogies." *Yale Journal of Law and Feminism* 17: 133–37.

Khanna, Ranjanna. 2003. *Dark Continents: Psychoanalysis and Colonialism*. Durham: Duke University Press.

Lenon, Suzanne. 2005. "Marrying Citizens! Raced Subjects? Re-Thinking the Terrain of Equal Marriage Discourse." *Canadian Journal of Women and the Law* 17 (2): 405–21.

Lenon, Suzanne, and OmiSoore H. Dryden. 2015. "Introduction: Interventions, Iterations, and Interrogations that Disturb the (Homo)Nation." In *Disrupting Queer Inclusion: Canadian Homonationalisms and the Politics of Belonging*, edited by OmiSoore H. Dryden and Suzanne Lenon, 3–18. Toronto: UBC Press.

Morgensen, Scott Lauria. 2011. *Spaces Between Us*. Minneapolis: University of Minnesota Press.

Mumford, K. 2005. "The Miscegenation Analogy Revisited: Same-Sex Marriage as a Civil Rights Story." *American Quarterly* 57 (2): 523–31.

Puar, Jasbir K. 2007. *Terrorist Assemblages: Homonationalism in Queer Times*. Durham: Duke University Press.

Richards, Graham. 2003. *Race, Racism and Psychology: Towards a Reflexive History*. New York: Routledge.

Riggs, Damien W. 2006. *Priscilla, (White) Queen of the Desert: Queer Rights/Race Privilege*. New York: Peter Lang.

———. 2013. "Anti-Asian Sentiment Amongst a Sample of White Australian Men on Gaydar." *Sex Roles* 68 (11–12): 768–78.

Riggs, Damien W., and Martha Augoustinos. 2005. "The Psychic Life of Colonial Power: Racialised Subjectivities, Bodies and Methods." *Journal of Community and Applied Social Psychology* 15(6): 461–77.

Snorton, C. Riley. 2014. *Nobody Is Supposed to Know: Black Sexuality on the Down Low*. Minneapolis: University of Minnesota Press.

ONE

Gay Racism

Denton Callander, Martin Holt, and Christy Newman

In 1983, a chapter entitled "Gay Racism" was published as part of a collection of short stories, poetry, essays, and photographs, which documented and unpacked the contentious relationship between sexuality and race in the USA (DeMarco 1983). Despite the incredible social, political, and economic changes that have taken place since the 1980s, it is a simple reality that many of the same challenges faced by DeMarco and other gay men of that time are as relevant today as they were then. While enduring, the specifics of gay racism—its configurations, implications, and responses—have changed quite dramatically, inviting renewed attention to how race shapes and is shaped by gay life. Here, we redeploy the expression "gay racism" to refer to the enactment of racist practices among and between gay men, which can perhaps be most usefully conceived as situated racism. Considering gay racism as part of a much larger picture allows us to explore how it is produced and enabled by specific social worlds, but also to consider its relationship to the enactment of racism more generally. For while there are some important characteristics that distinguish gay racism, it is in the similarities with general racism that we can get some sense of its potential impact.

Just as in its other forms, the racism expressed and experienced by gay men can be located at the level of individuals and it can operate within the broader social and political institutions of gay life. Gay racism is similar to general racism in that it can be expressed in blatant and easily identifiable ways but also, and far more commonly, in ways that are subtle and indirect. Individually or institutionally, blatantly or subtly, gay racism is ultimately about the operation and maintenance of power.

1

Exploring power in this way means considering not just concepts of race, but also a multitude of intersecting factors that either privilege or oppress individuals and groups of people. The inequities that these relations produce can be particularly confronting for individuals and institutions invested in the notion of a "gay community," wrapped in the ideals (but not always the reality) of diversity and inclusivity. Drawing attention to forms of exclusion and marginalization within gay life is, therefore, essential to understanding how racism is enacted and how it is experienced in settings that lay claim to safety from discrimination.

In this chapter, we explore the institutional enactment of gay racism by reviewing how race relations have been (mis)managed within gay advocacy organizations. We also examine the individual nature of gay racism, reviewing research that has documented experiences of gay racism in predominantly Western countries, including some of our own research in Australia. While there are a number of evocative ways to conceptualize racism, in this chapter we are most influenced by theories of intersectionality, which permit an appreciation of multiple and overlapping forms of oppression and exclusion (Crenshaw 1991). As a framing device, intersectionality also provides a much-needed panacea to the imagined homogeneity of social groups, which has particular significance for understanding racism within a group who have themselves experienced systematic discrimination, trauma, and oppression (Anthias 2013). Our approach to discussing this issue is also informed by critical whiteness studies, of use for understanding how white privilege within gay communities has permitted the concurrent establishment of a gay rights movement alongside the denial of racial inequality within (Ahmed 2007). Theories of intersectionality and whiteness permit recognition of the complex manifestations of gay racism among both individuals and institutions, and in their interactions with other social and material worlds.

THE INSTITUTIONAL ENACTMENT OF GAY RACISM

Understanding the dynamics of gay racism requires an understanding of the social and political movements that underpin contemporary gay life. Many of the largest and most influential gay institutions have roots in the gay rights and advocacy movements of the Western world, and the norms and culture of these movements are notably white. In an essay on gay racism in the 1990s, American political insider Keith Boykin (1996) recalled touring the country's largest gay rights organizations based in Washington, DC, and finding them staffed, almost exclusively, by those racialized as white. This disparity in staffing was particularly jarring given that the District's population at the time was predominantly black. Others have highlighted a dearth of racial minorities in positions of leadership across gay organizations in Western countries (Han 2007). Of course, diversity in representation and leadership is not an issue for gay organizations alone, but it is poignant that whiteness so clearly prevails in a domain associated with promoting the rights of a subjugated minority. Writing from the USA, lawyer and activist Urvashi Vaid (1995) put it this way: "If gay organizations at the national and state level wrap themselves in the mantle of civil rights language and history, they must take clear stands on the civil rights of blacks, people of color, immigrants and women" (126).

Historians of what many now call the "gay rights movement" often characterize it as a disruptive, protest-driven approach that borrowed liberally from the playbook of the American Civil Rights Movement of the 1950s and 1960s (Adam, Duyvendak, and Krouwel 2009). Interestingly, in spite of the strong parallels between these movements, they were rarely seen to be in alignment, and in fact some have argued that American political discourse in the 1960s through to the 1980s sought to pit black and gay issues and their respective supporters against each other (Mookas 1995), in the aim of separating potential allies while galvanizing the anger of white, middle-class voters (Frank 2013). Understanding this broader political context and relevant contexts in other countries is vital in understanding the history of race and racism within Western gay rights movements.

The onslaught of HIV and AIDS in the 1980s and 1990s represents a key turning point for gay life in the West, one that both mobilized and devastated the gay rights movement. To an even greater degree than the gay rights protests seen in major urban centers in the 1970s, AIDS inspired a new brand of disruptive political organization driven by a literal life-or-death imperative. Aside from employing innovative and captivating protest techniques, the HIV and AIDS activism embodied by ACT UP and other groups around the world demanded cooperation between the diverse populations affected by the virus, which included women and people of color. Jeffrey Edwards (2000) quotes a letter signed on behalf of the ACT UP/New York membership in 1989, which read:

> The inequities endemic in the AIDS crisis have made clear to gay white men in the group that their marginality is akin to that of women, people of color, the poor and intravenous drug users, communities long aware of the life-threatening consequences of being ignored. The ensuing mix of concerns, as well as the changing demographics of the crisis, provoke constant consciousness-raising at ACT UP's Monday night meetings, pushing us to address the major issues of our day: racism, sexism, disablism, homophobia, economic disenfranchisement, homelessness and unequal access to decent health care, among other issues. (492)

This excerpt reveals two things that contribute to our understanding of the institutional enactment of gay racism. First, there was a conscious and concerted effort by the (largely white male) membership of ACT UP to address racism within their organization, including as it related to health and equity. By all accounts, ACT UP successfully challenged many race-related issues in the response to HIV and AIDS, such as the inclusion of people of color in drug trials and the availability of treatment for people in prisons (Gould 2012). Second, however, is what this quotation reveals about the nature of privilege and power within ACT UP and similar organizations of the time. Although the intent of this letter can be read as one of solidarity and empathy, in setting up gay white men as a category distinct from others, the letter's authors reveal a degree of othering that separates from their ranks gay men of color, poor gay men, gay men who use drugs, and so on.

This fragmentation of people and issues came to define how ACT UP members were organized and the agendas they separately pursued. It was not uncommon, for example, for ACT UP chapters to have committees devoted to issues of race and racism but with less resourcing and attention than other committees, notably those devoted to HIV treatment that were populated predominantly by white men (Fuss 1991). Ultimately, this fragmentation, along with the ongoing loss and grief of the epidemic's early years, fostered conflict, particularly given that "some people within the lesbian and gay press and within ACT UP chapters themselves, mostly white men, charged that ACT UP had become excessively focused on fighting racism, sexism, heterosexism, and even capitalism" (Edwards 2000, 494). Such a charge can be characterized as an exercise in othering: they have *their* issues, we have *our* issues. It was, as Deborah Gould (2012) argues, difficult for many previously apolitical white men to recognize the privileges afforded by their gender, race, and class. Indeed, it was difficult for these men (many of whom were leaders in ACT UP) to grasp that with different levels of privilege came different kinds of needs. Ultimately, members' differing perspectives on a range of issues, of which race was only one, led to the dissolution of the ACT UP model in the early 1990s (Edwards 2000).

Our brief description of this pivotal period of HIV and AIDS activism cannot do justice to the story of how race was enacted in gay advocacy organizations of that time. It, nevertheless, provides some key insights for understanding how gay organizations try (and sometimes fail) to recognize and unite diverse racial identities under the banner of shared sexual politics. As Gould (2012) has argued, ACT UP was really no more or less racist than any other organization of its time, but because it represented a diverse membership united by a single issue, it had to contend more explicitly with the conflicts created by multiple, intersecting identities. Here, intersectionality as a frame of analysis helps demonstrate the institutional enactment of gay racism: although ACT UP tried to address the highly intersectional nature of the oppressions experienced by its members, when the needs of different identity combinations were in conflict it was ultimately those with the most power — white men — that took precedence (Edwards 2000). This does not imply that the needs of one group were more or less compelling than the needs of others, but it does suggest that in the history of the gay advocacy movement, a broader hierarchy of racial constructs has been deployed to empower some while oppressing others.

Beyond helping us to understand how race influences power relations within the institutions of gay life, intersectionality also invites us to question how or if these institutions can account for the plurality of the members they purport to represent. The example of ACT UP demonstrates just how difficult it can be to serve the needs of diverse people even in relation to a singular cause, such as HIV. Another relevant outcome of ACT UP was the formation of splinter groups that chose to focus on "gay" issues beyond HIV and AIDS (Edwards 2000). Today, Western countries typically boast multiple organizations devoted to gay advocacy at local, jurisdictional, and national levels. The fact that these organizations exist and commonly enjoy at least some public funding is a testament to decades of hard work and persistence. As with ACT UP, however, such organizations also face what we might call an intersectional crisis in trying to address the diverse needs and interests of their membership. Race is one defining feature of this complexity, but for the most part there is little evidence of modern gay advocacy organizations confronting race or racism either within or without. Indeed, the public face of such organizations tends to focus on symbols of inclusion and unity, as evidenced by seasonal themes such as San Francisco Lesbian, Gay, Bisexual, Transgender Pride's 2012 celebration "Global Equality," Sydney Gay and Lesbian Mardi Gras's 2014 theme "Kaleidoscope," and the 2015 theme from Birmingham Pride, "#FREEDOM — Together United." These themes are meant to inspire and excite revelers attending parties, parades, and other events, and, to be fair, they are more effective in that aim than a theme like "Racism is imbedded our social institutions." Yet, while they are meant to imply unity, these slogans do little to address or resolve the underlying complexities of race and inclusion. And to a degree they demonstrate that, as Antonio Pastrana Jr. (2006) put it in his study of gay and lesbian leaders of color, "lesbian and gay organizing efforts make strategic use of identity politics, sometimes suppressing notions of identity while at other time celebrating them" (223).

The complexity of managing and representing multiple identities at an institutional level can produce what we have referred to as an "intersectional crisis." These crises and responses to them have been shown time and again to reproduce and reinforce the racial demarcations that exist in our social world, and, as with ACT UP, it has been difficult for these organizations (and the white gay men who are typically in charge) to recognize the striking similarities between homophobia, racism, and sexism (Barnard 1999). One more recent example of this can be found in examining the gay advocacy and event organization Toronto Pride. Toronto Pride is the largest organization of its kind in Canada and one of the largest internationally, with a multimillion-dollar annual budget funded by both public and private sponsorship. In 2016, the festival adopted a theme of inclusivity, titled "You Can Sit with Us." This theme was artfully repurposed as a tool of protest when the advocacy organization Black Lives Matter staged a sit-in, challenging, among other things, Toronto Pride's failure to "honour . . . black queer/trans communities, and other marginalised communities" (Canadian Broadcasting Corporation News 2016). This intervention represented a significant and very public challenge to the perception of racial unity within an important gay institution and led to organizational restructuring, most notably in positions of leadership. While in 2012, seven out of eight directorships on the Toronto Pride Board of Directors were filled by men racialized as white, in 2017 this had fallen to two out of twelve spots. The organization's leadership also agreed to a list of demands from Black Lives Matter, the most contentious of which was the exclusion of Toronto's city police force from the 2017 festival (Canadian Broadcasting Corporation News 2017).

As gay institutions, neither ACT UP nor Toronto Pride are unique in their treatment of racial issues. Rather, they exemplify an institutionalized reproduction of racialized practices evident in gay organizations and the spaces they create across the Western world (Barnard 1999; Riggs 2006). Drawing on Sara Ahmed's (2007) work, these organizations have inherited what we might consider a history of whiteness, a way of orienting themselves that is maintained through the "repetition of decisions made over time, which shapes the surface of institutional spaces" (157). As illustrated by ACT UP and similar organizations around the world, history from both within and outside gay life speaks to how whiteness is constructed and reinforced within spaces for gay advocacy (Riggs 2006), which are ultimately just examples of what we have been calling "gay institutions." Ahmed's description of inherited whiteness as a process is important because it reminds us that whiteness is not fixed, that it continues, and that it can be changed. Since the 1980s, however, there has been little change or challenge to the whiteness of gay institutions, a process that has continued unhindered and even encouraged by what were likely the good intentions of some to distinguish between the gay rights movements and the civil rights movement. Boundaries between race and sexual orientation have made it difficult for gay advocacy institutions to address issues that are relevant to gay people but are also racialized in some way (Pastrana Jr. 2006), and they have created tangible gaps in agendas of gay social and political advocacy (Teunis 2007). Not only have these gaps contributed to racial inequity and racism, but, as the example from

Toronto demonstrates, they have also exacerbated a sense of community alienation among gay men of color.

While whiteness has remained the dominant orientation for many gay organizations, parallel institutions positioned specifically at the intersection of sexual orientation and race have arisen. In the USA, for example, the National Black Justice Coalition sits as a racialized counterweight to the Human Rights Campaign, which itself has faced criticisms over what was perceived as a homogeneous leadership of white gay men (Geidner 2015). Parallel organizations have long offered a way for minority groups to shift focus to different sets of issues (Boykin 1996), and for gay men they make sense given the fragmentation of social issues and the enduring whiteness of many organizations meant to represent their interests. Indeed, the very existence of parallel, race-based organizations makes clear the whiteness of those organizations that explicitly claim to represent *all* gay people. As Ahmed (2004) has argued, whiteness is invisible really only to white people; the active denial of that whiteness—particularly among institutions invested in a human rights agenda—represents a violent act of invisibility. In this way, Toronto Pride has diverged from ACT UP by undertaking tangible steps to address its problems of perpetuating white privilege by changing the way that race features in the organization. Whether or not this will resolve the organization's intersectional crisis remains to be seen, but it will no doubt serve as a future lesson for other institutions of gay life.

The final point to be made about the institutional enactment of gay racism relates to the notion of a "gay community." While many have argued that the idea of a single community is overly simplistic (Epstein 1999), it nonetheless persists as a social construct with an enduring currency and symbolism in the Western world. The institutions that are part of a gay community are not limited to Pride groups and HIV/AIDS organizations but extend to include everyday spaces, places, and products of gay life. It is, therefore, possible to see enactments of gay racism throughout bars, clubs, events, websites, mobile applications, magazines, pornography, advocacy agendas, health priorities, and neighborhoods that express and organize gay life, things that have long been racialized, but often in unrecognized ways (Boykin 1996; DeMarco 1983). If we, therefore, conceive of the "gay community" in the West as an institution itself, then the institutionalization of racism becomes something much more than the sum of racism within several discrete parts, the total force of which, as we explore in the next section, intersects closely with the lives of individuals.

THE INDIVIDUAL ENACTMENT OF GAY RACISM

Exploring how gay racism is institutionalized allows us to address the systemic expressions of racial inequality, but it does not provide much insight into the experiences of individuals. While examining "big picture" institutional dynamics has value, it runs the risk of obscuring how individuals produce, experience, and navigate racism. There are a number of relevant questions in this domain. How do men experience racism as a feature of gay life? In what ways do they seek to mitigate its impact? And what are the effects of gay racism, including on how men see themselves? These are not simple questions. While intersectionality remains a useful tool in addressing them, its application here requires that we shift our focus away from the collective and towards what Anthias (2012) called "concrete social relations."

Previous work has identified a number of ways that men experience racism in the context of gay life. Much of this work has assessed personal experience, and revealed that most racism experienced or produced by gay men is subtle and, at times, difficult to identify. Writing from Australia, Tony Ayres (1999) described it in this way: "For the most part, though, my experience in the gay scene has been characterized by neither outrageous abuse nor outrageous attention. Instead, it has involved a wearing, subtle, almost imperceptible feeling of exclusion" (89).

This idea of gay racism as "subtle" and nearly "imperceptible" has been echoed in personal accounts from Australia (Caluya 2006; Chuang 1999; Law 2012) and the USA (Han 2007; McBride 2005). This description of subtle racism is well-matched to how theorists have conceived of racism since the 1980s. Thomas Pettigrew (1989) called it "modern racism" and, like many of his contemporaries, defined it in large part by its subtlety and indirectness. Pettigrew highlighted the distinction between blatant and subtle expressions of racism while noting that in spite of these differences both remained, at the core, expressions of prejudice (Meertens and Pettigrew 1997). Modern racism is further defined by the explicit rejection of blatant prejudice, which has led to the myth that racism no longer exists or is irrelevant. The reality has not vanished but instead changed into something far more difficult to detect or report, particularly for those who experience it as part of their daily lives.

The subtlety of "modern gay racism" affects not only men's experiences but also their reactions. In 2012, we interviewed gay men of color living in Australia about racism they experienced while looking for sexual and romantic partners online (Callander, Holt, and Newman 2015). Reflecting the subtlety of modern gay racism, many men described being unsure if they had been excluded or rejected by potential partners because of their race or because of something else. In our analysis, we concluded that some men were reframing their experiences of racism, in part, to minimize racism's negative effects. Indeed, almost without exception, when the men in our study encountered gay racism they reacted by altering their own practices or thoughts rather than challenging racist practice, a practice observed when gay men experience racism in other settings as well (Choi et al. 2011; Poon and Ho 2008). The accommodation of racism is evident also in earlier explorations of gay racism, specifically the creation of separate social spaces (mainly bars and clubs) for gay men of color (Boykin 1996; DeMarco 1983). Collectively, this reveals that men typically only challenge or confront racism when it is at its most blatant; not only do men encounter different types of gay racism but they respond in different ways. These differences are significant because subtle racism is more common than blatant racism but is more difficult to identify and less likely to be challenged, which sustains its place as a normal part of gay life.

Beyond the strategies that men employ to deal with racism, it is also useful to explore how intersecting identities can alleviate or compound its impact. While there are some general features of identity that can intersect with race to compound oppression (poverty, for example), there are some that are of particular relevance to gay men. In his analysis of desirability among gay men in the USA, Jesus Gregorio Smith (2012) explored how features, such as having an athletic body, could work to overcome what he characterized as the inherent disadvantage of non-white skin while other factors, such as being HIV positive, accentuated racial disadvantage. Although his analysis was focused on desirability, we believe that from an intersectional perspective this has relevance for racism across gay life. Indeed, given the currency afforded to physical attractiveness among gay men, it is easy to imagine how desirability might intersect with race to accentuate or minimize the perception of oppression. That is not to suggest that racial fetishization is not experienced by men as a form of racism (it is), but that desirability can, in some cases, disguise racism in gay life. Conversely, other features—such as being HIV positive or displaying effeminate attributes—can work to compound racism. Ahmed (2006) argues that some individuals can approximate whiteness as a way to access and move within institutions that are, essentially, white. Features like attractiveness, normative masculinity, and wealth might allow gay men of color to "pass" within the institutions of gay life, while those marked with devalued characteristics are set even further apart from the expectations of whiteness. "Passing," of course, does nothing to address the underlying inequality. Overall, it is necessary to recognize that oppression and privilege among gay men can be experienced very differently even within what might loosely be considered racial groups, and those experiences—the negative and the positive—are ultimately a reaction to the whiteness that defines so much of gay life in the Western world.

Thus far we have reflected upon the ways that men experience and react to gay racism, but it is necessary to also touch upon some of its effects. Several studies have documented the immediate and long-term effects that racism in gay life can have on men. In our Australian interview study, for example, men described moments of anger and sadness, periods of anxiety, and the internalization of the racism they experienced (Callander et al. 2015). Researchers have identified other psychological effects, including depression (Chae and Yoshikawa 2008), difficulties with intimacy (Zamboni and Crawford 2007), and stress (Han et al. 2014). These are the kinds of effects produced by racism across populations— highlighting that gay racism has tangible, negative effects. Gay men experience racism not just in the general ways that people of color experience racism in Western countries, but also in ways that are specific to gay life.

The individual harms of gay racism share many similarities to those of general racism, but they carry a special significance because they manifest within a community that has been and continues to be defined by its diversity and supposed inclusivity. As discussed, this idea of a singular and inclusive gay community is often at odds with reality, but it remains a dominant feature in narratives of gay life in the West. It is, therefore, important to consider the tension fostered between racism and myths of an inclusive gay community, including the individual effects produced by that tension. Theorists have explored the ways that operations of power profoundly affect not just the experiences of individuals and institutions but also the ways in which identities and subjectivities are formed and understood (i.e., the ways in which people understand themselves as subjects), which Judith Butler (1997) described as the "psychic life of power." This idea of power as formative is important because it reveals that both the privileged and oppressive edges of power play some part in shaping individuals and groups. "Community" is central to not only the discourses of gay life but also the psychic life of gay racism because it is a symbol of inclusivity for those who enjoy intersectional privileges and a symbol of exclusion for those whose identities are rendered less valuable in the intersections that reproduce race. As individuals and organizations continue to grapple with racism within gay communities, attending to its psychic life has import for addressing the harmful effects described here.

RACISM ACROSS THE ACRONYM
AND AROUND THE WORLD

While we chose to focus this chapter on racism among gay men, it should be recognized that questions about race and racism are relevant to all who fall under the LGBTQIA umbrella. Many of the institutions we have discussed have relevance beyond just gay men and, importantly, it is necessary to recognize that from an intersectional perspective power is unequally distributed along gender lines as well. It has also been noted that lesbian women of color in the West face their own within-group challenges of representation, marginalization, and sexual stereotyping (Logie and Rwigema 2014), and race has featured in debates on access to health care among people with transgender experiences (Gehi and Arkles 2007). These examples demonstrate that race and racism remain challenging issues for all LGBTQIA people.

We focused our attention on racism as it is enacted and experienced by gay men in Western countries. Studies of race and racism require some form of geographic contextualization because their meaning and expression tend to vary widely around the world. With that being said, we believe it is useful to consider the racialization of gay life from this vantage point, given the ongoing influence of discourses of whiteness on gay life that have originated in the West. Indeed, almost all research and writing on gay racism has come from the USA, Australia, Canada, and the UK. Gaining some understanding of the work from these countries is important, but for us it also highlights the vital need for research on gay racism in other settings, particularly given the diverse organizations of gay life globally.

THE FUTURE OF GAY RACISM

Joe DeMarco concluded his 1983 essay on gay racism with a plan: confront discrimination when it arises, identify and be honest about the problem, establish and maintain communication, and provide ongoing support for gay men of all racial backgrounds. On the surface, these sound like simple strategies. Their complexity arises from the honesty they require about how race and racism feature across our social worlds, including the clever ways that racism disguises itself. Denial remains a popular reaction to any suggestion that racism might exist among gay men, but significant (albeit jarring) organizational shifts like those witnessed in Toronto provide some hope for progress. Institutions of gay life must take note of this example, because the disconnection and discontent fostered by ignoring race is not going away, and addressing institutional racism is an essential first step towards gaining ground on racism among individuals as well. Ultimately, while questions about race and racism remain as relevant to gay life today as they did thirty years ago, there is hope for a renewed willingness to critique race and question its place within communities of gay men.

REFERENCES

Adam, Barry, Jan Willem Duyvendak, and André Krouwel. 2009. *The Global Emergence of Gay and Lesbian Politics: National Imprints of a Worldwide Movement.* Philadelphia: Temple University Press.

Ahmed, Sara. 2007. "A Phenomenology of Whiteness." *Feminist Theory* 8 (2): 149–68.
Anthias, Floya. 2013. "Intersectional What? Social Divisions, Intersectionality and Levels of Analysis." *Ethnicities* 13 (1): 3–19.
Ayres, Tony. 1999. "China Doll—The Experience of Being a Gay Chinese Australian." *Journal of Homosexuality* 36 (3–4): 87–97.
Barnard, Ian. 1999. "Queer Race." *Social Semiotics* 9 (2): 199–212.
Boykin, Keith. 1996. *One More River to Cross: Black and Gay in America.* New York: Anchor.
Butler, Judith. 1997. *The Psychic Life of Power: Theories in Subjection.* Palo Alto: Stanford University Press.
Callander, Denton, Martin Holt, and Christy E. Newman. 2005. "'Not Everyone's Gonna Like Me': Accounting for Race and Racism in Australian Sex and Dating Webservices for Gay and Bisexual Men." *Ethnicities* 16 (1): 3–21.
Caluya, Gilbert. 2006. "The (Gay) Scene of Racism: Face, Shame and Gay Asian Males." *Australian Critical Race and Whiteness Studies Association e-Journal* 2 (2).
Canadian Broadcasting Corporation (CBC). 2016. "Black Lives Matter Toronto Stalls Pride Parade." *CBC News*, July 3.
———. 2017. "Pride Toronto AGM Vote Reaffirms Black Lives Matter Request for No Police Floats at Parade." *CBC News*, January 18.
Chae, David H., and Hirokazu Yoshikawa. 2008. "Perceived Group Devaluation, Depression, and HIV-Risk Behavior among Asian Gay Men." *Health Psychology* 27 (2): 140–48.
Choi, Kyung-Hee, Chong-suk Han, Jay Paul, and George Ayala. 2011. "Strategies for Managing Racism and Homophobia among U.S. Ethnic and Racial Minority Men Who Have Sex with Men." *AIDS Education and Prevention* 23 (2): 145–58.
Chuang, Kent. 1999. "Using Chopsticks to Eat Steak." *Journal of Homosexuality* 36 (3–4): 29–41.
Crenshaw, Kimberlé. 1991. "Mapping the margins: Intersectionality, Identity Politics, and Violence Against Women of Color." *Stanford Law Review* 43 (6): 1241–99.
DeMarco, Joe. 1983. "Gay Racism." In *Black Men/White Men: A Gay Anthology*, edited by Michael J. Smith, 109–18. San Francisco: Gay Sunshine Press.
Edwards, Jeffrey. 2000. "AIDS, Race, and the Rise and Decline of a Militant Oppositional Lesbian and Gay Politics in the US." *New Political Science* 22 (4): 485–506.
Epstein, Steven G. 2009. "Gay and Lesbian Movements in the United States: Dilemmas of Identity, Diversity, and Political Strategy." In *The Global Emergence of Gay and Lesbian Politics: National Imprints of a Worldwide Movement*, edited by Barry Adam, Jan Willem Duyvendak, and André Krouwel, 30–90. Philadelphia: Temple University Press.
Frank, Gillian. 2013. "'The Civil Rights of Parents': Race and Conservative Politics in Anita Bryant's Campaign against Gay Rights in 1970s Florida." *Journal of the History of Sexuality* 22 (1): 126–60.
Fuss, Diana. 1991. *Inside/Out: Lesbian Theories, Gay Theories.* Abingdon: Routledge.
Gehi, Pooja S., and Gabriel Arkles. 2007. "Unraveling Injustice: Race and Class Impact of Medicaid Exclusions of Transition-Related Health Care for Transgender People." *Sexuality Research & Social Policy* 4 (4): 7–35.
Geidner, Chris. 2015. "Internal Report: Major Diversity, Organizational Problems at Human Rights Campaign." *Buzzfeed*, June 4. https://www.buzzfeed.com/chrisgeidner/internal-report-major-diversity-organizational-problems-at-h?utm_term=.sakGJXLQBO#.lcv4xmNBD2.
Gould, Deborah B., 2012. "ACT UP, Racism, and the Question of How to Use History." *Quarterly Journal of Speech* 98 (1): 54–62.
Han, Chong-suk. 2007. "They Don't Want to Cruise your Type: Gay Men of Color and the Racial Politics of Exclusion." *Social Identities* 13 (1): 51–67.
Han, Chong-suk, George Ayala, Jay Paul, Ross Boylan, Steven E. Gregorich, and Kyung-Hee Choi. 2014. "Stress and Coping with Racism and Their Role in Sexual

Risk for HIV among African American, Asian/Pacific Islander, and Latino Men Who Have Sex with Men." *Archives of Sexual Behavior* 44 (2): 411–20.

Law, Benjamin. 2012. "Race-based Attraction." *Sydney Morning Herald*, March 26.

Logie, Carmen H., and Mari-Jolie Rwigema. 2014. "'The Normative Idea of Queer is a White Person': Understanding Perceptions of White Privilege among Lesbian, Bisexual, and Queer Women of Color in Toronto, Canada." *Journal of Lesbian Studies* 18 (2): 174–91.

McBride, Dwight A. 2005. *Why I Hate Abercrombie & Fitch*. New York: NYU Press.

Meertens, Roel W., and Thomas F. Pettigrew. 1997. "Is Subtle Prejudice Really Prejudice?" *The Public Opinion Quarterly* 61 (1): 54–71.

Mookas, Ioannis. 1995. "Faultlines: Homophobic Innovation in Gay Rights, Special Rights." *Afterimage* 22 (7–8): 14–18.

Pastrana Jr., Antonio. 2006. "The Intersectional Imagination: What Do Lesbian and Gay Leaders of Color Have to Do with It?" *Race, Gender & Class* 13 (3–4): 218–38.

Pettigrew, Thomas F. (1989). "The Nature of Modern Racism in the United States." *Revue Internationale de Psychologie Sociale* 2 (3): 291–303.

Poon, Maurice Kwong-Lai, and Peter Trung-Thu Ho. 2008. "Negotiating Social Stigma among Gay Asian Men." *Sexualities* 11 (1–2): 245–68.

Riggs, Damien W. 2006. *Priscilla, (White) Queen of the Desert: Queer Rights/Race Privilege*. Bern: Peter Lang.

Smith, Jesus Gregorio. 2012. "Sexual Racism in a Gay Community on the US-Mexico Border: Revisiting the Latin Americanization Thesis Online." Master's dissertation, University of Texas at El Paso.

Teunis, Neil. 2007. "Sexual Objectification and the Construction of Whiteness in the Gay Male Community." *Culture, Health & Sexuality* 9 (3): 263–75.

Vaid, Urvashi. 1996. *Virtual Equality: The Mainstreaming of Gay and Lesbian Liberation*. New York: Anchor.

Zamboni, Brian D., and Isiaah Crawford. 2007. "Minority Stress and Sexual Problems among African-American Gay and Bisexual Men." *Archives of Sexual Behavior* 36 (4): 569–78.

TWO

Islamophobia, Racialization, and Mis-Interpellation in Gay Men's Communities

Ibrahim Abraham

In the aftermath of the Pulse Nightclub shooting in Florida, in June 2016, in which a "lone wolf" terrorist who claimed affiliation to the Islamic State group killed forty-nine people in a gay venue, a leading scholar of Islam and homosexuality, Samar Habib (2016), wrote:

> Homophobia can emerge organically from religious beliefs and practice; it can also emerge without them. A tendency towards violence can emerge through religious institutions or ideologies; it can equally emerge without them. Sensible gun control and a public mental health-care system that works will curtail some of this maniacal violence. What will not help is the continued perception of Islam and Muslims as a global threat. That myopic confusion is the real danger. It is what radicalizes both some Muslims and those who fear or hate them.

Without seeking to minimize the impact of violence of this sort, this chapter seeks to address this "myopic confusion" that construes Muslims as inherently violent and fanatical. Focusing on debates around the idea of "Islamophobia" as a form of racism, emerging through a process of "racialization," this chapter will apply this growing body of literature to experiences of religious and racial discrimination in gay men's communities in the Anglophone West, primarily Britain and Australia. This chapter will make particular use of the psychoanalytically inspired work of anthropologists Pnina Werbner and Ghassan Hage, as well as empirical studies of everyday Muslim experience, from the disciplines of anthropology, sociology, and psychology.

A significant body of literature now exists on the experiences of gay, lesbian, and bisexual Muslims, primarily and understandably focusing on conflict, tensions, and negotiations with Muslim communities, and Islamic texts and traditions, as well as the particular nature of ethnic minority communities in the West. In addition to the material cited in this chapter, the collections edited by Habib (2010) and Hunt (2015) are informative, as is Kugle's (2014) study of the lives of gay, lesbian, and transgender Muslims. This should not preclude analysis of other forms of prejudice that inform the "intersectional" coordinates of gay Muslim identity and experience, as theorized by Momin Rahman (2010, 2014). The consequences of Islamophobia range from the anticipation of basic "incivility" in everyday life (Dunn, Klocker, and Salaby 2007, 582), to physical attacks, "to racial profiling and the tightening of security measures to contain, restrain and at times, ban" (Allen 2007, 57); this latter point has become most prominent since the election of President Trump, who promised precisely this. Further, since Islamophobia often manifests through interpersonal interactions and examples of "everyday racism" (Essed 1991), it can lead to the loss of self-esteem and a growing sense of alienation, as well as curtailing mobility and social interactions for fear of prejudicial encounters (Moosavi 2015, 47–48), similar to the psychologically devastating effects of closeting one's sexual identity, fostering fear and shame (Seidman 2002, 30–31). As Ghassan Hage (2014, 232) argues in analyzing Australian racism, the task of scholars is not to contest whether some societies or communities are more or less racist than others, but to understand how racism circulates, and how it "hurts and sometimes even destroys people."

This chapter will begin with an extended analysis of debates around the term "Islamophobia," noting the emergence of the term in analyses of the complexities of contemporary British racism. The chapter will then look at examples of Islamophobic racialization and racism in practice, focusing on the experiences of Islamophobia's non-Muslim victims and the impact of Islam on whiteness. This will be followed with an overview of Pnina Werbner's psychoanalytically inspired analysis of Islamophobia, understood as the fear of an overactive religious superego. The focus will then turn to experiences of Islamophobia in gay men's communities, utilizing existing empirical studies from Britain and Australia, theorized as examples of "mis-interpellation" or false egalitarianism.

ISLAMOPHOBIA, RACISM, AND RACIALIZATION

The term "Islamophobia" is of uncertain origins, but emerged in public discourse in Europe in the 1990s, and in the United States and elsewhere in the years following the attacks of September 11, 2001, and the subsequent "War on Terror." The linguistic ambiguities of "Islamophobia" are apparent, with both the "Islam" and "phobia" parts reasonably critiqued. Fred Halliday (1999, 898) criticizes "*Islam*ophobia" for suggesting the problem is theological opposition to "*Islam* as a religion," rather than prejudice against "*Muslims* as a people," implying religious conflicts of past centuries are still current in the "West." Similar to Celia Kitzinger's (1996, 11) criticism of the term "homophobia," for de-emphasizing the "heterosexist system" within which "discrete acts of harassment" labeled homophobic occur, Steve Garner and Saher Selod (2015, 17) criticize "Islamo*phobia*" for suggesting we are dealing with the "deviant psychological responses" of individuals rather than a social process with its own cultural and political logic. Nasar Meer and Tariq Modood (2009, 353), moreover, cite various reasons why there "may be little sympathy" for the idea of Muslims as victims of racism in public debate, including hostility to Islam being a liberal virtue in some intellectual circles. It is nevertheless clear that the term addresses a "new reality that needed naming," the "rapid" rise in anti-Muslim prejudice (Runnymede Trust 1997, 4).

The idea of Islamophobia is predicated on the emergence of distinct, public Muslim identities, which is itself predicated on the breakdown of earlier identity categories. In the British context, this meant political Blackness (Allen 2010, 7–11). As recently as 1994, Tariq Modood (1994), a leading scholar on British Muslims and multiculturalism, was arguing against what remained of the idea of Blackness as an inclusive identity for "all non-white groups" in the UK, emphasizing that people in Britain with different ethnic backgrounds experience prejudice in different ways. His emphasis at the time was a politicized British Asian identity, but in doing so he implies a politicized British Muslim identity by focusing on the Salman Rushdie affair, British Muslim protests against the controversial author in 1988 and 1989, around the same time as *l'affaire du foulard*, the French headscarves-in-school affair, was developing across the Channel. With these events, even before the 9/11 attacks, Muslims stopped being "out-there and external" to Europe and its settler colonies, and started being important political topics in the West; people who were "once remote and distant now have the ability, irrespective of geographical location, to infiltrate the lives, homes and relative security of each and every front room in the West" (Allen 2010, 41, 45).

A foundational text is the 1997 report *Islamophobia: A Challenge for Us All*, produced by the British anti-racist think tank the Runnymede Trust. The report emerged after a similar study on contemporary anti-Semitism underlined Modood's argument that racism cannot be understood simply along color lines (Allen 2010, 65–66). While recognizing the term "Islamophobia" is "not ideal," the report argues that that it is nevertheless a "useful shorthand way of referring to dread or hatred of Islam — and, therefore, to fear or dislike of all or most Muslims" (Runnymede

Trust 1997, 1). This basic definition of Islamophobia emerges from what the report calls a "closed" view of Islam as monolithic, alien, and perpetually in conflict with "superior" societies—an example of what has been termed an "Orientalist" approach to understanding Islam (Said 1979, 1997)—and a related view of Muslims as generally untrustworthy individuals who, given this understanding of Islam, are quite justifiably discriminated against (Runnymede Trust 1997, 4–11). A clear contemporary example of the Runnymede Trust's approach to Islamophobia can be found in *The Washington Post*'s overview of the attitude of President Trump's leading advisors:

> They describe a "long history of the Judeo-Christian West struggle against Islam," as [Stephen] Bannon put it, or "a world war against a messianic mass movement of evil people," as [Michael] Flynn, the incoming national security adviser, has written. Bush and Obama were careful to distinguish the terrorists of al-Qaeda and the Islamic State from Islam itself, which they described as a great religion worthy of respect. Not Flynn. Islam, he has said, is a cancer, a political movement masquerading as a religion and the product of an inferior culture. (Diehl 2016)

To recognize the movement from a certain attitude towards Islam to a certain attitude towards Muslims, is to recognize a process of *racialization* taking place. There is much more to say about the racialization of Muslim identity, and resistance to the idea of Islamophobia as racism, but we can posit the idea of Islamophobia as racialization by recognizing Islamophobia as "a set of ideas and practices that amalgamate all Muslims into one group and the characteristics associated with Muslims (violence, misogyny, political allegiance/disloyalty, incompatibility with Western values, etc.) are treated as if they are innate" (Garner and Selod 2015, 13). The result is that Muslims are both "homogenized and degraded by Islamophobic discourse and practices in their everyday lives" (Garner and Selod 2015, 17).

A leading scholar of Islamophobia, Chris Allen (2010, 14–15), detects three scholarly approaches to Islamophobia in the West; firstly, that Islamophobia has been present in the West for a millennium or more in a largely unchanged form, secondly, that Islamophobia has had a persistent presence, but (like anti-Semitism) has changed over time, and thirdly, that Islamophobia is a recent phenomenon, perhaps unique to this century. Fred Halliday (1999, 895–96) criticizes the first approach for failing to recognize the profound changes that have taken place since the days of the Crusades, and makes the practical point that if anti-Muslim attitudes are so ancient and persistent, then there is little that can be done. The second view of Islamophobia places it squarely within Howard Winant's (2015, 319) vulgar Marxist metaphor of the "world-historical shitpile of race," consisting of the detritus of centuries of imperialist oppression and exploitation. For example, Junaid Rana (2011) offers an anthropological study of the stigmatization of Muslim bodies as part of the racist system of contemporary global capitalism, focusing on Pakistani migrant workers, but takes his argument back to the racial regimes of the Spanish *Reconquista* and earlier. The idea of Islamophobia as an abidingly contemporary phenomenon has run into difficulty around ideas about the legitimacy of nominally anti-religious ideology, which we shall come to, as well as the problem that the term "Islamophobia" can give the impression that anti-Muslim attitudes are independent of other forms of prejudice, such as more conventionally understood ideas of racism or xenophobia (Allen 2010, 136). With reference to Louis Althusser's (1971, 170–83) psychoanalytically inspired notion of interpellative hailing, also made use of later in this chapter, Steve Garner and Saher Selod similarly argue that within the discourse of Islamophobia people may be wrongly interpellated "solely as Muslims," forgetting the complexity and intersectionality of individual identity and discrimination (Garner and Selod 2015, 17). In the British case, in particular, Allen observes that it can be difficult to conclusively demonstrate "a distinct and differentiable Islamophobia," since public acts of violence can appear to be based on ethnicity (Allen 2010, 62–63).

More combative debate has developed around the idea of Islamophobia as racism, with a clear divide between contemporary academic and quotidian "common sense" understandings of racism (Essed 1991, 146–47). As the American Anthropological Association's (1998) statement on race makes clear, "Both scholars and the general public have been conditioned to viewing human races as natural and separate divisions within the human species based on visible physical differences." Analyzing contemporary public debate around extending British anti-discrimination legislation to cover Muslims *qua* Muslims, Nasar Meer (2008, 76) is struck by how ubiquitous the "uncritical acceptance of racial biology" appears to be amongst public intellectuals and political commentators. While individuals understand that it is unacceptable to be racist, it seems there is limited understanding of the racialization that underlies racism. As such, Tyrer's (2013, 53) psychoanalytic study of Islamophobia argues that the denial of Islamophobia as racism relies on the continual "fantasy" of a "pure racial subject"—a fantasy rejecting the idea of both racialization and cultural racism which, while still a question of assigning superiority, asks whether one's "origin, parentage, religion, [or] culture" makes one an equal member of society or not (Allen 2010, 154).

With racism most commonly identifiable along Black/white lines in everyday discourse in the Anglophone West, with skin color in some way referencing one's biological racial belonging, the idea of anti-Muslim racism can be conceptually challenging (Allen 2010, 137, 152). But what the *Parekh Report* into British multiculturalism calls "West-East" or "Europe-Orient" cultural racism is recognizably similar to the "North-South" biological or phenotypical racism most associated with the Black/white divide, as both forms of prejudice imagine human variations to be "fixed and final" (Parekh 2000, 60). Indeed, looking at the history of imperialism and inequality more broadly reveals similar examples of "racism without race" within conceivably religious conflicts, such as in anti-Semitism or anti-Irish racism in Britain, wherein historical religious practices or heritage creates a racialized identity (Allen 2010, 153, 159). Given this continuity between racisms, Ash Amin sees contemporary Islamophobia as continuing earlier phenotypical ideas of racism insofar as Islamophobia is grounded in visual, often physical symbols that denote a set of uniform characteristics. A visual symbol might be skin color, or, in the case of Muslims of South Asian ancestry in the United Kingdom, "prayer caps, beards, baggy trousers, rucksacks, Yorkshire accents, loud music, shiny cars and shabby dwellings" (Amin 2010, 8).

In addition to troubling the commonsense idea of racism in the Anglophone West as predicated on one's biological grouping, the idea of Islamophobia also troubles the contemporary idea of religion as a voluntary identity. As Nasar Meer and Tariq Modood (2009, 345) observe, "It is frequently stated that, while gendered, racial and sexual identities are ascribed or involuntary categories of birth, being a Muslim is about chosen beliefs." The authors reject this idea, since individuals do not choose the family or the society in which they are born, and there is also a clear (Evangelical Protestant) Christian assumption about religious identity as conversion underpinning this idea. I suspect the sort of attitudes Meer and Modood critique are more common in gay communities in the Anglophone West than in their parent societies. A strong secularism operates such that religious identities may be normatively considered not only voluntary identities, but unnecessary identities, and the imperative placed upon "coming out," problematized in studies of gay Muslims indexed in the introduction and cited below, almost presupposes a rupture with family and community.

A number of American scholars suggest a willful misrecognition of the racialization of Muslim identities and of Islamophobia as a form of racism. As Todd Green (2015, 27) argues, Islamophobia has been intensified by the widespread public perception that, since Muslims are not a race, racializing discourse about Muslims is acceptable. The irony is that racialization is a process that never reaches its conclusion; Muslims are perpetually racialized, but never a "race," which remains defined in the pseudoscientific biological terms of the past. If this permanent racialization should succeed in Muslims discursively becoming a "race," only then will the racialization become unacceptable. Steve Garner (2010, 164, 173) recognizes a consciously contradictory aspect to Islamophobia, as perpetrators—especially elements of the liberal intelligentsia—know how racist discourse works, and know where the limits of acceptable racial discourse lie (Selod and Embrick 2013, 652). Individuals are capable of moving between discourses that recognize the diversity of Muslim belief and behavior (what the Runnymede Trust calls an "open" attitude) and racialized discourses focused on terrorism and uniform otherness (a "closed" attitude) (Runnymede Trust 1997, 4–11). The movement between these can be triggered by the phenotypical symbols that Ash Amin (2010, 8) cites, above, "prayer caps, beards," etcetera. This comes close to the psychoanalytic idea of disavowal in contemporary ideology, popularized by Slavoj Žižek (1989) from Peter Sloterdijk's (1987) idea of "cynical reason." Few people sincerely believe that all Muslims are bloodthirsty fanatics, but they sometimes act as if they do; "[t]hey know very well how things really are, but still they are doing it as if they did not know" (Žižek 1989, 33).

EVERYDAY ISLAMOPHOBIA

To understand how Islamophobia functions as a form of racialization, it is instructive to look at victims of Islamophobia who are not, in fact, Muslims, as well as victims of Islamophobia who otherwise experience the privileges of whiteness. In his psychoanalytic study of Islamophobia, David Tyrer (2013, 65–66) analyzes the shooting by London police of the non-Muslim Brazilian Jean Charles de Menezes—alleged to have "'looked' Muslim" (Allen 2010, 155)—not long after the "7/7" terrorist attacks in July 2005, to demonstrate the way in which Muslims upset existing racial tropes. He notes the wildly contradictory witness statements that offer wildly contradictory misrepresentations, including police officers as "fanatics" hijacking the train. There are various "traditional phenotypal markers of difference" referred to by eyewitnesses, and he argues that "Islamophobia emerges as a way of finding a language to speak of a presence that is difficult to place within a conventional racial grammar," as Muslims "resist proper symbolization" and the mere presence of Muslims produces a racial "excess" that makes it difficult to conventionally classify anyone else, either (Tyrer 2013, 65–66).

This racial "excess" spills over in different ways; one of the first victims of retaliatory violence after the 9/11 attacks was a gay Latino man who was attacked in San Francisco by men who thought his absence of *machismo* meant he was an Arab (Arondekar 2005, 242–43). Sikhs have also been the victims of Islamophobic attacks in the US, as well as Europe, because their turbans are viewed as Islamic symbols (Green 2015, 286–87; Tyrer 2013, 48–51). Speaking in early 2016, as Donald Trump's campaign was well under way and he had already called for a ban on Muslims entering the United States, the legal director of the Sikh Coalition, Harsimran Kaur, explained that "[o]ver the last few weeks, the level of intimidation is worse than it was after [September] 11th. . . . Then, people were angry at the terrorists and now they're angry at Muslims, anyone who is seen as Muslim, or anyone who is perceived as being 'other.' It's not just a case of mistaken identity" (Holley 2016).

Analyzing the experiences of nominally white Muslims, in particular white Muslim converts, demonstrates the way in which race is an "unstable" category subject to change (Moosavi 2015, 45). For just as European Jews, Italians, and the Irish have been "promoted" to the status of whiteness, through social changes over time, so we can see that white Muslim converts are "demoted" or "rejected" from whiteness (Selod and Embrick 2013, 652). A study of white British converts shows how they are "re-racialized" through conversion, leading to a loss of white privilege, above all the loss of their status as "unmarked subjects" who have no noticeable racial identity (Moosavi 2015, 42–43). Oishee Alam's (2012, 131) study of white Australian converts lists the "assets" that "unmarked" carriers of white privilege enjoy, and which one research participant, Tara, loses as soon as she wears her *hijab*, including "not being stared at, being treated well in stores, 'sailing through airport security,' and not being asked about 'politics on the other side of the world, in a country you've never visited.'" White converts are nevertheless aware of the residual privilege they enjoy; as Tara explained, "If I ever wanted to take off my headscarf and walk down the street, all white privileges would ultimately, instantly return" (Alam 2012, 134–35). A Jordanian American man in a similar study discussed his ability to pass as of Southern European ancestry, "unless he is in the company of his wife, a white American convert to Islam who wears the *hijab*" (Selod 2015, 84).

THE FANTASY OF ISLAMOPHOBIA

One of the most interesting approaches to Islamophobia in the West has come from the anthropologist Pnina Werbner (2013, 451–52), who offers a psychoanalytic approach to racial "fantasies, fears, symbols [and] folk devils" which change over time along with the broader changes in the "social imaginary." Werbner (2005, 8–9; 2013, 457–58) offers three archetypal figures of racist fear in Euro-American history: the "slave," the unrestrained black male body who embodies the id, especially as it pertains to unrestrained sexuality; the "witch," the financier or middleman embodying the ego and scheming his way to personal enrichment, the Jew in the European racist imagination; and the "Grand Inquisitor," embodying "the super-ego gone wild." She argues this last category forms the key basis for contemporary Islamophobia. Drawing further on psychoanalytic theories of racism, notably those of Frantz Fanon (2008) that note the inescapable connection between the self and the other, the figure of the Muslim as the religious authoritarian is not just a fear of cultural practices from the Orient being imposed on the Occident, but a recognition that Islam "evokes the specter of puritanical Christianity, a moral crusade, European sectarian wars, the Crusaders, the Inquisition," and above all, "the attack on the permissive society" (Werbner 2005, 8–9; 2013, 457–58). She argues that in contemporary liberal capitalism, the other archetypes of racist fear, the slave and the witch, are no longer frightening since unrestrained sexuality and scheming self-interest is tolerable or laudable. The Grand Inquisitor, on the other hand, represents a threat to the tolerant society, and must be "ghettoized or preferably expelled" from society, according to this logic, and as racialized subjects, so must all Muslims (Werbner 2013, 458–59).

Recalling Allen's (2010, 14–15) earlier typology of theories of Islamophobia, we can read this kind of analysis as thoroughly contemporary, suggesting that there is, as Garner (2010, 168) argues, "something specific to the historical moment" and the confluence of local and global sociopolitical currents that makes Islamophobia so virulent. Or, recalling the metaphorical "world-historical shitpile of race" (Winant 2015, 319), we can think of this with Werbner (2013, 457, emphasis in original) as "a very *postmodern* kind of fear," that has its roots in the past, but rearranges historical tropes as it regurgitates them in a different form. Or, we can think of contemporary Islamophobia as more closely contiguous with prejudice of the past, as critical race scholar David Theo Goldberg (2006, 331) does, in his slightly less phantasmagoric rendering of the tripartite focus of European racial fantasies, "the Black, the Jew, and the Muslim." Acknowledging that the European racist imagination has shifted its focus, and that Islamophobia addresses contemporary anxieties, he locates this idea of the Muslim "haunting" Europe very early (Goldberg 2006, 344). The figure of the Muslim represents not just the threat of religious persecution, as in Werbner's schema, but "the fear of violent death, the paranoia of Europe's cultural demise [and] of European integrity" (Goldberg 2006, 346)—geopolitical examples of the racial "excess" of the Muslim presence which upsets existing racial categorizations (Tyrer 2013, 65–66).

Goldberg's (2006, 346) depiction of the figure of the Muslim in the "dominant European imaginary" is in line with Werbner's figure of the Grand Inquisitor; Islam, he argues, is seen "to represent a collection of lacks: of freedom; of a disposition of scientific inquiry; of civility and manners; of love of life; of human worth; of equal respect for women and gay people." This latter point is of obvious relevance, and Goldberg places it within and alongside the idea of Islam "spurning individuality, spurred on by manic collective excitability," which stands in stark contrast to the emphasis on individuality in the West, including in religious matters (Goldberg 2006, 346). That individual rights are comparatively curtailed in most Muslim-majority countries is no doubt true, but this is hardly unique or unanimously supported, although it does offer a stark contrast on matters of sexuality; Gabriele Marranci (2016, 85) notes that "[w]hile Muslim majority countries are introducing more restrictive legislation against homosexuality, Muslim communities in the West are finding themselves living in societies that are fast approaching the total normalization of non-heterosexual life." This likely exacerbates the idea of the Muslim as the "Grand Inquisitor" figure which is noticeable as an aspect of everyday prejudice by non-Muslims who act as "informal gate-keepers of social membership," acting out versions of official state practices (Selod 2015, 91). This includes the idea of confronting Muslims—typically women—about "how their cultural values are a threat to American values" (Alam 2012, 132) It is also an aspect of everyday Islamophobia experienced in gay communities, to which this chapter will now turn.

GAY ISLAMOPHOBIA AS MIS-INTERPELLATION

The impact of Islamophobia in gay communities is, of course, far less severe than the impact of homophobia in Muslim-majority societies. This said, gay Islamophobia does have an impact, relating to broader patterns of prejudice within gay communities and within broader society. Gay Islamophobia manifests in three ways, firstly as discourse, secondly as everyday experience that I will refer to as a process of mis-interpellation, and thirdly as the consequential restraining or reorganizing of social life. As discourse, gay Islamophobia manifests as "homonationalism," as theorized by Jasbir Puar (2007), which replicates the kind of racialized Islamophobic discourse analyzed above—with particular focus on the discourse of the Inquisitor—but, within the broader framework of what Lisa Duggan (2002) labels "homonormativity," which seeks to present an image of queer life in accordance with the hegemonic values of twenty-first-century American liberal capitalism. This includes its various overseas entanglements and dependents, and the underlying racial system that justifies such global inequality, attracting criticism from Joseph Massad (2007, 2015), who takes aim at what he calls the "Gay International" which he views as a cultural imperialist movement seeking to impose contemporary Euro-American liberalism on the world, an approach criticized for, *inter alia*, radically overestimating the influence gay rights groups have over foreign policy (Rahman 2014, 79–82). I am less interested in the abstract discourse of Islamophobia than what empirical studies of gay communities reveal of everyday experiences, however, but they are of course related and can be understood like other forms of racism as a network of political principles, prejudices, and everyday practices (Allen 2010, 160–63; Wieviorka 1995), and we will nevertheless return to these ideas in analyzing the consequential reorganization of gay social life.

Focusing on examples of everyday experience of Islamophobia in literature on gay men's communities is instructive for revealing the thoroughly intersectional nature of identity and discrimination, as emphasized by Momin Rahman (2010). This is especially evident in the British context where there is constant slippage between a sense of discrimination against Muslims and of discrimination against (South) Asians (Jaspal and Cinnirella 2012). Explicit hostility is typically directed towards Muslims *qua* Muslims, in keeping with earlier discussion of the recognition of what is and is not acceptable racist language. This emerges in two forms, direct Islamophobic acts triggered by the phenotypical signs of Muslim identity (Amin 2010, 8) and indirect Islamophobic acts in the presence of Muslims who are not recognized as such, following Selod's (2015, 83–87) observation that, unlike Muslim women in headscarves, Muslim men who lack phenotypical Muslim (or Sikh) signifiers are unlikely to be accosted in public, and then only accosted in private if a conceivably Muslim name is revealed.

Direct Islamophobic acts typically focus on the issue of terrorism and Islamic fundamentalism. The founder of the UK branch of the queer Muslim organization al Fatiha, Adnan Ali, complained of widespread Islamophobia in the British queer community, saying that "to them [non-Muslims], everyone is like the Taliban" (Arondekar 2005, 243–44). The experiences of an Egyptian-Australian gay man, interviewed as part of my own research on this topic, are instructive; a devout Muslim who grew a beard as part of his religious identity, he said that "the first time I went out to an openly gay place—and that was a major step for me—there were a few people who did make comments about my beard making me look like a terrorist" (Abraham 2009, 86). The association with terrorism was something that all the other research participants in the study of queer Muslims in Australia felt, and most had encountered, but at a distance. A Malaysian-born man said, "9/11 has had so much impact not only on the Islamic world but on the gay world as well. People didn't know anything about Islam, and now they just know Muslims are all terrorists!" (Abraham 2009, 84).

An Indonesian-born gay Muslim in Australia explained the ability to hide his religious identity, since as someone from Southeast Asia he was not immediately thought of as a Muslim. He suggested that even people who may carry the phenotypical signs of Muslim identity could nevertheless deny this:

> Despite your physical appearance, you can always deny what you are. It's the same with before we came out; we'd always deny it, no matter how camp we are, no matter how much of a queen we are. With some Middle Eastern people who aren't the stereotype, I'm sure it's a lot easier for them to hide their religious identity. I don't think it's because they're ashamed of it, just that if I reveal it, it will create more trouble for me. It's more like a choice that they have to make. (Abraham 2009, 86)

This close association of Muslim religious identity with certain ethnic identities, and connection to certain ideas about how sexuality is embodied and performed, was experienced by a white Australian convert in Sydney, who explained:

> Friends and people that I meet are always totally shocked to find out that I'm a Muslim. I hear them going on about "fucking Muslims" and all that and I ask, "oh, really? You think so? Well, I'm a Muslim," and they go, "nooo!" It used to be like that with being queer. It's the same thing. Friends would be telling gay jokes and not realize that I was gay. (Abraham 2009, 89)

This is similar to the experiences of a white British convert reminding us of Tyrer's suggestion that the presence of Muslims upsets conventional categorizations (Tyrer 2013, 65–66): "I was at a wedding once and there was a guy sat next to me and about twenty times he must have said: 'You're Muslim but you're a white man?' . . . he wasn't even saying it to me, he was just shocked and couldn't believe it" (Moosavi 2015, 44–45). Finally, the Malaysian-born gay Muslim in Australia, quoted earlier, explained that he felt fortunate not to "look" Muslim so as to be the target of prejudice in the gay community. "They don't think I'm a Muslim," he said. "They think I could be Buddhist or a Filipino boy and a Christian. They don't think I look Muslim, they think of Arabic guys, they think that they're Muslim; they'll be racist to them" (Abraham 2009, 86).

I want to think of such experiences as examples of "mis-interpellation," as theorized by the anthropologist Ghassan Hage (2010), under the influence of Frantz Fanon (2008) and Louis Althusser (1971). Hage (2010, 122) describes the experience of racial mis-interpellation as a two-act drama:

> [I]n the first instance the racialized person is interpellated as belonging to a collectivity "like everybody else." S/he is hailed by the cultural group or the nation, or even by modernity which claims to be addressing "everyone." . . . Yet, no sooner do they answer the call and claim their spot than the symbolic order brutally reminds them that they are not part of everyone: "No, I wasn't talking to you. Piss off. You are not part of us."

This is most dramatic in the case of the Egyptian-Australian, quoted earlier, who experiences racial mis-interpellation "the first time I went out to an openly gay place" (Abraham 2009, 86). His situation is similar to the passage in Fanon (2008, 83–84) that inspires Hage here; where the "real world," understood by Fanon as the "white world," challenges his claims to be a participant in the European progressive project. A child yelling "Mama, see the Negro! I'm frightened!" indexes the "legends, stories, history, and above all *historicity*" (emphasis in original) that makes Fanon acutely aware of his racialized body.

The example Hage (2010, 123–24) uses to illustrate Fanon's experience is that of a Lebanese-American girl who considers herself "just another white American girl who happens to have Lebanese origins," until she is confronted with a portrait by a caricaturist that was "what I expected a Saudi to look like. . . . It kind of dawned on me that maybe I was not who I thought I was." The victim of this kind of racial mis-interpellation becomes "conscious of their body in a debilitating way," Hage argues after Fanon, such that the body becomes "dysfunctional" (Hage 2010, 126). As the Egyptian-Australian man quoted earlier reflected on this experience, "There's some things about yourself that you just can't change. . . . With me, in some ways I distinctively look Muslim. I can't change the way I look or change my ethnicity, so you've just got to deal with it. That's the way I look at it—I just have to deal with it; it's just there" (Abraham 2009, 86).

Hage's (2010, 123–24) understanding of racial mis-interpellation follows closely on Fanon's critical work, analyzing the residual impact of the false universal system on the mis-interpellated subject who develops "an emotionally ambivalent relation to the source of their mis-interpellation" which becomes a "source of rejection" in their life. He sees racial mis-interpellation as a way of understanding the broad experiences of alienation of elements of ironically-named "second generation" Muslim immigrant youth who experience racism growing up in the West, and a sense that they are not welcome in the society in which they were born (Hage 2011). He notes that these mis-interpellated subjects can look to Islam—or hip hop—for an alternative sense of identity and belonging. This is true also for some gay Muslims in the West, even in the ideological form of oppositional—sometimes labeled Occidentalist—religion, with the idea that homosexuality truly is a purely contemporary Western phenomena, a product of secularization and liberal permissiveness and unknown in the Muslim world. Statements like "I haven't heard of any gays in our village" illustrate this as one way that same-sex-attracted Muslims can try to make sense of their situation (Jaspal and Cinnirella 2010, 108).

Another consequence of mis-interpellation is the restriction of gay social life to ethnic subcultures, religiously organized or otherwise. There can be a "reciprocal and bi-dimensional" process of exclusion and "othering" insofar as gay men who are Muslim, or of a particular minority ethnic background, may stereotype or avoid gay men from the dominant ethnic group on the assumption that cultural differences are too great (Jaspal and Cinnirella 2012, 234). Several of the gay British Muslims in Andrew K. T. Yip's (2004, 343) study argued that family is a key division; "[t]hey're a lot more important to us than [to] white people," a Muslim of South Asian ancestry argued. While this idea emphasizes the social consequences for an extended family of the individual non-fulfillment of the expectation of heterosexual marriage and family embedded in the idea of honor (*izzat*) among Muslim, Hindu, and Sikh communities from South Asia (Jaspal 2012, 769–70), it is often expressed in ways that make liberal individualism appear a personal choice for selfishness. Other approaches contextualize gay Islamophobia within more subtle critiques of hegemonic aspects of local "homonormativity" (Duggan 2002), recognizing discriminatory practices impact on many people on many grounds, including religion in general (Abraham 2010, 404–7).

Imitating Fanon, once again, there are also new desires to develop some different kind of universality emerging in a number of scholarly studies of Islam and homosexuality. These are attempts to work through the experience of mis-interpellation, or a critical theorization of cultural and sexual difference. The most radical approach comes from Joseph Massad (2007; 2015), emphasizing the alterity of Muslim and non-Western culture and sexuality. The most sophisticated example of this thought is Momin Rahman's (2014) study *Homosexualities, Muslim Cultures and Modernity* that moves beyond his earlier study of queer Muslims as intersectional identities, citing the need to "imagine different terms and concepts that avoid such reifications" as have been outlined in this section (Rahman 2010, 954). It is an attempt to deal with the subjective fragmentation and embodied dysfunction that Hage argues is produced by the process of mis-interpellation, as well as the process of "compartmentalization" or "closeting" experienced by both gay and Muslim subjects.

CONCLUSION

Focusing on the experiences of Muslims in the Anglophone West, this chapter has sought to apply contemporary literature on Islamophobia as racism and racialization to the study of gay men's communities. Demonstrating the significance of these debates, the latter part of this chapter has focused on the idea of Islamophobia and some attendant aspects of reciprocal prejudice as a process of "mis-interpellation," suggesting that same-sex-attracted Muslims can experience a sense of alienation and disillusion after failing to find acceptance in gay men's communities. Beginning with an extensive analysis of debate around the idea of Islamophobia as a form of racism, predicated on a process of racialization, this chapter has sought to expand the understanding of forms of racism that circulate within gay men's communities by focusing, in particular, on psychoanalytically inspired theories of Islamophobia and other racisms. As such, this chapter has made use of Pnina Werbner's theorization of Islamophobia as a discourse of the "Grand Inquisitor," emphasizing the fear of Islam and Muslims as the fear of the return of the repressed in the form of religious repression considered long eradicated from the West. It was suggested that this fear is particularly acute in gay communities, but that reproducing Islamophobic discourse can only contribute to the "myopic confusion" that exacerbates conflict (Habib 2016).

REFERENCES

Abraham, Ibrahim. 2009. "'Out to Get Us': Queer Muslims and the Clash of Sexual Civilisations in Australia." *Contemporary Islam* 3 (1): 79–97.

———. 2010. "'Everywhere You Turn You Have to Jump into Another Closet': Hegemony, Hybridity and Queer Australian Muslims." In *Islam and Homosexuality, Volume 2*, edited by Samar Habib, 395–418. Santa Barbara: Praeger.

Alam, Oishee. 2012. "'Islam is a Blackfella Religion, Whatchya Trying to Prove?': Race in the Lives of White Muslim Converts in Australia." *La Trobe Journal* 89 (May): 124–39.

Allen, Chris. 2007. "Islamophobia and its Consequences." In *European Islam: Challenges for Public Policy and Society*, edited by Samir Amghar, Amel Boubekeur, and Michael Emerson, 144–67. Brussels: Centre for European Policy Studies.

———. 2010. *Islamophobia*. Farnham: Ashgate.

Althusser, Louis. 1971. *Lenin and Philosophy and Other Essays*. New York: Monthly Review Books.

American Anthropological Association. 1998. "AAA Statement on Race." Accessed February 1, 2017. http://www.americananthro.org/ConnectWithAAA/Content. aspx?ItemNumber=2583.

Amin, Ash. 2010. "The Remainders of Race." *Theory, Culture & Society* 27 (1): 1–23.

Arondekar, Anjali. 2005. "Border/line Sex: Queer Postcolonialities, or How Race Matters Outside the United States." *Interventions* 7 (2): 236–50.

Diehl, Jackson. 2016. "Trump's Coming War against Islam." *The Washington Post*, December 11. Accessed February 1, 2017. https://www.washingtonpost.com/opinions/global-opinions/trumps-coming-war-against-islam/2016/12/11/edf3241c-bd60-11e6-91ee-1adddfe36cbe_story.html.

Duggan, Lisa. 2002. "The New Homonormativity: The Sexual Politics of Neoliberalism." In *Materializing Democracy: Toward a Revitalized Cultural Politics*, edited by Russ Castronovo and Dana D. Nelson, 175–94. Durham: Duke University Press.

Dunn, Kevin M., Natascha Klocker, and Tanya Salabay. 2007. "Contemporary Racism and Islamophobia in Australia: Racializing Religion." *Ethnicities* 7 (4): 564–89.

Essed, Philomena. 1991. *Understanding Everyday Racism: An Interdisciplinary Theory*. London: SAGE.

Fanon, Frantz. 2008. *Black Skin, White Masks*. London: Pluto Press.

Garner, Steve. 2010. *Racisms: An Introduction*. London: SAGE.

Garner, Steve, and Saher Selod. 2015. "The Racialization of Muslims: Empirical Studies of Islamophobia." *Critical Sociology* 41 (1): 9–19.

Goldberg, David Theo. 2006. "Racial Europeanization." *Ethnic and Racial Studies* 29 (2): 331–64.

Green, Todd H. 2015. *The Fear of Islam: An Introduction to Islamophobia in the West*. Minneapolis: Fortress Press.

Habib, Samar, ed. 2010. *Islam and Homosexuality*. Santa Barbara: Praeger.

Habib, Samar. 2016. "Here's the Truth about the History of Islam's Relationship with Homosexuality." *New York Daily News*, June 13. Accessed February 1, 2017. http://www.nydailynews.com/opinion/history-islam-relationship-homosexuality-article-1.2672573.

Hage, Ghassan. 2010. "The Affective Politics of Racial Mis-interpellation." *Theory, Culture and Society* 27 (7–8): 112–29.

———. 2011. "Multiculturalism and the Ungovernable Muslim." In *Essays on Muslims and Multiculturalism*, edited by Raimond Gaita, 155–86. Melbourne: Text Publishing.

————. 2014. "Continuity and Change in Australian Racism." *Journal of Intercultural Studies* 35 (3): 232–37.

Halliday, Fred. 1999. "'Islamophobia' Reconsidered." *Ethnic and Racial Studies* 22 (5): 892–902.

Holley, Peter. 2016. "Obama White House Sends Highest-ever Official to Sikh House of Worship Following Attacks." *The Washington Post*, January 11. Accessed February 1, 2017. https://www.washingtonpost.com/news/acts-of-faith/wp/2015/12/28/americans-are-still-attacking-sikhs-because-they-think-theyre-muslims/.

Hunt, Stephen, ed. 2015. *Religion and LGBTQ Sexualities: Critical Essays.* Farnham: Ashgate.

Jaspal, Rusi. 2012. "'I Never Faced Up to Being Gay': Sexual, Religious and Ethnic Identities Among British Indian and British Pakistani Gay Men." *Culture, Health & Sexuality* 14 (7): 767–80.

Jaspal, Rusi, and Marco Cinnirella. 2010. "Coping with Potentially Incompatible Identities: Accounts of Religious, Ethnic, and Sexual Identities from British Pakistani Men who Identify as Muslim and Gay." *British Journal of Social Psychology* 49 (4): 849–70.

————. 2012. "Identity Processes, Threat, and Interpersonal Relations: Accounts from British Muslim Gay Men." *Journal of Homosexuality* 59 (2): 215–40.

Kitzinger, Celia. 1996. "Speaking of Oppression: Psychology, Politics, and the Language of Power." In *Preventing Heterosexism and Homophobia*, edited by Esther D. Rothblum and Lynne A. Bond, 3–19. London: SAGE.

Kugle, Scott Siraj al-Haqq. 2014. *Living Out Islam: Voices of Gay, Lesbian, and Transgender Muslims.* New York: New York University Press.

Marranci, Gabriele. 2016. *Wars of Terror.* London: Bloomsbury Academic.

Massad, Joseph. 2007. *Desiring Arabs.* Chicago: University of Chicago Press.

————. 2015. *Islam in Liberalism.* Chicago: University of Chicago Press.

Meer, Nasar. 2008. "The Politics of Voluntary and Involuntary Identities: Are Muslims in Britain an Ethnic, Racial or Religious Minority?" *Patterns of Prejudice* 42 (1): 61–81.

Meer, Nasar, and Tariq Modood. 2009. "Refutations of Racism in the 'Muslim Question.'" *Patterns of Prejudice* 43 (3–4): 335–54.

Modood, Tariq. 1994. "Political Blackness and British Asians." *Sociology* 28 (4): 859–86.

Moosavi, Leon. 2015. "The Racialization of Muslim Converts in Britain and Their Experiences of Islamophobia." *Critical Sociology* 41 (1): 41–56.

Parekh, Bhikhu. 2000. *The Future of Multi-Ethnic Britain: Report of the Commission on the Future of Multi-Ethnic Britain.* London: Profile Books.

Puar, Jasbir K. 2007. *Terrorist Assemblages: Homonationalism in Queer Times.* Durham: Duke University Press.

Rahman, Momin. 2010. "Queer as Intersectionality: Theorizing Gay Muslim Identities." *Sociology* 44 (5): 944–61.

————. 2014. *Homosexualities, Muslim Cultures and Modernity.* Basingstoke: Palgrave Macmillan.

Rana, Junaid. 2011. *Terrifying Muslims: Race and Labor in the South Asian Diaspora.* Durham: Duke University Press.

Runnymede Trust. 1997. *Islamophobia: A Challenge for Us All.* London: Runnymede Trust.

Said, Edward W. 1979. *Orientalism.* Harmondsworth: Penguin.

————. 1997. *Covering Islam, Revised Edition.* London: Vintage.

Seidman, Steven. 2002. *Beyond the Closet: The Transformation of Gay and Lesbian Life.* New York: Routledge.

Selod, Saher. 2015. "Citizenship Denied: The Racialization of Muslim American Men and Women post–9/11." *Critical Sociology* 41 (1): 77–95.

Selod, Saher, and David G. Embrick. 2013. "Racialization and Muslims: Situating the Muslim Experience in Race Scholarship." *Sociology Compass* 7 (8): 644–55.

Sloterdijk, Peter. 1987. *Critique of Cynical Reason.* Minneapolis: University of Minnesota Press.

Tyrer, David. 2013. *The Politics of Islamophobia: Race, Power and Fantasy.* London: Pluto.

Werbner, Pnina. 2005. "Islamophobia: Incitement to Religious Hatred—Legislating for a New Fear." *Anthropology Today* 21 (1): 5–9.

———. 2013. "Folk Devils and Racist Imaginaries in a Global Prism: Islamophobia and Anti-Semitism in the Twenty-First Century." *Ethnic and Racial Studies* 36 (3): 450–67.

Wieviorka, Michel. 1995. *The Arena of Racism.* London: SAGE.

Winant, Howard. 2015. "The Dark Matter: Race and Racism in the 21st Century." *Critical Sociology* 41 (2): 313–24.

Yip, Andrew K. T. 2004. "Negotiating Space with Family and Kin in Identity Construction: The Narratives of British Non-Heterosexual Muslims." *Sociological Review* 52 (3): 336–50.

Žižek, Slavoj. 1989. *The Sublime Object of Ideology.* London: Verso.

THREE

Gay Orientalism

Jacks Cheng

No rice, no curry, no spice and the use of other ethnoracial clichés within the gay community as a substitution for what are viewed as sexual "preferences" have been well documented in popular media across the globe (Cho 2016; Donnelly 2016; Jones 2016; Rupiah 2016). Most often observed on mobile and online dating applications for gay men, these words conjure stigmatizing images of men of color of Asian descent by associating them with the food items stereotypically representative of their respective cultures: East and Southeast Asian men who eat rice as their main diet, South Asian men who frequently consume curry, and West Asian men who enjoy food with a myriad of spices. These caricatures are used to characterize sexual preferences by objectifying men of color of Asian descent, reducing them to Western assumptions about their cultures of origin.

The patronizing and essentializing of Asians is certainly not new in the Western world, nor unique to gay communities. In his seminal work, Edward Said (1978) redefined *Orientalism* as an understanding of Eastern cultures shaped by historical and continuous colonization and exoticization as a tool of imperial control and power assertion. Said (1978) further described *Orientalism* as beyond just imagination; rather it is "an integral part of European material civilization and culture [. . .] and expresses and represents that part culturally and even ideologically as a mode of discourse with supporting institutions, vocabulary, scholarship, imagery, doctrines, even colonial bureaucracies and colonial styles" (2). Riggs and Augoustinos (2005) provided a similar argument that racism and the conceptualization of racialized bodies is a product that extends beyond interpersonal and concrete acts; these ideologies emerge as a transfusion,

33

as the psychic life of white colonial power that represents racially biased practices and preferences that the Western world embodies and draws from culturally.

In this chapter, I attempt to use a lens informed by Said's (1978) *Orientalism* and Riggs and Augoustinos' (2005) *Psychic Life of Colonial Power* to construct a framework to understand the experiences of racism among Asian men in relation to their white counterparts across the globe. More specifically, I seek to (a) better define the scope of what I refer to as "gay orientalism" as a superlative phenomenon vis-à-vis sexual racism against Asian men in gay men's communitities currently, (b) explore and illustrate gay orientalism historically, interpersonally, and institutionally, and (c) discuss issues of gay orientalism among Asian men. I conclude the chapter with comments on the utility of understanding gay orientalism as a tool for anti-racism in the gay community.

THE LANDSCAPE OF GAY ORIENTALISM

From Ancient Egypt's Khnumhotep and Niankhkhnum, Ancient Greece's pederasty and Sappho's love poems for women, to Ancient China's Emperor Ai of Han and his lover Dong Xian, it is not difficult to find evidence of same-gender attraction throughout history around the globe. Nonetheless, scholars across disciplines have argued that the contemporary global discourse on gayness has predominantly placed emphasis on the narratives of white middle-class young men, to the detriment of the representation of people of color (Bérubé 2001; Moradi, DeBlaere, and Huang 2010; Ward 2008). In *Not Gay: Sex between Straight White Men*, Jane Ward (2015) further argues that the emergence of gayness is related to the act of defining white heterosexuality and masculinity. In other words, discourses of homosexuality function as tools for white middle-class young men to form their racial, gender, and sexual identities: by delineating the power structure between heterosexual and gay narratives, white heterosexual men are able to prove their endurance and repudiation of same-gender relationships and activities, where they come out a stronger and more masculine man.

In *Geisha of a Different Kind: Race and Sexuality in Gaysian America*, C. Winter Han (2015) argued that this defining form of masculinity for white middle-class young straight men creates a hegemonic standard of appropriate masculinity. Han contended that this standard not only renders white masculinity and sexuality more desirable, it also creates a norm for all men, and seeks to police those who fail to conform to the standard. Indeed, Han argues that the transposition of white masculinity over men of color's masculine agency differentially assigns men of color to inappropriate levels of masculinity: whereas black, Latino, and Arab men are hypermasculinized and hypersexualized, Asian men from East,

South, and Southeast Asia are emasculated and desexualized. Consequently, men of color are forced to fail the masculine standard by default, which ultimately helps white masculinity to remain in perpetual control and dominance.

The process of using gayness to interpret white heterosexuality and create hegemonic masculinity is reminiscent of how Said (1978) described Orientalism as "a Western style for dominating, restricting, and having authority over the Orient" (3) that makes an "ineradicable distinction between Western superiority and Oriental inferiority" (42) by way of a "political vision of reality whose structure promoted the difference between the familiar (Europe, the West, 'us') and the strange (the Orient, the East, 'them')" (43). Certainly, the advent of Orientalism and of gayness both demonstrate the need for the West, and white European cultures specifically, to use the racial Other as a surrogate to establish and empower their own strength and identity.

The need for a repudiated Other against which to shape the self-definition of the West in turn engenders a necessary desire and curiosity that instigates continued discovery of the racial Other. Through the globalization of individualistic capitalism and consumerism, white European cultures are further able to reach the farthest corners of the Orient in their quest to develop identity and imperial control. As a consequence, the scope of Orientalism as a construct has expanded from an interpretation of the Near East, now better known as the Middle East or West Asia, to also include the Far East, which refers to East, Southeast, and South Asia. The Orient has even evolved as an almost exclusive and identifying synonym for the Far East, as has the word *Asian*, in vernacular English.

Gayness has also seen its own similar process of expansion in meaning. From describing same-gender attractions and activities, it has morphed into a larger and more inclusive *queer* identity that represents an ensemble of experiences that include sexual orientation, gender identity and expression, and sexual activities (Butler 2003; Halperin 1995). For men, gayness as a concept can range from attraction, romantic relationships, and sexual behaviors between men, as well as resemblance to and membership in gay subcultures such as bear, leather, HIV gifting, and drag queen communities (Hajek 2012). Within this chapter, I use this notion of a broader gayness to both refer to sexual minority men's identity and experiences, as well as the sexual and gender minority community, in its position of the Other.

The above premises showcase the compatibility of Orientalism and gayness as a unified construct for racialization and masculinization within the global gay community. As a product of racism and hegemonic masculinity, gay Orientalism combines the simultaneous need to associate with two Others, the Orient and the inappropriately masculine. Gay Orientalism can thus be conceptualized as white gay men's attempt to politicize and enshrine their racial and sexual narratives to assert imperial power, while still maintaining connections with gay Asian men on their own terms, and without compromising their assumed supremacy.

HISTORICAL BACKGROUND TO
ORIENTALIST FANTASIES

Gay Orientalism is a powerful and insidious colonial tool, because it produces narratives of racial Others that are easily malleable to the needs and desires of the West over time. As Said (1978) described, the tacit command of Orientalism is that "[o]nly an Occidental could speak of Orientals [. . .] just as it was the [w]hite man who could designate and name the coloreds, or nonwhites" (228), and that "no Oriental was ever allowed to be independent and rule himself" (228). Orientalism and gayness as colonial constructs allow for white European cultures to dictate and manipulate ideas, images, and experiences of racial Others, and in so doing render white European cultures as the sole legitimate cognizance of these Others at their leisure. Such a narrative serves to minimize or render invisible the evolutions and changes of cultures in the East and the West; the West retains the prerogative to restructure and reinvent their versions of the Orient to maintain their superior position between the West and the East.

As encounters with the East increase, the Orient became a quasi-synonym for all of Asia and associated Eastern cultures. This definitional expansion not only creates a fully juxtaposed Occident, the West, in sharp contrast with the Orient, the East, but it also inevitably triggers the need for Occidental narratives of the Orient to also account for the differences that exist between Eastern populations, the Orientals, who come from different cultures and geographical locations within the East (Said 1978, 117, 251). Keeping Orientals selectively organized and disorganized positions the West as the privileged observer that objectifies and governs Orientals for their own benefit (Said 1978, 228, 251)

One notable shift is demonstrated in changes in narratives from the "Yellow Peril" to the "Model Minority" for the Far East, namely for East Asian countries such as China and Japan. Indeed, the West's initial curiosity and romance for conquering the Far East started to dissipate as the West began to see the consequences of colonizing the Far East. The Far East became an increasing threat as anti-colonialist and expansionist movements rose in the Far East against white European control, and as Far Easterners immigrated to Western countries such as the United States, Canada, Australia, and New Zealand (Marchetti 1993; Shim 1998).

Initially, white entrepreneurs saw Chinese and Japanese immigrants as inexpensive solutions to shortages in the labor market during rapid industrialization in the mid to late nineteenth century, and employed immigrants in positions such as cooks, laundry workers, miners, and domestic staff (Shim 1998, 387; Sue and Kitano 1973). However, as these laborers often performed the most intensive and unwanted work for minimal wage, Westerners began to fear eventual economic dislocation, which developed into exaggerated fear about possible invasion and extortion on witnessing their diligence and endurance (Shim 1998, 387; Sue and Kitano 1973, 87–88).

Such fears lead to the development of a narrative of the "Yellow Peril," namely that the influx of Chinese and Japanese immigrants in the West was a predatory phenomenon orchestrated to destroy white civilization (Shim 1998, 388). These East Asian immigrants were described as morally corrupt and treacherous, with a low intellect and naturally cowardly, therefore incapable of assimilation to a superior white civilization (Sue and Kitano 1973). They were also further portrayed as nefarious sexual seducers: East Asian men sought to rape and desecrate white women to undermine the purity of whiteness, and East Asian women were skilled in compromising the efforts of white heroes to save their cultures from the allegedly contaminating influences of the East (Marchetti 1993).

The urgency to neutralize the threat and aggression of the "Yellow Peril" was partially resolved by exclusion and sequestration: for example, Chinese immigrants were forced to return to China or live in specific areas called Chinatown, and, during wartime, by the internment of Japanese Americans (Sue and Kitano 1973, 85–86). Fear of "Yellow Peril" in the West, however, began to decline post–Second World War given the wartime alliance of China and the defeat of Japan. The West began to develop more favorable images of East Asians given their low rates of crime, divorce, illness, high educational attainment, and willingness to assimilate to white cultures (Sue and Kitano 1973, 87–88).

Despite the increasing amicable relationships with Far Eastern immigrants domestically, the West was facing developing tensions with different parts of Asia. In criticizing the foreign policies of the United States, social activist and professor Noam Chomsky (2009) identified how the United States' growing conflict with the former Soviet Union during the Cold War period had implications for the West's relationship with the Middle East. Like Chomsky, other scholars similarly described the multiplicity of the Cold War struggle: as the United States inherited the historical popularity of anti-Arab and anti-Islamic prejudice from Europe and took alliance with Israel in its efforts against neighboring Arab countries, the Soviet Union maintained strong diplomatic ties with many Middle Eastern Arab countries such as Syria and Egypt in collective opposition to the West (Kreutz 2007, 12–13, 111; Little 2008, 94, 96; Said 1978, 294).

Furthermore, Chomsky (2009) highlights how United States–Middle East relations were further complicated by the United States' mounting attention on the Middle East as a source of strategic power, given their rising economic power based in the oil industry. In the interest of legiti-

mizing their interventions in the Middle East, the West seized the opportunity to capitalize on the ameliorated image of the East Asian immigrants to create the narrative of a Model Minority, against which other
people of color are compared.

In this Occidental narrative of the Orient, even the previously aggressive and perilous East Asians were eventually rehabilitated and assimilated into upright citizens of the West via their continued exposure to
what were viewed as more sophisticated and civilized Western cultures.
The sexual image of Far Eastern Asians, especially for men, had also
shifted during this time. While previously seen as sexual predators, Far
Eastern Asian men were now seen as less athletic, muscular, and sexually
competent, which would also translate into being less masculine and
more domestic and asexual (Cheng 1996; Cheng et al. 2016; Chua and
Fujino 1999; Iwamoto and Liu 2009; Liu and Wong 2016).

The West also simultaneously exercised its role to speak for the Orient
by reinterpreting the economic growth in the Middle East as representative of Arabs and Muslim countries' thirst for power and success (Said
1978, 306). With this reinterpretation, the West sought to enhance the
existing negative stereotypes of Arabs and Muslims as primitive, dishon-
est, violent, and without humanity as qualities informed by the religion
of Islam, viewed as too political and not accepting or developed enough
to be capable of being secular (Said 1978). The West further explained
that the oppressive Islamic ideals of sexuality cause a powerful and unre-
alized undercurrent of sexual appetite and exaggeration for Arabs and
Muslims (Said 1978).

COMMISSIONING GAY ORIENTALIST FANTASIES

Concurrent with some of the latter developments described above, the
gay West adopted a self-image of sexual inclusion and diversity through
the feminist and homophile movements (Puar 2006). Through recourse to
what Puar has referred to as homonationalism, the acceptance of sexual
and gender diversity became an evaluative criterion for the legitimacy
and capacity for national sovereignty. In this way, the West framed what
was seen as Islamic "backwardness" as the cause for "Muslim homophobia" viewed as exclusive to the Middle East, necessitating the need to
combat it and liberate the sexually repressed to uphold Western gay
pride (Mepschen, Duyvendak, and Tonkens 2010; Puar 2006; Rahman
2014).

With this Islamophobic and anti-terrorist narrative, the West invokes
the Model Minority narrative ascribed to East Asians as a standard, a
means to encouraging Arabs and Muslim countries to relinquish their
purportedly uncivilized and unprogressive customs and conform to
Western ideals. There are two consequent choices for Arabs and Muslim

countries: those who do as they are told are good Arabs, whereas those who do not are bad Arabs, the terrorists (Said 1978, 306). Yet Arabs and Muslims, like East Asians and all the Orientals, can only "become repetitious pseudo-incarnations of some great original (Christ, Europe, the West) they were supposed to have been imitating" (Said 1978, 62), regardless of whatever choice they make.

The narrative specific to white gay men in this context is the interaction between a racial majority and a sexual minority identity. Law professor and civil rights advocate Kimberlé Crenshaw (1989) pioneered the idea of intersectionality, in which social identities are seen as overlapping and interlocking to create a uniquely synergetic experience. Despite Crenshaw's original intent to use intersectionality to explain the multiple marginalized experiences of people who hold more than one minority identity, this framework could also explain the liberty that white gayness takes to endorse gay Orientalism.

Gayness as a concept, as I have demonstrated earlier, is embedded within heterosexuality to help define heterosexuality through its opposite qualities. Indeed, queer theorist David M. Halperin (1995) purported the idea that gayness uses a positionality of resistance to the norm, heterosexuality in this case, as a means to define sexual identity. I would argue that white gay men and white gay institutions use this oppositionality to rationalize their embrace of gay Orientalism. In other words, even though white gay men are representatives of a privileged race and gender, their perception of being the Other given their sexual orientation acts as a handicap to their position of power, laying ground for the claim that they cannot be discriminatory when they are also subject to discrimination. This skewed perception equally allows white gay men to theoretically conceptualize themselves as equivalent to the Orient as a sexual Other, which further provides justification for them to exercise gay sexual racism.

The implications of white gay men's perception of their power and sexuality is manyfold. As social epidemiologist and physician Camara P. Jones (2000) suggested, discrimination is a culmination of invisible levels of agency that interpret the power structure and its corresponding prototypes and ideological narratives. Jones theorized three levels through which discrimination is manifested: (a) at the systemic level, the society creates and maintains discriminatory narratives in its approach to multiculturalism and diversity, policies and services, as well as regulatory institutions; (b) at the personally mediated level, individuals with membership to the majority act as interpreters and agents of the system through their thoughts, beliefs, and comportment; and finally, (c) at the internal level, minorities who are the object of these discriminatory institutions and acts internalize them as factually reflective of who they genuinely are.

Gay Orientalism as a white oppressive institution also is manifest at these three levels. For example, white community and governmental organizations actively interpret the psychic life of colonial heroism and gay sexual racism at an international and systemic level, even if they may have benevolent intent. Political scientist and professor Joseph Massad (2002) argued that the problematics of the universalization of gay rights and the proliferation of gay international organizations to advocate and defend these rights in "areas in need" were rooted in Orientalist views of the Middle East. Massad further contended that organizations such as the International Lesbian and Gay Association (ILGA) and the International Gay and Lesbian Human Rights Commission (IGLHRC), referred to as the "Gay International" by Massad, were largely dominated by white Western men with the mandate "to liberate Arab and Muslim 'gays and lesbians' from the oppression under which they allegedly live" (362).

For Massad, the Gay International's mission revealed its assumption that the repression of gay sexuality in the Middle East was a function of Islamic intolerance and fear of organized sexuality (Massad 2002), which is consistent with Orientalist understanding that Islamic beliefs were aggressive, inhumane, irrational to personal rights, and in need of modernization (Said 1978). As with the oil industry, the West invented a nonexistent sexual repression to intervene and attack Arab and Muslim sexual discourses as underdeveloped (Massad 2002, 363; Sabsay 2012). As I mentioned previously, the homonationalistic antagonization of the Orient has politicized same-gender behaviors in these Middle Eastern countries, which inevitably alienates and dislocates the sexual citizenship of those who did not wish to be assimilated into this identity (Massad 2002, 363; Sabsay 2012).

A compulsory Western gay identity is also entrenched in the policies and legislations in Western countries in immigration and employment for Eastern gay men, an artefact that contradicts the Gay International's efforts to promote global gay freedom and equality. For one, even though the West claims that sexual orientation and gender identity can be grounds for seeking refuge, sexual and gender minority refugee claimants in Western countries often face heightened scrutiny through the vetting process (Fassin and Salcedo 2015; Lee and Brotman 2011). Western countries such as Australia, Canada, the United Kingdom, and the United States require that refugee claimants prove the genuineness of their claim, which involves demonstrating reasonable evidence of the cause of persecution in their home country and the consequent imminent danger for their safety (Morgan 2006).

In other words, sexual and gender minority refugee claimants of color would need to testify that they are "gay enough" before a potentially racist and homophobic immigration officer in the West. As such, sexual and gender minority refugee claimants of color in these Western countries may resort to conforming to gay Orientalism where they are forced to describe themselves in an essentialist identity narrative that reflects Western gay stereotypes, and their home countries in colonialist imagery, to substantiate their credibility as a bona fide gay refugee (Berg and Millbank 2009; Heller 2009; Lee and Brotman 2011; Morgan 2006). Evidently, not only does so-called gay equality and freedom fail to protect sexual and gender minorities from persecution, but it also further reinforces the gay Orientalist narratives that occlude and make invisible their genuine experiences and agency.

The coercive nature of the gay Orientalist identity also affects couples in same-gender marriages. Immigrating partners from the East in same-gender binational relationships and marriages may often feel forced to immigrate to the West because of the lack of recognition in their home country and the legitimacy of the gay identity in the West (Nakamura, Kassan, and Suehn 2017). Once immigrated, these gay men from the East experience a heightened level of psychosocial distress because of racially motivated exclusion by the local gay community, as well as incomplete employment acceptance and protection for same-gender couples in society at large (Cheng et al., forthcoming; Nakamura, Kassan, and Suehn 2017).

The gay Orientalist narratives of heroism and conquest are also interpreted and enacted at the interpersonal level. This phenomenon is particularly exemplified by white gay men's travels to East and West Asia. Gay tourism promotes the globalization of white gay consumerism and desire, as travelers hold strong beliefs about the sexual minority identities and behaviors at home and what to expect at their destinations (Collins 2009; Puar 2002). With these gay Orientalist ideals, white gay tourists are able to facilitate the construction of their own white gay identity through escaping home restrictions and accessing homonormative spaces overseas (Collins 2009; Hughes 1997; Puar 2002).

In studying white gay expatriates' experiences in Manila, the Philippines, Dana Collins (2009) clarified how white gay men believed they could leave the heteronormative and heterosexist regulations in the West and not be subjected to the social control of the Eastern host country given their transient foreigner existence. Indeed, Westerners live in an Orientalist bubble that separates them from the host culture, and watch through a voyeuristic looking glass that creates an urban sexual place where they lived and exoticized the local Asian men, without having to renounce their home identity (Collins 2009; Lary 2006). Collins also found that these white gay men felt entitled to use their foreignness to increase sexual attention and desirability by relying on the gay Orientalist construction of Asian men's submission to and attraction for Western gay masculinities.

Some scholars have suggested that white gay men who are specifically attracted to Far Eastern Asians, often referred to as *rice queens*, may be disenfranchised as unattractive and disloyal in white gay institutions given their lack of desire for white partners (Daroya 2013; Jackson 2000; Rafalow, Feliciano, and Robnett 2017). As such, by molding their Far Eastern Asian hosts and host countries in their own imagination, and by transposing the hyposexualization of Far Eastern Asian men in the West to the East, white gay men expatriated in the East build an expatriate persona that conquers the East through sexual exploitation; they reassert the racial power dynamics that exist in their home countries, and escape the image of a powerless traitor.

As white gay men perpetuate the myth of Far Eastern Asian men as passive actors in sexual and romantic relationships to regain power and popularity, Ghassan Moussawi (2013) put forward a similar modus operandi for white gay men in the Middle East. Moussawi described the rise of fame for Beirut as a gay tourist destination as related to the gay Orientalist representation that the Middle East presents a simultaneous ambiguity for gay experience that is safe but dangerous, glamorous but war-torn and unprogressive.

Indeed, Beirut's existence in the Middle East as a legitimate white space is affirmed given its compliance to homonationalistic ideology and the Western ideals of sexual acceptance and freedom of gay people (Moussawi 2013; Puar 2006). However, what makes the Middle East more thrilling than the Far East sexually is that white gay men can revive the narrative of colonial heroism in exhibiting extraordinary courage to embrace danger and mystery in the Middle East. After all, the endurance and conquest of unknown and dangerous sexuality are the ultimate proof of white masculinity (Ward 2015), the delineation of which not only allows the continuity of white gay masculine hegemony, but also legitimizes the place of gayness in white heterosexuality.

RECLAIMING GAY ORIENTALISM

While I have suggested through previous passages that white gay men continue to be holders and enactors of a gay Orientalist legacy, the larger Asian gay community and its member groups can also be its active interpreters. Indeed, Asian members of gay communities can act on the intimate knowledge and experiences they have of being the Other and being objects of gay Orientalism. Within these Oriental narratives of gay Orientalism, the gay Orientalist *us versus them* dichotomy is similarly produced: there are Asian men who conform to and enforce gay Orientalism, while others range from silent dissent to active resistance.

As I discussed in the previous section, white gay men are attracted by the sexual mystique of the East and impose their gay Orientalist desires through personal travels to, and residence in, the East. Gay Far Eastern Asian men are also consistently portrayed as youthful, naïve, and effeminate bottoms whose function is to be sexually objectified and penetrated for the sole pleasure of dominant white tops (Daroya 2013; Nguyen 2014). Clearly, sexuality is at the forefront of the experiences of gay Orientalism, not only because white gayness is always co-defined by sexuality, but also because the West has historically been sexually intrigued by the East (Halperin 1995; Said 1978).

Over time, it may appear that Asian gay men of various ethnicities have accepted and subscribed to the white narrative of gay Orientalism to affirm and protect their sexual experiences within their legacy cultures. A search on Google quickly reveals a plethora of gay organizations that cater to the rights and socialization of Asian gay men across the globe, as well as personal dating profiles that endorse stereotypical and static criteria of an Orientalist gay identity. Despite the colonialist and apparent objectification, messages like "submissive Asian bottom looking for dominant white daddy" or "muscular and virile Arab for your sexual fantasy" on dating profiles exemplify the many Asian men who conform to gay Orientalist narratives and are like the model Asian gays as prescribed by the West.

The acceptance of such an oppressive narrative is likely partially sponsored by the congruence of racialization and colorism within Asian cultures. There is an internal version of Orientalism in the East that assumes a natural hierarchy where Asians with lighter skin, namely East Asians, are superior to ethnicities with darker skin, such as South, Southeast, and West Asians (Lary 2006). Asians with lighter skin are associated with the upper class and seen as more beautiful, intelligent, and fortunate, while Asians with darker skin are associated with the working class, uncivilized, and undesirable (Chanbonpin 2015; Rondilla and Spickard 2007). Many Asians strive to be white to either maintain or gain higher status; in actuality, it is encouraged that people avoid the sun at all costs and use whitening products to lighten skin tone (Chanbonpin 2015; Rondilla and Spickard 2007, 1–2).

For some Asian gay men, both in the East and in the West, internalizing Orientalist messages can be analogous to the way Asians attempt to climb the colorist ladder. Their subscription to gay Orientalism not only transforms their sexual and racial experience into a defined and visible identity that has legitimacy in the superior white society, but it also provides an opportunity to ascend to higher social and economic status via the Model Minority Myth and the attention from the white gay men who desire them.

With that said, recent scholarship has provided evidence for a need to reinterpret these apparent narratives of internalized gay Orientalism. Media scholars and professors Maxime Cervulle and Nick Rees-Roberts (2008) examined the transition from an Orientalist to a postcolonial pornography production in France. Cervulle and Rees-Roberts focused on the release from a studio with a Maghrebi French founder, Citébeur, whose mission was to revolutionize the self-presentation of French men of Maghrebi origin to provide a counter-discourse to a gay Orientalist gaze of white gay culture. To empower Maghrebi French men, Citébeur's films subtly alter the gay Orientalist narrative and power structure through parodying stereotypical cues attributed to Arab men, such as hypersexuality, aggressiveness, and barbarity, against the backdrop of recognizable French territories and surroundings (Cervulle and Rees-Roberts 2008). Not only does this agentic change force white gay consumers to repatriate their Orientalist imagery of Arab men from the Orient back to their home, it also uses the resources of these white gay observers to fund more organic portrayals of Arab men (Cervulle and Rees-Roberts 2008).

There is also some evidence to suggest that Far Eastern Asian gay men use a similar strategy to subvert gay Orientalism as a viable tool of imperial control. Han (2015) echoed the power of storytelling as a way for Asian gay men to expose the myth of gay Orientalism and to regain the ability to use counter-narratives to shape their own racial and sexual experiences. For example, Han noted that Kim Chi on season 8 of *Ru-Paul's Drag Race* actively infused narratives of her heritage culture, such as anime and Korean pop references, as well reclaiming ascriptions of fatness, femmeness, and Asianness as a genuine experience and expression for her being (Kornhaber 2016). This form of agency negates the Occident's ability to assign identities and narratives to the Orient and undermines the Occident's identity as it loses its Other to help define itself.

Far Eastern gay men also reappropriate gay Orientalism in the social and sexual spheres. In a qualitative study about sexual minority men of color and their experiences of racism on Grindr, researchers found that Asian men overwhelming reported that they used the phenomenon of *no rice, no curry, no spice* and other forms of ethnoracial objectification and rejection as a sorting strategy on their journey of sexual agency and discovery on geolocational mobile dating applications (Cheng, Sandil, and Breslow 2015). These Asian participants used sexually racist messages to sieve out undesirable partners and used sexually objectifying messages to identify partners from whom they could gain what they want, including monetary and sexual favors; they explained that this process allowed them to use the white gay men's Orientalist desire as a mean to control the interactions that happen between them (Cheng, Sandil, and Breslow 2015).

Beyond Asian gay men in the West, resistance to gay Orientalist identity and discourse can also be witnessed in the East. For example, Taiwanese scholar Pei Jean Chen (2006) discussed that introducing direct linguistic transliteration of the Western queer terminology is problematic because not only do these terms have no locally invested sociohistorical context, but they also inevitably reinforce the Orient's need to mimic their colonizer's culture. The gay community in Taiwan has largely chosen to retain culturally significant terms for self-expression, and has innovated terms such as *rayray* (from a corrupted form of *gay*), as a way to bridge Eastern and Western gay culture (Chen 2006; Zhongtian Television, 2014).

CONCLUSION

In this chapter I endeavored to introduce gay Orientalism as a form of imperially established sexual racism that seeks to objectify and narrate the lives of Asian gay men through a Eurocentric and heterosexist interpretation of the relationship between the racial norm and the Other. I wanted to emphasise the importance of understanding gay Orientalism as a superlative construct both in its intersectional and metasocial nature. Gay Orientalism is more than just a concoction of two ideas; it is a ubiquitous, timeless, and intelligent system of power and oppression with a psychic life of its own that has the capacity to independently change and adapt to serve the interests of the oligarchical white European cultures, as Riggs and Augoustinos (2005) proposed.

While existing beyond us, gay Orientalism is an integrated product of the racist, heterosexist, hegemonic masculine, and colonialist narrative that we live and participate in. As Crenshaw (1989) suggested, we must recognise issues arising at the crossroads of identity and experiences if we want to dismantle a system of differential power assignment based on multiple social identities and experiences. As scholars and activists, I sincerely hope that we can use the information in this chapter to help us be conscious of how our own identities and experiences can interact with each other and those around us to create difficulties and blind spots to better address and advance our social justice efforts to combating sexual racism and other forms of discrimination

REFERENCES

Berg, Laurie, and Jenni Millbank. 2009. "Constructing the Personal Narratives of Lesbian, Gay and Bisexual Asylum Claimants." *Journal of Refugee Studies* 22 (2): 195–223.

Bérubé, Allan. 2001. "How Gay Stays White and What Kind of White it Stays." In *The Making and Unmaking of Whiteness*, edited by Birgit Brander Rasmussen, Eric Klinenberg, Irene J. Nexica, and Matt Wray, 234–65. Durham, NC: Duke University Press.

Butler, Judith. 2003. "Critically Queer." *GLQ: A Journal of Lesbian and Gay Studies* 1 (1): 17–32.

Cervulle, Maxime, and Nick Rees-Roberts. 2008. "Queering the Orientalist Porn Package: Arab Men in French Gay Pornography." *New Cinemas: Journal of Contemporary Film* 6 (3): 197–208.

Chanbonpin, Kim D. 2015. "Between Black and White: The Coloring of Asian Americans." *Washington University Global Studies Law Review* 14 (4): 609–36.

Chen, Pei Jean 陳佩甄, 2006. "Taiwan tongzhilunshu zhong de wenhua fanyi yu ku'er shengcheng" 台灣同志論述中的文化翻譯與酷兒生成 [Cultural Translation and

Queer Formations of Homosexual Discourses in Taiwan]. Master's diss. National Chiao Tung University.

Cheng, Cliff. 1996. "'We Choose Not To Compete': The 'Merit' Discourse in the Selection Process, and Asian and Asian American Men and Their Masculinity." In *Masculinities in Organizations*, by Cliff Cheng, 177–200. Thousand Oaks, CA: Sage Publications.

Cheng, Hsiu-Lan, Ryon C. McDermott, Y. Joel Wong, and Susanna La. 2016. "Drive for Muscularity in Asian American Men: Sociocultural and Racial/Ethnic Factors as Correlates." *Psychology of Men & Masculinity* 17 (3): 215–27.

Cheng, Jacks, Elyssa M. Klann, Nelson O. O. Zounlome, and Y. Barry Chung. Forthcoming. "Promoting Affirmative Career Development and Work Environment for LGBT Individuals." In *Psychology of Career Adaptability, Employability and Resilience*, edited by Jacobus G. Maree. Dordrecht: Springer.

Cheng, Jacks, Riddhi Sandil, and Aaron S. Breslow. 2015. "'No Fried Chicken, Tacos, Rice, or Curry!': The Experiences of Men of Color on Grindr." Presentation at the Annual Convention of the American Psychological Association, Toronto, ON, August 6–9.

Cho, Wancy Young. 2016. "Vanilla Only: That's Right, No Rice, No Spice, No Chocolate, No Curry." *Salon.* November 14. http://www.salon.com/2016/11/14/vanilla-only-thats-right-no-rice-no-spice-no-chocolate-no-curry/.

Chomsky, Noam. 2009. "The Unipolar Moment and the Culture of Imperialism." Lecture, Edward Said Memorial Lecture, Columbia University, New York, December 3.

Chua, Peter, and Dune C. Fujino. 1999. "Negotiating New Asian-American Masculinities: Attitudes and Gender Expectations." *The Journal of Men's Studies* 7 (3): 391–413.

Collins, Dana. 2009. "'We're There and Queer': Homonormative Mobility and Lived Experience among Gay Expatriates in Manila." *Gender & Society* 23 (4): 465–93.

Crenshaw, Kimberlé. 1989. "Demarginalizing the Intersection of Race and Sex: A Black Feminist Critique of Antidiscrimination Doctrine, Feminist Theory and Antiracist Politics." *University of Chicago Legal Forum* 140: 139–67.

Daroya, Emerich. 2013. "Potatoes and Rice: Exploring the Racial Politics of Gay Men's Desires and Desirability." *Critical Race and Whiteness Studies* 9 (2): 1–13.

Donnelly, Beau. 2016. "Gay Minorities Speak Out Against Racists [sic] Slurs on Grindr." *The Sydney Morning Herald.* April 18. http://www.smh.com.au/national/gay-aboriginal-man-publishes-racist-slurs-on-dating-app-20160418-go8zov.html.

Fassin, Eric, and Manuela Salcedo. 2015. "Becoming Gay? Immigration Policies and the Truth of Sexual Identity." *Archives of Sexual Behaviors* 44: 1117–25.

Hajek, Christopher. 2012. "Communications and Identities Characterized by Male Sexual Orientation." In *The Handbook of Intergroup Communication*, edited by Howard Giles, 211–22. New York, NY: Routledge.

Halperin, David M. 1995. *Saint Foucault: Towards a Gay Hagiography.* New York: Oxford University Press.

Han, C. Winter. 2015. *Geisha of a Different Kind: Race and Sexuality in Gaysian America.* New York: New York University Press.

Heller, Pamela. 2009. "Challenges Facing LGBT Asylum-Seekers: The Role of Social Work in Correcting Oppressive Immigration Processes." *Journal of Gay & Lesbian Social Services* 21 (2–3): 294–308.

Hughes, Howard. 1997. "Holidays and Homosexual Identity." *Tourism Management* 18 (1): 3–7.

Iwamoto, Derek Kenji, and William Ming Liu. 2009. "Asian American Men and Asianized Attribution: Intersections of Masculinity, Race, and Sexuality." In *Asian American Psychology: Current Perspectives*, edited by Nita Tewari and Alvin N. Alvarez, 211–32. New York: Routledge.

Jackson, Peter A. 2000. "'That's What Rice Queens Study!' White Gay Desire and Representing Asian Homosexualities." *Journal of Australian Studies* 24 (65): 181–88.

Jones, Camara Phyllis. 2000. "Levels of Racism: A Theoretic Framework and a Gardener's Tale." *American Journal of Public Health* 90 (8): 1212–15.

Jones, Owen. 2016. "No Asians, No Black People. Why Do Gay People Tolerate Blatant Racism?" *The Guardian*. November 24. https://www.theguardian.com/comment isfree/2016/nov/24/no-asians-no-blacks-gay-people-racism.

Kornhaber, Spencer. 2016. "The Fierceness of 'Femme, Fat, and Asian.'" *The Atlantic*. May 19. https://www.theatlantic.com/entertainment/archive/2016/05/kim-chi-rupauls-drag-race-femme-fat-asian-c-winter-han-interview-middlebury/483527/.

Kreutz, Andrej. 2007. *Russia in the Middle East: Friend or Foe?* Westport, CT: Praeger Security International.

Lary, Diana. 2006. "Edward Said: Orientalism and Occidentalism." *Journal of the Canadian Historical Association* 17 (2): 3–15.

Lee, Edward Ou Jin, and Shari Brotman. 2011. "Identity, Refugeeness, Belonging: Experiences of Sexual Minority Refugees in Canada." *Candian Review of Sociology/ Revue canadienne de sociologie* 48 (3): 241–74.

Little, Douglas. 2008. *American Orientalism: The United States and the Middle East Since 1945*. Chapel Hill: University of North Carolina Press.

Liu, Tao, and Y. Joel Wong. 2016. "The Intersection of Race and Gender: Asian American Men's Experience of Discrimination." *Psychology of Men & Masculinity* Advance Online Publication. doi: 10.1037/men0000084.

Marchetti, Gina. 1993. *Romance and the "Yellow Peril": Race, Sex, and Discursive Strategies in Hollywood Fiction*. Berkeley: University of California Press.

Massad, Joseph Andoni. 2002. "Re-Orienting Desire: The Gay International and the Arab World." *Public Culture* 14 (2): 361–85.

Mepschen, Paul, Jan Willem Duyvendak, and Evelien H. Tonkens. 2010. "Sexual Politics, Orientalism and Multicultural Citizenship in the Netherlands." *Sociology* 44 (5): 962–79.

Moradi, Bonnie, Cirleen DeBlaere, and Yu-Ping Huang. 2010. "Centralizing the Experiences of LGB People of Color in Counseling Psychology." *The Counseling Psychologist* 38 (3): 322–30.

Morgan, Deborah A. 2006. "Not Gay Enough for the Government: Racial and Sexual Stereotypes in Sexual Orientation Asylum Cases." *Law & Sexuality: Review of Lesbian, Gay, Bisexual & Transgender Legal Issues* 15: 135–75.

Moussawi, Ghassan. 2013. "Queering Beirut, the 'Paris of the Middle East': Fractal Orientalism and Essentialized Masculinities in Contemporary Gay Travelogues." *Gender, Place and Culture* 20 (7): 858–75.

Nakamura, Nadine, Anusha Kassan, and Megan Suehn. 2017. "Resilience and Migration: Experiences of Same-Sex Binational Couples in Canada." *Journal of Gay & Lesbian Social Services* 29 (2): 201–19.

Nguyen, Tan Hoang. 2014. *A View from the Bottom: Asian American Masculinity and Sexual Representation*. Durham, NC: Duke University Press.

Puar, Jasbir K. 2002. "Circuits of Queer Mobility: Tourism, Travel, and Globalization." *GLQ: A Journal of Lesbian and Gay Studies* 8 (1): 101–37.

———. 2006. "Mapping US Homonormativities." *Gender, Place and Culture* 13 (1): 67–88.

Rafalow, Matthew H., Cynthia Feliciano, and Belinda Robnett. 2017. "Racialized Femininity and Masculinity in the Preferences of Online Same-sex Daters." *Social Currents* 4 (4): 1–16.

Rahman, Momin. 2014. "Queer Rights and the Triangulation of Western Exceptionalism." *Journal of Human Rights* 13 (3): 274–89.

Riggs, Damien W., and Martha Augoustinos. 2005. "The Psychic Life of Colonial Power: Racialised Subjectivities, Bodies, and Methods." *Journal of Community and Applied Social Psychology* 15 (6): 461–77.

Rondilla, Joanne L., and Paul Spickard. 2007. *Is Lighter Better?: Skin-Tone Discrimination among Asian Americans*. Lanham, MD: Rowman & Littlefield.

Rupiah, Kiri. 2016. "No Fats, No Femmes, No Blacks: The Unbearable Racism of Grindr in South Africa." *Mail & Guardian*. November 2. https://mg.co.za/article/

2016-11-02-no-fats-no-femmes-no-blacks-the-unbearable-racism-of-grindr-in-south-africa.

Sabsay, Leticia. 2012. "The Emergence of the Other Sexual Citizen: Orientalism and the Modernisation of Sexuality." *Citizenship Studies* 16 (5–6): 605–23.

Said, Edward W. 1978. *Orientalism*. New York: Pantheon Books.

Shim, Doobo. 1998. "From Yellow Peril through Model Minority to Renewed Yellow Peril." *Journal of Communication Inquiry* 22 (4): 385–409.

Sue, Stanley, and Harry H. L. Kitano. 1973. "Stereotypes as a Measure of Success." *Journal of Social Issues* 29 (2): 83–98.

Ward, Jane. 2008. "White Normativity: The Cultural Dimensions of Whiteness in a Racially Diverse LGBT Organization." *Sociological Perspectives* 51 (3): 563–86.

———. 2015. *Not Gay: Sex Between Straight White Men*. New York: New York University Press.

Zhongtian Television. "2014.03.25 Daxueshenglemei wanzhenban wobushi rayray yebushi nansheng! Kuaxingbiezhe de xinsuanxielei" 2014.03.25大學生了沒完整版我不是RAYRAY也不是男生！跨性別者的心酸血淚 [2014.03.25 Are you a college student yet full version I am not rayray nor a boy! The blood and tears of trans people]. YouTube video, 44:59, March 25, 2014.

FOUR

Homonationalism and Failure to Interpellate

The "Queer Muslim Woman" in Ontario's "Sex-Ed Debates"

Sonny Dhoot

Where are queers of color within the queer times of *homonationalism*?[1] Scholarship grounded in Jasbir Puar's (2007) framework of homonationalism has interrogated queer praxes that collaborate with state racism and other structures of violence, particularly how white queers secure life through participation in violence against non-white populations, but what of the unique and varying locations of queers of color specifically? Within analyses of homonationalism there remains a need to theorize under what new conditions queers of color, across different locations, are located within recently queer-friendly nations, as well as how these locations can both be vastly uneven and produce antagonisms between queers of color in the name of inclusion. This chapter is a modest contribution to locate some queers of color in the discussion of Canadian homonationalism, particularly as they intersect with questions about the psychic power of interpellation.

Following with the spirit of this collection, my chapter actively pursues the psychic and affective processes under homonationalism, while actively locating queers of color in the discussion. I contend that within queers of color's interpellation into economies of homonationalism, they sustain a psychic blow of homonormative racial power. I question how queer Muslims, queer Muslim women in particular, are *differently* interpellated by homonationalism, and what happens to queer Muslims who fail to be interpellated properly. To read this question more open-endedly, this chapter seeks to answer what might theorization of the psychic life of homonationalism look like? While discussions have clearly attended to the affective mappings of homonationalism, less has been said about the interpellative affects of homonationalism. I take up this point by reading the locations and nonappearances of queer Muslim women within Canadian homonationalism.

My discussion is grounded in the Canadian context, and as I elaborate in the following section on homonationalism, I situate homonationalism as a project aligned to Canadian racial projects of citizenship, borders/detention and the foundational settler logic itself. "Nationalism" should not be read as substitute for "racism"; rather, nationalism advances racisms, particularly nationalist articulations attached to the racial power of the state, police, and military violence, including the racial logics of *border imperialism* (i.e., detention, deportation, and dispossession/occupation) (Walia 2013). This chapter pays close attention to Orientalism as it connects with other modalities of power, particularly with relevance to reading across queer Muslim diasporas.

My analysis focuses on protests that began in 2015 (continuing into 2016) in response to the province of Ontario's unveiling of an updated Health and Physical Education Curriculum. Pulling from both LGBT and mainstream media sources (with a mixture of left- and right-leaning news sources), I analyze a variety of politician, activist, and academic commentaries. Though I focus on Canadian homonationalism, this chapter has broad implications for other "western" states, especially other white settler states such as Australia, Israel, and the US. I situate the analysis of Canadian homonationalism as inflected simultaneously by multiple racial logics and anxieties, much of which seems to be a trajectory or extension of Canadian multiculturalism, which I expand on in the following section where I briefly contextualize homonationalism within the Canadian state. The second section examines how the debates over the curriculum moved from discussions about the province's conservative political party and its use of homophobia to a shift and convergence with Islamophobic and xenophobic homonational iterations of so-called "Muslim homophobia." I then move to consider what a properly interpellated non-white queer subject looks like within the homonormative nation; in particular, I examine the conditions for which queer Muslims may gain status as legible subjects under homonationalism. Lastly, I consider what the subject positions of queer Muslim women are who "fail" proper homonormative interpellation. Borrowing from Gayatri Gopinath's (2005) work, I consider how the queer Muslim woman, as located within multiple diasporas, becomes unthinkable and unintelligible but also disruptive within homonationalism due to her multiple locations and failure to defer to homonational narratives of Islamic incompatibility with queerness, wherein queerness stands as the marker of (sexual) modernity. The intent of this discussion is to locate queer women of color subjectivities within discussions of homonationalism, partly because of their frequent absence but also to offer a critique of activist and queer practices that collaborate with homonationalism. I undertake this by reading queer Muslim women into the moment of ethnic and queer liberalism that attempts to demarcate them as unintelligible. As I will discuss, the queer Muslim woman serves as one subject who disrupts and reveals the limitations of inclusion proffered by twin constellations of state power: multiculturalism and homonationalism.

Two notes on praxes. While I occasionally used the term "queers of color" above, I actively break up this term in my discussion. Although politically useful, this moniker can be reductive or deceptive in intersectional analytics between differently racialized queers of color—particularly when dis/articulating differently located queers of color in their vastly uneven locations, shifting over time and across events, within homonationalism. Second, though I write specifically of queer Muslim women's locations within homonationalism, I do so as a non-Muslim queer (Sikh) man. Writing from this position, I want to reinforce my purpose is not to narrate queer Muslim women's lives or describe the psychic interiority of their experiences. My discussion is meant to disturb the racial, gendered, and national parameters of inclusion within homonationalism, and simultaneously center questions about queer Muslim women's absent subjectivity within discussions of Canadian homonationalism and queer politics broadly.

HOMONATIONALISM AND SEXUAL CITIZENSHIP

Taking up Jasbir Puar's (2007) theorization in *Terrorist Assemblages*, I use homonationalism to denote the collusion of gay and lesbian populations, interests, and politics with the nation-state via "bio-necro-political collaborations." These collaborations incorporate some gay and lesbian populations into the fold of the nation (sexual citizenship) through the cooperation with war on terror regimes, including surveillance, militarism, securitization, and the state's monopoly over violence to safeguard national life (Reddy 2011). For Puar this collusion is evidenced by the increase of US state and governmental collaborations with gay and lesbian rights politics parallel with the war on terror. This incorporation of some gay and lesbian bodies is produced via a (perversely) queer-racial counterpoint, the "terrorist-look-alikes" (Arab, Muslim, and turbaned Sikh men), who is marked for death in the name of national life-making.

Homonationalism does not refer to particular politics, activists, or persons who engage a "bad" or co-opted brand of queerness. Rather, homonationalism refers to an assemblage or matrix of affects, which is not escapable via "good politics" nor can queer sexual subjects transgress homonational temporalities, given all subjects are interpellated by homonationalism (Puar 2013). As I will demonstrate in the following section, non-heterosexual subjects are not all hailed in the same way, nor do they respond to this hailing in the same ways as queer locations cut across multiple axes—including citizenship, race, indigeneity, serostatus, mental health and dis/ability, legality of work (e.g., sex work), class location and housing in/security, gender-identity, and whether one is on the inside or outside of the prison—with some queer people themselves marked for death so the nation/al can live (Edelman 2014).

Grounding homonationalism within a particular national context is crucial to contextualize the operations and affects of homonationalism as they are nationally specific, and simultaneously shifting over time. This chapter's discussion of interpellation and networks of affects is grounded within Canadian homonational formations. The most comprehensive examination of Canadian homonationalism is perhaps located in the edited volume *Canadian Homonationalisms and the Politics of Belonging*. The editors of the volume, OmiSoore H. Dryden and Suzanne Lenon (2015, 5), trace Canadian homonationalisms as "predicated on foundational Canadian national mythologies that inscribe whiteness as the embodiments of legitimate citizenship and belonging." This line of thinking expands earlier theorizations by anti-racist feminists, such as Sunera Thobani and Himani Bannerji, and diaspora scholars, in particular Rinaldo Walcott, who have extensively demonstrated how Canada has continuously produced itself in the eyes of the global community and its own (white) national populace to be tolerant, accepting, and inclusive via its official multiculturalism policy and liberalism, despite Canada remaining structured by settler colonial practices of belonging and racist institutions of citizenship.

While multiculturalism is often touted as progressive and inclusive, such interpretations prevail through a national amnesia. As an official policy, it was a response to 1970s anti-racist organizing, economic demands for labor, and global shifts towards postcolonialism (Thobani 2007, 145–47). The policy also follows from prior foundational structures and logics including the 1876 Indian Act preceded by centuries of Indigenous land dispossession and the disavowal of a Black presence that predates Canadian confederation dating back to Upper and Lower Canada's involvement in slavery. The multicultural project of ethnic inclusion has continued to exist alongside Canada's maintenance of a white national identity, marked as distinctly English and French in origin. State multiculturalism has largely sought to prop up select heterosexual males within various *cultural* communities as representatives. These heteropatriarchal figures have acquired national legitimacy to discipline and police community members and values vis-à-vis a multicultural heteronormativity, whereby ethnic subjects gain national legibility through sexual-straightening secured through the nuclear family and immigrant labor. Puar does consider how capitalist markets leave room (albeit often out of necessity) for varying kinship structures that deviate from heteronormativity. Despite these considerations, I would move to suggest that subjects at the negative confluence of gender, race, sexuality, and class (particularly, Indigenous and diasporic queer and trans women) are seen simultaneously through the market, nation, and mainstream queer politics as "wasted life" (Bauman 2004) within "sexual modernity" (see also Ferguson 2004); that is, as failing to achieve normative class, racial, gender, and sexual affiliations.

The rise of Canadian homonationalism fuses to the aforementioned foundational white settler matrix of Canadian belonging rather than apart from it. This marks an (homonormative) ascendancy of whiteness for gay and lesbian populations to become incorporated into the nation's life-making practices (marriage, juridical/carceral protection, and health care), which not only excludes Indigenous, Black, and particular migrant populations from life-making, but targets them for death often through their spatialization, into what Achille Mbembe (2003) calls "death worlds," such as prisons, detention centers, reservations and other ghettoized areas, and deportation sites, undertaken for the securitization of the nation's border and defense of the citizenry's life. But as recent scholarship on queer necropolitics has noted, queer and trans people of color are also pushed into death worlds alongside their non-white heterosexual and cisgender counterparts, to produce and secure life-making chances for white (settler) queers (see Haritaworn, Kuntsman, and Posocco's 2014 *Queer Necropolitics*).

While this chapter is only able to focus on one facet of homonationalism and interpellation, Canadian homonationalism performs an interpellative function for homonormative subjects distinctly linked to multiculturalism through three intersecting sites: cultural recognition in lieu of sovereignty and continued dispossession for Indigenous peoples; inclusion and celebration of some im/migrants while maintaining strict border controls against migrants marked as "threats" and participation in imperial ventures narrated as democratic (e.g., Somalia and Afghanistan); and nostalgia of the Underground Railroad as a disavowal of a Black presence in Canada, including Canada's history of slavery and persisting violence against Black communities.[2] The remainder of this chapter explores how homonationalism interpellates (or fails to interpellate) queer Muslim women, and how the queer Muslim woman is situated within homonationalism (multiculturalism).

"SEX-ED" DEBATES

In late February 2015 debates arose over the province of Ontario's updated Health and Physical Education Curriculum (hereafter HPEC), dubbed by media, politicians, and protestors the "Sex-Ed Curriculum." Initial controversy stemmed from the province's oppositional party, the Progressive Conservatives, who objected to the new curriculum unveiled under the Liberal Party (a center-left party). Much of these earlier debates were laced with homophobia directed at the Liberal government's leader Kathleen Wynne who was identified in the media as an "out lesbian." On February 24, 2015, Progressive Conservative MPP Monte McNaughton was accused of inciting homophobic hysteria over the HPEC during a legislative proceeding when he indicated that Liberal premier Wynne was "especially" unqualified for producing the new HPEC proposal, without an explanation for why she was unqualified. The following day McNaughton denied that homophobia was behind his specific concerns about Wynne, but remained ambiguous about what his concerns with Wynne were. The same day, he and another Progressive Conservative MPP spoke at a demonstration against the new HPEC; the other speakers included a member of the Catholic parents' group and the Ontario Campaign Life Coalition. The Ontario Campaign Life Coalition is most well known as a vocal anti-abortionist group but became a vocal "Christian family" opposition to the proposed HPEC. On the organization's website there is statement titled "Ontario's Radical Sex Ed Curriculum," which details "Christian"/"Catholic" concerns about HPEC's promotion of homosexuality, anal and oral sex, HIV and STI information, and pedophilia (Campaign Life Coalition n.d.). At the demonstration where these groups and MPPs spoke, protestors frequently associated Wynne with homosexuality and pedophilia in interviews and on posters (see CTV 2015).

In the following weeks, several HPEC conservative critics pointed to the involvement of Benjamin Levin in creating the new HPEC. Levin was once an acclaimed education professor at the University of Toronto who in 2013 was arrested on child pornography charges. Many HPEC critics often drew ambiguous parallels between homosexuality and pedophilia. For example, during a March 2015 interview, MPP McNaughton characterized his own and his constituency's concerns with the HPEC in the following way: "This [Levin] is a convicted criminal who was very close to this Premier [Wynne], played a huge role in the 2010 curriculum. There are well-documented details about that" (Watson 2015). While specific concerns remained ambiguous by McNaughton and conservative commentators, the association of Wynne with Levin played into conservative fears of the sexual exploitation of children by (sexual) deviants, which drew pedophilia and homosexuality together as joint concerns.

Despite Christian conservatives and fundamentalists leading the HPEC protests, much of the media engagement on the matter, including Toronto's LGBT media *Daily Xtra* which interviewed McNaughton, paid little attention to Christians, white conservatives, or the Progressive Conservative government's mobilization during the HPEC frenzy. By the onset of May 2015 public protests to the curriculum continued, but media attention had completely shifted from mild concerns about government conservatives and Christian groups to new and distinct concerns over the (sexual) backwardness and conservativism of Muslim migrants. The shift also marked a discursive change from a debate between conservatism and liberalism into what the National Post called a "multicultural affair" (Selley 2015). These discursive shifts revitalized economies of Orientalism and Islamophobia.

Despite obvious contradictions in the dominant narrative of homophobic and sexually primitive Muslims versus secular Canadians and "inclusive" Christians, the debates were used to refuel a Huntington-style "clash of civilization" narrative hinged on racialized discourses of sexual modernity. For instance, David Rayside, a Director Emeritus of Sexual Diversity Studies and political scientist at the University of Toronto, commented on the debates that "there is a somewhat stronger current of what we might call *family traditionalism among Muslims*," elaborating further that "the vast majority of Canadian Muslims are first generation, and *they come from very traditional parts of the world*" (Selley 2015, emphasis added). Such an account dehistoricizes the HPEC, eliding Christian conservative responses that delayed the curriculum dating back to the province's previous leadership. When articles referenced homophobia at protests it was within articles about Muslim protestors, linking Muslims and homophobia, thus eliding an interrogation of the long-standing Christian ideologies embedded within primary education curricula, the opposition Progressive Conservative party, and the nation itself.

In naming the opposition to the curriculum as a Muslim problem, a web of homonational affects was produced, whereby politician, academic, and (white) LGBT responses recreated a "clash of civilization" frame, mobilizing gay inclusion as a marker of sexual modernity that provided a dividing line to separate Canada as modern from the "very traditional parts of the world" where Muslims are said to come from. Such practices rely on what Jin Haritaworn (2015, 3) has called the new *queer regeneration*—an affect that produces "queer bodies [as] a lovely site in the shadow of racialised Others." In the era of homonationalism, the "homophobic Muslim" becomes the new "folk devil" (ibid.). Following Edward Said's theorization of Orientalism, during the HPEC debates Muslims were once again confronted with pathologizing knowledge of barbarism (homophobia) and sexual backwardness (against consent, safer sex practices, and basic knowledge of the body), perhaps most significantly as too traditional to be part of the nation, questions that were never once raised over the vocal white Christians, including those in office.

"NATIVE INFORMANTS" IN QUEER TIMES

Co-founder of the Safra Project, a group for lesbian, bisexual, and trans Muslim women in the UK, Tamsila Tauqir highlights a salient theme within conversations about sexuality and Islam where access to speaking is not necessarily afforded to those at the intersection of queer and Muslim:

> Authority to speak is a significant issue. Often the apologetics or non-Muslims are seen by the media as "impartial" enough to speak about Muslims but those of us in the movements are not seen as objective enough [. . .] we are seen as too controversial to be given a voice. This happens despite that fact that it is our organisation and similarly others which are embedded in the Muslim communities we work with [. . .] We are on the frontline when backlash comes after the whims and ignorance of others are often given voice in the media, it doesn't affect them as they're not part of the Muslim communities, but it affects us, our families, neighbours and community. (Tauqir n.d.)

As Tauqir notes, those deemed "outside" of Muslim communities are handed speaking positions and afforded legibility as credible sources, while queer Muslims are often ignored, particularly by media. Tauqir names this partly in the problematic frames of impartiality, objectivity, and controversy. Agreeing with these points, I want to consider what happens in these moments of rendering queer Muslim women as non-speaking subjects. And secondly, how queer Muslim women are necessarily unintelligible within nationalist and mainstream queer discourses, a point I will take up in the final section.

During the Ontario HPEC debates, queer and Muslim subjects were hailed by homonational discourses of sexual exceptionalism and Islamophobia, often through speaking positions. However, the outcomes of hailing are not predetermined as subjects are interpellated differently, and consequently different subjectivities are produced. During the debate, the frames of legibility for Muslim commentators became narrowed to one of either bad Muslims (traditional) or good Muslims (progressive) who respond to the bad Muslims' claims. The media coverage sought to interpellate queer, feminist, and otherwise HPEC-supporting Muslims into "native informants" — good Muslims worthy of national belonging who could replay the civilization narrative of Western modernity as well as shame "bad Muslims."

One commonly cited voice within Toronto who has been assigned authority to speak on the "problem" of Muslims is anonymous blogger Eiynah Mohammed-Smith, self-described as an "ex-Muslim atheist" "who writes and draws about sexuality in South Asia (mostly Pakistan), religion, politics, feminism, godlessness" (CBC 2016; Mohammed-Smith n.d.). A year after the HPEC debates began, she published for a local newspaper and was interviewed by the CBC (a national public radio and television network). She began her publication by declaring, "In my community, religious orthodoxy is violently lashing out. *Modernity*, science and internet-connectivity take us forward and water down strict adherence to religion—but they also trigger reactionary pushback" (Mohamed-Smith 2016, emphasis added). In a colloquial move, she declares herself an *ex*-Muslim but claims Islam as "my community," legitimating her insider knowledge over membership that she no longer claims. Reminiscent of orientalist authorship, she is not part of the problematic orientalized community, but instead claims insider knowledge establishing herself as a proper modern subject having rejected Islam for atheism. She runs through a list of issues with Muslims, including homophobia and HPEC rejection, but lastly, she ends her article by focusing on Muslim feminists who claim that wearing a hijab or niqab can be a feminist choice and declares the "hijab/niqab [. . .] a garment used exclusively in its original form to ensure women cover up lest they provoke the lust of men." While she starts by posing a "Liberal Muslim" critique of "religious orthodoxy," she concludes by admonishing Muslim feminists who do not follow the narrative that both the hijab and niqab are inherently oppressive patriarchal devices. Thus, she links the homophobic HPEC protestors with Muslim women who wear the hijab or niqab as a choice linked under the failure to adapt to modernity (along with "science and internet-connectivity").

In her interview with the CBC (2016), when asked whether Muslim children need "more" sex education than other students, Mohammed-Smith replies, "absolutely" and elaborating, "Some people thinking they're going to be harmed by masturbation, that it could lead to their death, some people don't understand what things can get them pregnant [. . .] teaching kids about consent, teaching them about preventing STDs, teaching them about preventing pregnancy" (quotation is retrieved from the audio not the edited transcription). Despite these items being prevalent in the Christian opposition, the narrative offered by Mohammed-Smith and the CBC pathologizes Muslims as disproportionately lacking knowledge about what masturbation, consent, pregnancy, or STIs are. In other words, the revised HPEC would serve to help educate Muslims into sexual modernity. Jasbir Puar (2007) notes a similar trope in the war on terror, whereby Muslims are depicted as sexually perverse and requiring intervention; in Canada, Muslims are represented as lacking an understanding of sexual education and thus in need of intervention.

In these rhetorical framings, conservativism (across religious and secular contexts) is exchanged for Muslims and Islam generally. "Muslim" and "conservative," to borrow from Sara Ahmed (2014, 98–99), become stuck together, whereby they become interchangeable, to the point that they become iterations of each other. Mohammed-Smith's position as a feminist and sexuality commentator, once on the inside of Islam, allows her to position herself as a *subaltern-queer-native-informant*. Despite not identifying as queer she is afforded credibility to inform a white Western audience of the violence queers face and the sexual knowledge lacking under Islam.

Groups such as Muslims for Ontario's Health and Physical Education that formed in support of the HPEC tended to not replay oriental scripts of good versus bad Muslims; however, liberal and LGBT media tended to either ignore the group or depict them as marginal Muslim voices of dissent within a larger homophobic Muslim world. While the HPEC debates are a recent event, a more well-known homonational interpellation occurred with the earlier international attention of Canadian lesbian author Irshad Manji. Acclaimed for her publication *The Trouble with Islam*, Manji became an authority in the media on Islam and what became its unique problems. While depicting Islam "today" as monolithically homophobic, misogynistic as well as anti-Semitic, she positioned herself as a reformist and outsider to Islam. Like Mohammed-Smith, she identified herself as close enough to the troubled religion that she could be called upon as an expert. Manji has often turned to white settler projects as superior and only minimally problematic, such as the white settler mythologies of Israeli Zionism and Canadian settler nationalism, as opposed to dominant Islamic interpretation which she positions as far more problematic (see Haritaworn, Tauqir, and Erdem 2008). Not to conflate these two figures, Manji sees herself as a liberal/reformist Muslim who publicly evokes her Muslim faith as part of her life and identity, which does critique some facets of homonationalism that view Islam and queerness as incompatible. However, the positioning of her queer-Muslim identity as unique has served to further make her exceptional as if no other queer Muslims exist or are capable to speak. Unlike other perspectives, Manji has gained notoriety across North America and Europe as the subaltern-queer-native-informant who could attest to Islam's backwardness and homophobia and the superiority of a progressive "west" (ibid.). Manji's popularity in both conservative and liberal circuits marked an earlier shift in interpellative power, at the onset homonationalism rooted in the war on terror; while both queer and a woman, questions of sexuality have gained primacy over gender with a focus on homophobia in Islam and her remarkable ability to reconcile a queer identity with Islamic faith.

With the HPEC debates, the figure of the dangerous Muslim extended beyond the Muslim man to heterosexual Muslims, including the Muslim woman. While less common during the height of Manji's popularity, during the HPEC debates a large portion of the media focus was on the figure of the migrant Muslim woman, as she appears more than the Muslim man as a representation of Islamic sexual backwardness. For instance, the *Toronto Star*'s coverage of the HPEC debates used more than once a provocative photograph of a Muslim woman in a niqab pushing a stroller with a child walking by her side as they passed a school, the school's exterior spray-painted with the words "shame on you," as a (white) staff member stands in front of the graffiti (see, for example, Rushowy 2015). The photograph reproduces the metonymic association of "Islam"—signified by the niqab wearing woman who has also become the "cultural excess" that tests the limits of multiculturalism—with homophobia, depicted through the graffiti supposedly aimed at the school for its support of the HPEC. The photograph also performs to pull the "veiled Muslim woman" from her location in orientalist iconography as a culpable subject of "Islamic patriarchy" in need of saving into a new location of (perverse) heterosexual barbarity and sexual backwardness. Linked with homophobic sexual perversity in resistance to the HPEC, and criminality (graffiti) to accomplish goals, the niqab wearing woman becomes a *terrorist* figure, or more aptly, the new folk-devil of Canadian homonationalism and queer modernity. This helped to shift a primacy of sexuality over gender as "the trouble with Islam."

In this section, by connecting Tamsila Tauqir's statement with Puar's theorization, I have extended theorizations of homonationalism to consider these modalities of power operating through economies of interpellation. First, I have contended that these modalities further cement an orientalist pathology and a homonational (queer necropolitical) narrative of the nation/al in need of securitization from Muslim migrants. For instance, in a PinkNews article on the HPEC debates, one commenter wrote,

> Having spent 5 years in Toronto I can safely say it is the immigrant communities that are at the heart of homophobia in the city having aligned with the local religious nut jobs. *The simple solution would be to deport all those people* who have religious objections back to the countries they came from so they can practice their religion freely and hopefully be oppressed and slaughtered by it. *These people have no place in the civilized world.* (Payton 2016, emphasis added)

While many responses attempted to paint Muslims as outside modernity for failing to join the liberal nation, other responses evoked the violence of detention and deportation for Muslims as effective solutions to homophobia. Ignoring larger homonormative-patriarchal structures and ideals of the nation, individuals made implicit turns to "racialized psychic and libidinal economies" of securitization and state violence (Agathangelou, Bassichis, and Spira 2008, 128), which properly disciplined queer subjects stake a claim to, facilitating their entry into the nation and citizenship.

Second, these aforementioned modalities of power assign legibility to certain queer and Muslim subjects such as Mohammed-Smith and Manji

over and against others, namely queer Muslim women who fail homonational interpellation and are made unthinkable in existing as queer wom-
en within Islam. The following section considers the queer Muslim woman who fails to be properly interpellated into her subject position of subaltern-queer-native-informant; for instance, one who wears a hijab as part
of her queer Muslim identity, views her queer Muslim identity as part of
the Muslim community, identifies as a queer Muslim to her Muslim family, visits a queer/trans-friendly Imam, or simply challenges the conditions of queer inclusion.

QUEER-MUSLIM-WOMAN

Unlike the interpellated subaltern-queer-native-informant, the improperly interpellated queer Muslim who does not replay Orientalist narratives
of Western superiority (rendered unproductive to the national consciousness) becomes unintelligible. In Gayatri Gopinath's (2005) incisive work,
Impossible Desires, she demonstrates how the "queer South Asian female"
is rendered an impossible and unthinkable subject within South Asian
diasporas. While (heterosexual) female subjectivity appears particularly
within (ethno)nationalist discourses of "homeland," and gay male South
Asian subjectivity emerges often as subordinated, these subjectivities
nonetheless are imaginable and legible (Gopinath 19, 83, 181), unlike the
queer South Asian woman who cannot be read legible through conventional diaspora texts/reading practices. To extend Gopinath's theorization
to the queer Muslim woman, I contend that she is an "unthinkable" and
"impossible" subject position under homonationalism. In the moment of
the HPEC debates the heterosexual Muslim woman appeared as a homophobic migrant dangerous to the national (a terrorist figure herself), or
marginally as a good modern/moderate Muslim. The gay Muslim man,
though seldom appearing himself, emerged over (though not necessarily
against) the queer Muslim woman, as an ideal informant and subject of
intervention (gay refugees, transnational rights advocate, or otherwise
diversity performances), and generally as a legible "queer Muslim subject."

Controversy swirled around a children's book published by Eiynah
Mohammed-Smith titled *My Chacha* [paternal uncle] *Is Gay* (Mohammed-
Smith 2014). The text follows a young boy and his uncle's relationship in
a Muslim country. Cathected through conventional racial and sexual
norms of Western and late-colonial South Asian and Middle Eastern national discourses (i.e., the uncle is monogamous, upper/middle-class, and
non-Black) and laced with a few exotic narratives (e.g., the uncle takes the
nephew to ride a camel), the text follows a nephew's otherwise normative
relationship with his uncle. Toward the end of the story, in a parental-like
union, the uncle's partner who is an airline pilot joins them after work.

Borrowing from Gopinath's reading, the text follows a narrative of queer women of color as unthinkable. The queer Muslim woman's presence could disturb the convivial homosociality upon which *My Chacha Is Gay* is dependent. The only women in the book are the boy's mother and (paternal) grandmother, who do not speak and hold only implicit significance in their reproductive function of producing the chacha and (grand)son. The centrality of the gay male subject and homosociality generally makes queer and feminist projects appears separate, as if one defers to the other within a single-axis field of liberal recognition. For a queer Muslim woman to become publicly legible, as with the uncle, would require a feminist, queer, and labor critique to disturb her invisibility in public space, existence outside the hetero-family which also stands as the primary source of security, and significance beyond reproduction.

Mohammed-Smith's text is certainly not exceptional in this move; rather, I draw from this children's book only due to its many appearances during the HPEC debates (both in support and opposition of the new curriculum). My point here is that while there are multiple times for the queer Muslim woman to appear, such as an in the book, the conditions of her impossibility are reinforced by the structural impossibilities of the state and the appearance of other figures: the homophobic Muslim man (or woman) and the (non-Black) gay Muslim male.

It is important to note that unlike a diasporic reading from "South Asian" geographies, there is hardly a constitution of something that can be called a "Muslim diaspora" (though I am aware of texts that attempt this move). Rather, what I'm interested in thinking through is queer Muslim women from various diasporas who converge in Canada and other white settler states and whose multiple locations contest the grounds of homonormative nationalism. Opening questions of queer Muslim diasporas (beyond Pakistan and Arab countries) destabilizes insular understandings of diaspora and nation reproduced in diasporic texts regarding queer Muslims. For instance, in thinking about queer Muslim women's impossibility within diasporas, we can note her disappearance in Indian and Filipino diasporas, assumed uniformly Hindu (*savarna*) and Catholic, respectively; queer Muslims from Kashmir and Palestine do not have necessarily legible or definable homeland for heteropatriarchal norms to refract; and queer Nigerian and Somali diasporas disturb silences around antiblackness within Muslim and queer spaces. Explaining diasporic reading practices centered on the diasporic queer woman, Gopinath (2005, 11) elaborates, "Queer diaspora enables a simultaneous critique of heterosexual and the national form while exploding the binary oppositions between nation and diaspora, heterosexuality and homosexuality." Taking this further, the queer Muslim woman read as multiply located in identity and geography, rather than a singular subject, critiques—transnationally—racist and ethnonationalist frames of legibility, but also the racial and sexual basis for homonational belonging or "sexual citizen-ship."

In Puar's reading of the ascendancy of whiteness and heteronormativ-ity, she notes the parameters of inclusion for queer subjects is via racially (and class) normative alliances and ethnic subjects via sexually normative alliances (in the nuclear family). Within Canada, ethnic subjects are inter-pellated by multicultural discourses that rely on heterosexual notions of the family, including the state's rejection of non-nuclear kinship struc-tures for immigration and family reunification (Thobani 2007, 137–38). These heteronormative immigration discourses interlock with neoliberal welfare policies (see also Reddy 2011), creating insecurity for (queer) migrant lives outside the heterosexual family. One facet that distin-guishes queer migrant men's locations from queer migrant women's lo-cations is the political utility of their gay legibility. Chandan Reddy (2011) notes that the figure of the "gay Pakistani immigrant" emerges as a contradiction between the national heteronormativity and occidental sex-ual exceptionalism. In November 2015, Canadian Prime Minister Justin Trudeau declared that the Canadian government would open itself to Syrian refugee families, but the government would exclude single-male refugee claimants as a matter of safety (the orientalized migrant male as rapist, terrorist, or otherwise "bogus" claimant). Critiques quickly fol-lowed, arguing that the exclusion would be harmful to gay men; conse-quently, the government reopened single-male claims for gay Syrian ref-ugees. Taking up Reddy's (2011) theorization, the gay refugee makes visible a contradiction in the homonational moment between Canadian multicultural heteronormativity and narratives of sexual exceptionalism, but he appears and is nonetheless incorporated into the nation. Reading this moment further through queer necropolitics of sexual exceptional-ism, the move to incorporate the gay migrant coincides with the in-creased incarceration via detention of migrants, including the increased securitization of the nation through incarceration of pregnant women and migrant children (as happened with the 2010 arrival of Tamil mi-grants).

The queer Muslim woman too is included but ambiguously incorpo-rated incidentally through the heteronormative framework of "refugee women as heterosexuals fleeing an Islamic country." When the queer Muslim woman attempts to assert her visibility, however unintelligible, or improperly interpellated—by either multiculturalism (as heterosexual) or homonationalism (as exception/informant)—she corrupts national identity (bio)politics. She delineates the sexual, gender, and racial limits of Western versions of liberal inclusion. In Kimberlé Crenshaw's (1989, 145) intersectional critique of juridical liberalism, she notes that liberal justice of the modern state is limited "to minor adjustments within an established hierarchy." The liberal manifestations of sexual freedom and immigration "openness" are predicated on small remedial changes like those in juridical forms of gender justice. The queer Muslim woman does not simply call into question her identitarian erasure within sexual libera-tion, multiculturalism, and gender justice paradigms; rather it is that her appearance questions *why* she is disappeared from them. The nation can-not name let alone elect to explicitly include queer migrant Muslim wom-en without contradicting *hetero*patriarchal structures of the welfare state and multiculturalism, imperial peacekeeping to "save women" through heteronormative class and gender formations (implantation of liberal capitalist economies predicated on the family), or the racially and class normative project of homonational incorporation. She reveals the nation-state's hetero/homo- and racial-normative organizing logics. In effect, the queer Muslim woman *queers* the notion of nation, home, and belonging embedded within the promises of homonationalism. Her subjectivity for-wards a critique that the Western nation-state can never be inhabitable as home as she can never be fully incorporated as she is always unimagin-able within it even while she persists inside of it.

CONCLUSION

Theorizing from the Ontario Health and Physical Education Curriculum debates, I have argued that the queer Muslim woman's subjectivity is largely unintelligible under homonationalism, particularly in her failure to properly interpellate into contemporary orientalist and Islamophobic discursive regimes. Her failure to interpellate, into what I have called the subaltern-queer-native-informant, occurs in tandem with her disappear-ance from national (ethnic and queer) legibility. Her subject location as an improper subject disrupts an interlocking system of nationalism delineat-ed by heteropatriarchy, white citizenship, and imperialism. She exists as an uneasily absorbed subject of either homonationalism or multicultural-ism, twin logics that uphold the liberal mythology of Canadian inclusion.

Against the repudiated frameworks of exceptionalism, I want to note that the "queer-Muslim woman" is not alone in her disruptive location to homonationalism (and multiculturalism). Black queer women as well as Two-Spirit and queer Indigenous people stand as disruptive subjects within white settler nations, primarily in contesting the legitimacy of liberalism grounded in settler colonial statehood, white supremacist structures of citizenship, and transnational imperial projects (see Holland 2012, 65–93; Driskill 2016, 154–65). There are likely other queer of color locations that contest the grounds of ethnic and sexual incorporation into Canadian belonging. I draw from the queer Muslim woman largely due to her disappearance during the HPEC debates and her properly interpel-lated counterparts' popularity within Canadian media.

In moving critiques of homonationalism further, and broadly modal-ities of queer and ethnic liberal inclusion, I want to suggest that theorists and activists work to not only center invisiblized subjectivities but also highlight the conditions of their invisibility. Such a move, I am suggesting, re-centers the racial and sexual limited nature of the liberal nation-state, which disperses its national hegemony by marking inclusivity as unrestricted despite securing and defending its liberal inclusion through racial and sexual securitization (i.e., border and carceral restrictions). Future work may also benefit from a consideration of the psychic dimensions of unintelligibility and legibility on queers of color. However, rather than turn to accounts of psychoanalysis that attempt to make the interiority of queer of color psyches "knowable" or "uncovered," I recommend a move to the affective relations under homonationalism that make apparent the homonational/multicultural demands on queers of color's subjectivities. Lastly, this discussion is a reminder that queers of color, cutting across multiple locations, are never necessarily located equally or the same within homonationalism and may have access to different forms of recognition and legibility, rendering some queers of color intelligible over and against other often more vulnerable queers of color.

NOTES

1. The author thanks Kiran Saili and Lynn Ly for comments on an earlier version of this chapter.
2. These should not be taken as three injured groups, especially as there is tremendous overlap between these groupings; instead it refers to three "problems" multiculturalism serves to manage, disavow, or disappear.

REFERENCES

Agathangelou, Ana, M. Daniel Bassichis, and Tamara L. Spira. 2008. "Intimate Investments: Homonormativity, Global Lockdown, and the Seductions of Empire." *Radical History Review* 100: 120–143.
Ahmed, Sara. 2014. *Cultural Politics of Emotion*. Edinburgh: Edinburgh University Press.
Bauman, Zygmunt. 2004. *Wasted Lives: Modernity and Its Outcasts*. Malden: Blackwell Publishing.
Campaign Life Coalition. n.d. "Ontario's Radical Sex Ed Curriculum." *Campaign Life Coalition*. Accessed December 3, 2016. http://campaignlifecoalition.com/index.php?p=Sex_Ed_Curriculum.
CBC. 2016. "Former Muslim Objects to Watered Down Sex-Ed at Toronto School." *CBC Radio*, March 22. Accessed December 3, 2016. http://cbc.ca/radio/the180/the-truth-about-gmos-accommodations-in-sex-ed-and-retiring-smokey-bear-1.3591155/former-muslim-objects-to-watered-down-sex-ed-at-toronto-school-1.3591261.
CTV. 2015. "Ontario's Revised Sex Ed Curriculum Sparks Debate, Rally at Queen's Park." *CTV*, February 24. Accessed December 3, 2016. http://ctvnews.ca/politics/ontario-s-revised-sex-ed-curriculum-sparks-debate-rally-at-queen-s-park-1.2251168.
Crenshaw, Kimberlé. 1989. "Demarginalizing the Intersection of Race and Sex: A Black Feminist Critique of Antidiscrimination Doctrine." *University of Chicago Legal Forum* 140: 139–167.

Driskill, Qwo-Li. 2016. *Asegi Stories: Cherokee Queer and Two-Spirit Memory.* Tucson: University of Arizona Press.

Dryden, OmiSoore H., and Suzanne Lenon, eds. 2015. *Disrupting Queer Inclusion: Canadian Homonationalisms and the Politics of Belonging.* Vancouver: University of British Columbia Press.

Edelman, Elijah A. 2014. "'Walking While Transgender': Necropolitical Regulations of Trans Feminine Bodies of Colour." In *Queer Necropolitics*, edited by Jin Haritaworn, Adi Kuntsman, and Silvia Posocco, 172–190. London: Routledge.

Ferguson, Roderick. 2004. *Aberrations in Black: Toward a Queer of Color Critique.* Minneapolis: University of Minnesota Press.

Gopinath, Gayatri. 2005. *Impossible Desires: Queer Diasporas and South Asian Public Cultures.* Durham: Duke University Press.

Haritaworn, Jin. 2015. *Queer Lovers and Hateful Others: Regenerating Violent Times and Places.* London: Pluto Press.

Haritaworn, Jin, Adi Kuntsman, and Silvia Posocco, eds. 2014. *Queer Necropolitics.* London: Routledge.

Haritaworn, Jin, Tamsila Tauqir, and Esra Erdem. 2008. "Gay Imperialism: Gender and Sexuality Discourse in the 'War on Terror.'" In *Out of Place: Interrogating Silences in Queerness/Raciality*, edited by Adi Kuntsman and Esperanza Miyake, 71–95. York: Raw Nerve Books.

Holland, Sharon P. 2012. *The Erotic Life of Racism.* Durham: Duke University Press.

Manji, Irshad. 2003. *The Trouble with Islam: A Wake-Up Call for Honesty and Change.* Toronto: Random House Canada.

Mbembe, Achille. 2003. "Necropolitics." Translated by Libby Meintjes. *Public Culture* 15 (1): 11–40.

Mohammed-Smith, Eiynah. 2016. "Liberal Muslims Face an Uphill Battle." *NOW Toronto*, October 25. Accessed December 3, 2016. https://nowtoronto.com/news/think-free-blog/liberal-muslims-face-an-uphill-battle.

———. 2014. *My Chacha Is Gay.* http://nicemangos.blogspot.ca/2014/02/my-chacha-is-gay.html?zx=4f572b5cb91cbf14.

———. n.d. "Nice Mangos." Accessed December 3, 2016. http://nicemangos.blogspot.ca/?zx=5964187d6a2009a1.

Payton, Nathan. 2015. "Ontario Parents Protest Inclusive Sex Education." *PinkNews*, April 17. Accessed December 3, 2016. http://pinknews.co.uk/2015/04/17/ontario-parents-protest-inclusive-sex-education/comments/#disqus_thread.

Puar, Jasbir K. 2013. "Rethinking Homonationalism." *International Journal of Middle East Studies* 45 (2): 336–339.

———. 2007. *Terrorist Assemblages: Homonationalism in Queer Times.* Durham: Duke University Press.

Reddy, Chandan. 2011. *Freedom with Violence.* Durham: Duke University Press.

Rushowy, Kristin. 2015. "Premier Visits School at Centre of Sex-Ed Controversy." *TheStar*, October 8. Accessed December 3, 2016. https://thestar.com/yourtoronto/education/2015/10/08/premier-visits-school-at-centre-of-sex-ed-controversy.html.

Selley, Chris. 2015. "Muslim Community Taking the Lead in Latest Round of Ontario Sex-Education Protests." *National Post*, May 5. Accessed December 3, 2016. http://news.nationalpost.com/news/canada/muslim-community-taking-the-lead-in-latest-round-o.f-ontario-sex-education-protests.

Tauqir, Tamsila. n.d. "Gender, Sexuality, & Islam: Empowering Muslim Lesbian, Bisexual and Trans Women." *Global Fund for Women*. Accessed December 8, 2017. http://muslima.globalfundforwomen.org/content/gender-sexuality-islam.

Thobani, Sunera. 2007. *Exalted Subjects: Studies in the Making of Race and Nation in Canada.* Toronto: University of Toronto Press.

Walia, Harsha. 2013. *Undoing Border Imperialism.* Oakland: AK Press.

Watson, H.G. 2015. "McNaughton Insists Ontario Sex Ed Linked to Criminal." *Daily Xtra*, March 26. Accessed December 3, 2016. http://dailyxtra.com/toronto/news-and-ideas/news/mcnaughton-insists-ontario-sex-ed-linked-criminal-101100.

FIVE

"Not Into Chopsticks or Curries"

Erotic Capital and the Psychic
Life of Racism on Grindr

Emerich Daroya

In 2017, Grindr, a geosocial networking application ("app") geared towards gay and bisexual men, marks the eighth year since its inception.
While Grindr and other online cruising technologies are believed to open
new sexual practices, intimacies, and attachments (Race 2015), others,
however, point to the ways in which Grindr and other similar apps have
perpetuated, rather than challenged, the racialized organization of desire
among gay and other homosexually active men (Raj 2011; Robinson
2015). For instance, using two smartphones to conduct a "Grindr experiment," a self-identified gay Asian man notes that identifying as white on
Grindr generates more response than identifying as Asian despite having
similar, arguably desirable, characteristics: "5'10", 170 lbs, muscular, 8"
uncut." Reflecting on his experiences on Grindr, the author of the blog
"Angry Homosexual" (2014) writes:

> As a hot white guy, you can expect a near 100% reply rate. In fact, you
> wind up with the problem that more guys are messaging you in a day
> than you can realistically sleep [with] within a month.
> In contrast, however:
> As an Asian, you can only hope to be so lucky to get the pleasure of a
> response [. . .]. There's an inherent bias against us and you need to
> know for all intents and purposes, you have no realistic chance of
> dating a hot white guy your own age. (Angry Homosexual)

The differences in response rate between white and Asian men that emerged from this Grindr experiment reverberates some academic studies on sexual racism among gay and other homosexually active men online (Daroya 2013; Gosine 2007; McBride 2005; Riggs 2013; White et al. 2014). That is, it reaffirms the dominance of whiteness as a desirable attribute among gay men and whiteness as the standard from which non-white gay men are measured, despite having similar desirable characteristics (see, for example, Han 2006; 2007; 2008). In this respect, it might be suggested that whiteness along with other attributes such as body type, gender expression, sexual position, cock size, and height become significant currencies in the economics of desire on Grindr. Put simply, whiteness is an important erotic capital, indeed a stable norm, in Grindr's marketplace of desire from which one's desirability is evaluated.

Whiteness is not an easy concept to define. In *Performing Whiteness*, Foster (2012) suggests that "whiteness does not exist at the biological level." Instead, "[i]t is a cultural construct" (2). Yet, it is a powerful social construct because it marks those who are non-white as *others*: "whites are not of a certain race, they're just the human race" (Dyer 1997). Whiteness, as Dyer elaborates, is powerful because it is invisible—it can speak for everyone, unlike non-whites who can only speak for their specific "race" (3). "If to be human is to be white," writes Sara Ahmed (2007, 161), "then to be not white is to inhabit the negative: it is to be 'not.'" For her, whiteness is an orientation: "a social and bodily orientation given that some bodies will be more at home in a world that is orientated towards whiteness" (Ahmed 2007, 160). Whiteness then is "not reducible to white skin, or even to 'something' we can have or be" (Ahmed 2007, 159). Instead, it is an effect of a repetition of a style of embodiment (ibid.), echoing Butler's theory of performativity in which identities are constituted through repetition of certain acts (Butler 1990). As Ahmed further explains, whiteness is a habit: "what bodies do, where the body takes the shape of the action" (2007, 156). In other words, whiteness must be performed, created, and managed in order to gain currency as that which is most desirable and desired by both white and non-white gay and other homosexually active men in certain spaces, such as Grindr. This echoes some of the ways in which I theorized the production of race and racialized markers through online cruising spaces where the display of "erotic capital" is understood as performative, reinforcing hegemonic norms of race (Daroya 2013).

In this chapter, I augment the notion of erotic capital through the concept of the "psychic life of racism" to illustrate how racialized discourses shape how desires and desirability are socially organized and how erotic value is differentially distributed among gay and other homosexually active men in online cruising spaces such as Grindr. By drawing on these theories, I suggest that what is considered erotically desirable by gay and other men who have sex with men on Grindr—that is, white, muscular, and masculine with a sizeable cock—can be understood as effects of hegemonic forms of race, constituting and regulating the ways in which erotic capital is played out in this specific sexual field. The first part of this chapter briefly discusses the notion of "erotic capital" as introduced by Adam Green (2008a, 2008b). Green's adaptation of Pierre Bourdieu's sociological concept of "habitus" makes a significant contribution in understanding how might the social help in the constitution and organization of desire. The second section of this chapter attempts to link Green's theorization of the social organization of desire with the notion of the "psychic life of racism" to better understand and explicate the power of racialized discourses in how desires are constituted. If, as Judith Butler (1997) argues, the psyche is an "effect of the regulatory, disciplinary and normative operation of power" (Campbell 2001, 39), then racialized desires, as I further argue, can also be rendered effects of power on the psyche. In this respect, the notion of erotic capital, expanded through the theorization of the psychic life of racism, contributes towards a better understanding, albeit limited, of how racialization has material effects in online gay cruising spaces such as Grindr. In the remainder of this chapter, I mobilize these theories to elucidate on the power of racialized discourses in shaping how erotic capital is differentially distributed among gay and other homosexually active men on Grindr. I propose that the material effects of racialized discourses can be discerned through analyzing the ways in which the desire for white men and unattraction towards Asian men are expressed. I support this by suggesting that Orientalist discourses about Asian men as soft, poorly endowed, and, most significantly, effeminate, affect how Asian men are described as undesirable, often rejected by both white and non-white men on Grindr because they do not conform to the idealized notion of "masc" (masculine). This brief analysis demonstrates that hegemonic discourses on race are imbued with power and have material effects in the lives of both white and non-white gay men through the differential distribution of erotic capital.

MARKET ANALOGY AND THE ECONOMIES OF DESIRE IN THE GAY COMMUNITY

Conceptualizing whiteness as a valuable capital on Grindr as an erotic marketplace echoes some of the ways in which desire in gay communities has been conceptualized. As McCaskell (1998) argues: "The gay community is a sexual marketplace" because "people aren't so likely to get frozen with one partner" (46). Similarly, in a study conducted by Thorne and Coupland (1998) on personal ads by gays and lesbians in newspapers, they argue that it is important to interpret personal ads "more specifically as commodified and marketised discourses" (234). In these

marketized and commodified "dating markets," personal ads are mod-
eled on the "small ads" paradigm, which principally serves to "sell sec-
ond-hand consumer goods" (235). According to Thorne and Coupland,
these personal ads only feature characteristics that are perceived to be
marketable to the target audience. In other words, the self is commodified in personal ads to become desirable and consumed as a sexual object
based on one's understanding of his/her value in the marketplace of desire. McBride (2005) expands that one's understanding of his/her erotic
value in the (gay) marketplace of desire is partly shaped and regulated by
ideals of race. For McBride (2005), however, one's value in the (gay)
marketplace of desire is tied to and regulated by ideals of race.

In his analysis of online gay personal ads, McBride (2005) suggests
that whiteness appears to be the most valuable attribute that some, if not
most, men find the most desirable and attractive. As McBride elaborates,
"whiteness is the all-around salient variable that increases one's value in
the gay marketplace of desire." "A white man [. . .] who is 'very good-
looking,' with a 'large penis,' a 'hot tight body,' and a masculine affect
[. . .] represents the ideal type, the sexy and desirable man that we should
all want in the personals world" (117). In this respect, whiteness is elevat-
ed "into a social and bodily ideal" (Ahmed 2004), which can be conceptualized as valuable "erotic capital" in the racialized gay marketplace of
desire. Following McBride, I suggest that one's erotic value on Grindr is
structured by ideals of race, producing specific modes of erotic capital.

By featuring only marketable attributes of the self, one's capacity to be
desired and become desirable can be understood through the paradigm
of exchange-value, wherein whiteness and other positive attributes (such
as one's body, masculinity and penis size) organize the ways in which
specific modalities of erotic capital can be performed or highlighted to
place oneself in the hierarchy of desires. Understanding Grindr as a specific gay marketplace of desire offers a way in understanding erotic capital "as the quality and quantity of attributes that an individual possesses,
[. . .] elicit[ing] an erotic response in another," regulated and constituted,
as I add, by hegemonic norms of race, which takes many forms including
"physical traits, affective presentations and socio-cultural styles" (Green
2008a, 29).

Green's (2008a) notion of erotic capital is a sociological concept derived from Pierre Bourdieu's theory of "habitus." While the aim of this
chapter is not to engage extensively with Green's theorization of erotic
capital, it is important to note that his adaptation of Bourdieu's theories
implicate the social, believed to supply a "cosmology of eroticized objects
and attendant thematics [. . .] that orients the undifferentiated biological
libido towards particular social forms" (Green 2008a, 614). In other
words, what is considered to be erotically desirable in the gay marketplace of desire—that is, white, good-looking with a body sculpted
through the gym, big cock, and masculine—can be understood as effects

of hegemonic forms of race, further constituting and regulating the ways in which erotic capital is expressed on this specific "sexual field." Grindr, a social networking app, can be thought as a site where "participants with more or less shared erotic appetites congregate in ways that put in high relief structured relations of social and sexual exchange constitutive of a sexual field." Indeed, the more specialized a given erotic world becomes, the more standardized its erotic prize, the more predictably ordered the relational patterns, and the more institutionalized the currency of a given form of erotic capital (Green 2008b, 29). On Grindr and other online websites and platforms, whiteness can be perceived as the most valuable erotic capital, organizing and stratifying relations between men. This is exemplified by Angry Homosexual's observations from his Grindr experiment where whiteness is considered the standard erotic prize due to the apparent high success rate in finding a potential sexual partner while presenting himself as white. In contrast, a man who identifies as Asian but with similar desirable characteristics will be half as successful in finding a desirable sexual partner.

What Angry Homosexual's Grindr experiment reveals, apart from the obvious, is that the desirability of whiteness in this particular sexual field is attached to a specific type of embodiment. Following Ahmed (2007), this embodied whiteness can be understood as an effect of a repetition of a certain "type," further shaping how participants interact with each other. Indeed, if what is considered the most valuable and desirable erotic capital on Grindr is a stylized repetition of whiteness, "an effect of racialization" (Ahmed 2007, 151), then whiteness also has material and lived effects. This is illustrated by Angry Homosexual's expression of frustration regarding Asian men's low prospects in attracting white men who are deemed to be desirable. In this respect, the embodiment of a masculine, muscular, and well-endowed whiteness as the most valuable erotic capital on Grindr has its own psychic life, permeated with power that affects how erotic racism is reproduced by and within online cruising spaces.

THE PSYCHIC LIFE OF RACISM IN THE DIGITAL AGE

Online spaces have been a favorite milieu for research on the effects of erotic racism among gay and other homosexually active men. For example, Gosine's (2007) earlier study of passing-as-white in a Canadian online chatroom reveals the same sort of effects as Angry Homosexual's experiences on Grindr: "Self-identification as white often serves as a qualifier to access conversations with other users" (Gosine 2007, 148). Gosine's and Angry Homosexual's passing-as-white online alludes to the power of racialized discourses in opening the possibility "to experience the material and cultural privileges afforded to white people" (Gosine

2007, 146). Passing-as-white in online spaces thus underscores not only the erotic value of whiteness, but also the psychic life of racism, where whiteness is understood to be imbued with power, shaping how access to erotic resources is afforded to some but not others, illustrated through the erotic economy on Grindr.

The notion of "psychic life" is drawn from Judith Butler's (1997) work in *The Psychic Life of Power* where she attempts to understand the relation of power and subjectivity. In this work, Butler theorizes, "What is the psychic form that power takes?" by rethinking subject formation as dependent "on a discourse we never chose but that, paradoxically, initiates and sustains our agency" (Butler 1997, 2). For Butler, it is not simply that power is internalized by the psyche, but that the psyche itself "is an effect of power, because it is an effect of the regulatory, disciplinary, and normative operation of power" (Campbell 2001, 39). Butler's intervention in providing a critical lens in explaining the psychic form that power takes also has significant contributions in other areas of subjective formation beyond gender and sexuality. For example, Riggs and Augoustinos (2005) draw inspiration from Butler to understand the "psychic life of colonial power" in shaping the subject of the Australian nation. They suggest that the question of the subjectivity in Australia is "shaped by the ongoing acts of colonization that configure the Australian nation" based on the disavowal of Indigenous sovereignty (Riggs and Augoustinos 2005, 467). That is, the construction of the Australian subject as white, middle-class, and heterosexual is formed concurrently with their investment in white belonging, an investment that is a "continuation of the acts of dispossession and genocide that are formative of the Australian national psyche" (ibid.). In other words, the unequal power relations that exist under colonialism between Indigenous and non-Indigenous Australians affect how racialized practices are performed by colonizing subjects who are invested in the maintenance of this power (ibid.).

The "psychic life of colonial power" is an idea borrowed by Riggs and Augoustinos (2005) from the work of Derek Hook (2012) in his engagement with the works of Frantz Fanon and the psychoanalysis of racism. Fanon, drawing on psychoanalytic theory, asks why it is that the "Negro myth" (that the black man stands for "evil") is so pervasive in European societies. Turning to the works of Carl Jung, Fanon suggests that there is a "collective unconscious," a reservoir of innate ideas that may explain "how racism may work in an unconscious [. . .] manner shared by a wide historical and geographical constituency of (white) Europeans" (Hook 2012, 115). For Hook, Fanon's intervention in linking racism to psychoanalysis sheds light on how it is that colonial investments on the "Negro myth" (in Europe and North America) or the disavowal of Indigenous sovereignty (in the Australian context) can be understood as effects of power on the psyche: "Racism [. . .] exists very much in the symbolic field [. . .], which of course contain profound 'extra-discursive' and psychological impacts" (Hook 2002, 123). To put it simply, understanding colonialism and racism as having a "psychic life" bridges the gap between racist discourses and subjectivity specifically in looking critically at how whiteness operates psychically to maintain power relations between white and non-white subjects.

If racialized discourses, as effects of power, equally affect the psyche in explaining the pervasiveness of whiteness as a site of racial privilege, is it possible that these very discourses also constitute the social organization of desire among gay and other homosexually active men? While not drawing on these theorizations, Green's (2008a, 2008b) attempt to explicate the social organization of desire through Bourdieu's notion of habitus echoes some of the ways in which the psychic life of racism is explicated. Indeed, as Green contends, erotic habitus is where "the social order and one's place within it have a somatic relationship to the unconscious," reverberating some of the ways in which Butler (1997) describes the psyche as an effect of power. Similarly, racialized desires may be rendered effects of racialized discourses in the unconscious, contributing towards the social organization of desire (Green 2008a, 614). In this respect, the formation of erotic habitus—an "orientation" towards "particular social forms" (ibid.)—can be understood as an effect of power on the psyche. If my argument is right, then the constructions of erotic capital on Grindr may elucidate on the psychic life of racism precisely by placing great value on whiteness as the most desirable attribute in this particular sexual field. In what follows, I draw on different accounts of racism on Grindr to demonstrate how hegemonic discourses on race shape how erotic capital is differentially distributed on Grindr.

GRINDR: "ONE OF THE LAST BASTIONS OF OPEN RACISM"

In her observations on Grindr, Manisha Krishnan (2016), a self-identified heterosexual female writer for *Vice*, a Canadian-American digital media, elaborates that the online app "is one of the last bastions of open racism (and fat-shaming and ageism) that exists in a relatively PC [politically correct] society." After hearing stories from some gay male friends about racism on Grindr, "white ones included," Krishnan decides to do some digging only to find that there is indeed an incredible bluntness about racism in some of the profiles on Grindr. According to her investigation, some men openly deploy racist discourses (using food metaphors, for example) to reject men who are non-white: "More into vanilla and spice than chocolate and rice," alluding to the desire for white and Latino men and the non-attraction for Black and Asian men. For Krishnan, her analysis of Grindr profiles reveals that many gay and other homosexually active men are openly racist on this online platform, often displayed "in the form of disclaimers [. . .] that sit front and centre on a person's profile."

Krishnan's observations regarding racism on Grindr echo some of the ways in which sexual racism has been found to be more commonly expressed and experienced in online spaces precisely due to the disinhibiting effects these technologies offer (Callander, Holt, and Newman 2012). As Suler (2004) observes, online spaces are anonymous, aphysical, and depersonalized, which may lead to online disinhibiting effects, promoting easier sharing of attitudes or perceptions with respect to race, gender presentation, age, body type, and other exclusionary caveats which may not be readily acceptable in offline settings. In these online spaces, "no Asians," "no Blacks," "no Indians," "no fats," "no femmes," "no oldies," and "no shorties," among others, proliferate, alluding to the differential distribution of erotic capital. While rejections based on physical characteristics are typical in this particular sexual field, Nguyen (2014) notes that the most common exclusion on Grindr is directed towards Asian men. Numerous examples of this can be found from the blog "Douchebags of Grindr":

> Aussie, fit, laid back guy. Easy going, masculine, friendly. No Asians/ unfit/unclean or above 50 years.
> Real boys with tatts and stuff. Not into femmes, fatties or furballs. I am not into Asians.
> No Asians, no Fems, and no Queens.

These excerpts, culled from profiles of white Grindr participants, capture how Asian men's erotic capital is valued less, indeed considered undesirable, on this online platform. Nguyen (2014) contends that Asian men are excluded from white men's imaginary on Grindr because they "appear to occupy the most unsexy, undesirable position of all, seen as soft, effeminate and poorly endowed" (2). In other words, Asian men's accrual of erotic capital is denied by some men on Grindr precisely because they are not seen to exhibit masculinity. This is clearly illustrated in the first quote from a self-identified "Aussie" who depicts himself as "masculine" and "fit," while Asians are shaped as "unfit" and "unclean," equally unattractive as men who are "above 50 years." The undesirable position of Asian men as feminine is further elaborated by the latter quotes, where Asian men are emasculated, considered "queens" rendered opposite of "real boys." These profiles further shed light on the link between racialization and gender expression, reiterating the role of Orientalist discourses, "a system of knowledge that delineates Asian men as the antithesis of white masculinity" (Daroya, 2013), in the social organization of desires.

These expressions of racialized desires, in particular the rejection of Asian men, may illustrate how erotic capital is played out on Grindr and how Grindr may be implicated in the materialization of the psychic life of racism. If, as I argued previously, Orientalist discourses affect the ways in which desires are racially organized (Daroya, 2013), then it is possible to consider that expressions of attraction towards white men and non-attraction towards Asian men on Grindr are effects of Orientalist discourses on the psyche. If so, in what forms do these effects of power materialize on Grindr as erotic capital?

Regarding this line of inquiry, David Eng (2001) proposes that fantasies and idealizations about Asian men cannot be separated from Orientalist discourses, where white men are placed in the position of masculinity (151). Similarly, Richard Fung (1991) also argues that Asianness and passivity are conflated because Asian men are portrayed as always taking the position of the bottom in gay male pornography, reiterating the domination of white men over the inferior and weak Oriental. As Edward Said (1977) writes, "Intercourse was always the Westerner's privilege; because his was the stronger culture, he could penetrate [. . .], he could give shape and meaning to the great Asiatic mystery" (44). Arguably, these discourses are also expressed on Grindr by some white men who deny the desirability of Asian men precisely due to their perceived femininity. For example, one white Grindr participant writes on his profile: "Sorry not into Asians. Masculine for masculine," suggesting that Asian men are not considered masculine, a possible effect of Orientalist discourses, which affects their "value" in the erotic economy of Grindr. In short, the repudiation of Asian masculinity by white men on Grindr also bars Asian men from accruing and negotiating any form of erotic capital. Because Asian men are always already rendered feminine, they are also always already shaped as undesirable, often grouped along with those who are deemed unattractive on Grindr: "No shorties, Asians, fats or fems."

The profiles presented here, although few and short, may provide some insights into how the psychic life of racism is materialized through expressions of desire and erotic capital on Grindr. Indeed, the examples convey that the emasculation of Asian men, partly informed by Orientalism, also shapes how their desirability is valued by other men on Grindr. Notably, erotic capital in this specific online cruising app is not dependent on one variable alone (e.g., race), but a combination of characteristics that are deemed to be desirable: that is, one must not only be white, but must also be tall, gym fit, and, most significantly, masculine. Thus, within this online space, the accrual of erotic capital intersects with class, gender, sexuality, ethnicity, etc. (Eng 2001). Moreover, these profiles reveal that embodied whiteness is a stable norm. The erotic value of whiteness on Grindr affect how gay men of color, particularly Asian men who are considered to be effeminate and asexual, are treated (read: excluded) in this space. In this respect, it is possible to suggest that Grindr, while it has been lauded by some commentators as a technology that reconfigures "the landscape of human relationships" partly because it enables online cruising (Vernon 2010), nonetheless helps in the reification of old categories of race which "allows for statements of racial preference to be made with less risk of negative social repercussions" (Ahlm 2017, 372). Indeed, a preference for a particular "race" is often defended by some men on Grindr as merely a matter of preference: "Only into white guys. Sorry, it's just a preference," "Not into Black or Asian—sorry guys!," "No Asian— 'solly,'" "I'm sorry not into Asian or Indian," and "No disrespect, but please don't waste your time if you're unattractive, out of shape, Asian, Black or fem[inine]." In the next section, I put these "preferences" through a critical lens by suggesting that these perceived expressions of racial "taste" is a form of "new racism" (Robinson 2015).

PERSONAL PREFERENCE AS NEW RACISM

Most significant about these so-called "preferences" for certain "races" on Grindr is that they are often accompanied by an apology. "Sorry, just a preference" seems to imply that erotic preferences based on race and stereotypes are perceived to be neutral, immune to the influences of power or racialized discourses that are prevalent in the society at large. This contention is echoed by Callander and colleagues (2015) in their research on online sexual racism among Australian gay and other homosexually active men where preference for a particular race is viewed not as an expression of racism, but simply as a way to articulate desire: "a matter of individual preference and taste" (8). Defending one's (un)attraction towards a particular group of men based on their race as merely a question of personal preference reflects how individual desires are recognized as an expression of "sexual freedom" in contemporary Western societies. That is, by describing disinterest towards Asian men (or Black men or Indian men, among others) as simply an affair of "personal taste" invokes, as Callander et al. expand, a key ideology in Western democracies where individuals are believed to have the ability to choose one's partner based on various characteristics. Indeed, while for some expressions of exclusion against racialized minorities by both white and non-white men are conceptualized as collective forms of racial prejudice, others deny these claims precisely by refuting accusations of racism. As Zachary Sire (2011), editor of *The Sword*, a gay news and lifestyle website covering the adult industry, puts it: "What's wrong with having a preference? Don't tell me I can't have a preference! I don't want to have sex with women. No hard feelings. Does that make me a misogynist? What makes someone an authority on how to delineate when and where something stops being a 'preference' and starts being racist? The hell?"

What is interesting in Sire's response against accusations of racism on Grindr is the analogy he utilizes between sexual orientation and racism: that being erotically and romantically attracted to men and not women is the same as having erotic and romantic gravitation towards white men and not men of color. Although it is impossible to engage in a lengthy discussion as to the fallacy of his argument, it is worth noting that analogizing sexual orientation to race not only implicitly alludes to essentialism (i.e., that there is a monolithic "gay experience" independent of other facets of experiences), but it also importantly highlights Sire's white privilege precisely by perpetuating white domination and obscuring the role that race plays in his desires as a white gay man. In other words, by questioning the limits of "racism" (i.e., that racial preferences are simply matters of individual taste), Sire legitimizes and even reiterates the power of racialized discourses precisely by masking racialized desires as expressions of sexual freedom.

As Robinson (2015) contends, the discourse of "personal preference" is "a form of new racism," where Grindr and other online cruising websites open the possibility "to openly disclose these racist remarks but not see them as racist" (326). "Sorry, just a preference" reveals the intersection between the liberal notion of choice and racialized discourses, where offensive language, such as "not into chopsticks or curries" to allude to the rejection of Asian men, is disavowed as racist because it is believed to be an expression of sexual freedom. To consider such choice as racist squarely puts individualism and choice with questions of exclusion and discrimination. Further, to conclude that racialized desire is not racist because being attracted to either male or female is not sexist takes back issues of racism from gay men of color and puts other issues (such as misogyny) front and center, as if each form of exclusion is separate and not mutually shaped by hegemonic power. By perpetuating the notion of racialized desires as simply personal preference, Grindr participants participate in the maintenance of the hegemony and normativity of whiteness as the most valuable erotic capital, embodied as muscular, well-endowed, and masculine.

CONCLUSION

The purpose of this chapter was to augment the concept of erotic capital through the theory of the psychic life of racism to elucidate on the role of racialized discourses in shaping the social organization of desire. By drawing on these theories, I considered how racialized discourses about Asian men based on Orientalism diminish their value in the erotic economy on Grindr. I suggested that what gay and other men who have sex with men on Grindr consider as erotically desirable—white, muscular, and masculine with a sizeable cock—might be considered effects of hegemonic forms of race, which, in turn, constitute and regulate the expression of erotic capital. In the first part of this chapter, I briefly discussed the notion of "erotic capital" as introduced by Adam Green (2008a, 2008b) by drawing on Pierre Bourdieu's concept of "habitus." Green's adaptation of Bourdieu's sociological concept makes a significant contribution in understanding how might the social help in the constitution and organization of desire by "supplying a cosmology of eroticized objects" (Green 2008a, 614). In the second part of this chapter, I attempted to reinforce Green's theorization of the social organization of desire with the notion of the "psychic life of racism" to better understand and explicate the power of racialized discourses in the construction of (racialized) desires. If Judith Butler (1997) considers the psyche as an "effect of the regulatory, disciplinary and normative operation of power" (Campbell 2001, 39), then racialized desires might also be acknowledged as effects of power on the psyche. In this respect, the notion of erotic capital augmented through the concept of the psychic life of racism may contribute towards a better understanding of racism in online gay cruising spaces such as Grindr.

In the rest of this chapter, I mobilized these ideas to illustrate the material effects of racialized discourses in constituting the differential distribution of erotic capital among gay and other homosexually active men on Grindr. I maintained that the effects of racialized discourses could be discerned by analyzing some of the ways in which the desire for white men and non-attraction towards Asian men were expressed on Grindr profiles. The analysis I presented attest to the role of Orientalism in shaping how Asian men were seen as soft, poorly endowed, and, most significantly, effeminate, materially affecting the ways in which other men described them as undesirable, rendering them repulsive along with other racialized men of color, men who are "fat" and "unfit," "short," "unclean," and older. Thus, along with whiteness, Orientalism has significant impacts in the lives of both white and non-white gay men through the distribution of erotic capital and in the constitution of who counts as desirable in the gay marketplace of desire.

Indeed, men on Grindr were found to openly reject Asian men precisely because they were considered feminine, the antithesis of the desirable white masculine. These were often expressed through the use of food metaphors—"no rice," "no sushi," "not into curries," "not into chopsticks," revealing that white gay men on Grindr openly conveyed racism through their rejection of Asian men. Yet, despite the offensive nature of these remarks, these racialized desires were often masked as "preferences" that reflect personal tastes, often accompanied by an apology. Apologizing for not being attracted to a particular race by openly rejecting them based on perceived stereotypes, yet disavowing the role of hegemonic discourses on race, might be considered as an investment of some of these men in the maintenance of white hegemony in the desires of gay men. The psychic life of racism is thus materialized through the differential distribution of erotic capital that was, and is continually, performed through the rejection of Asian men (and other men of color) via profiles on Grindr. These practices of exclusion may be an effort to marginalize and deny the desirability of Asian men and other non-white men, preserving the stratified and racialized economy of desire in online cruising spaces.

REFERENCES

Ahlm, Jody. 2017. "Respectable Promiscuity: Digital Cruising in an Era of Queer Liberalism." *Sexualities* 20 (3): 364–79.

Ahmed, Sara. 2004. "Declarations of Whiteness: The Non-Performativity of Anti-Racism." *Borderlands e-journal* 3 (2). Accessed January 1, 2017. http://www.border lands.net.au/vol3no2_2004/ahmed_declarations.htm.

———. 2007. "A Phenomenology of Whiteness." *Feminist Theory* 8 (2): 149–68.

Angry Homosexual. 2014. "Asian vs White Grindr Experiment: Why It's Great to be White." Accessed February 1, 2017. http://angryhomosexual.com/asian-vs-white-grindr-experiment-why-its-great-to-be-white/.

Butler, Judith. 1990. *Gender Trouble: Feminism and the Subversion of Identity.* New York: Routledge.

———. 1997. *The Psychic Life of Power: Theories in Subjection.* Stanford: Stanford University Press.

Callander, Denton, Martin Holt, and Christy E. Newman. 2012. "Just a Preference: Racialised Language in the Sex-Seeking Profiles of Gay and Bisexual Men." *Culture, Health & Sexuality* 14 (9): 1049–63.

Callander, Denton, Christy E. Newman, and Martin Holt. 2015. "Is Sexual Racism *Really* Racism? Distinguishing Attitudes Toward Sexual Racism and Generic Racism Among Gay and Bisexual Men." *Archives of Sexual Behavior* 44 (7): 1991–2000.

Campbell, Kirsten. 2001. "Theory: The Plague of the Subject: Psychoanalysis and Judith Butler's Psychic Life of Power." *International Journal of Sexuality and Gender Studies* 6 (1–2): 35–48.

Daroya, Emerich. 2013. "Potatoes and Rice: Exploring the Racial Politics of Gay Asian and White Men's Desires and Desirability." *Critical Race & Whiteness Studies* 9 (2).

Dyer, Richard. 1997. *White.* New York: Routledge.

Eng, David L. 2001. *Racial Castration: Managing Masculinity in Asian America.* Durham: Duke University Press.

Foster, Gwendolyn Audrey. 2012. *Performing Whiteness: Postmodern Re/constructions in the Cinema.* Albany: SUNY Press.

Fung, Richard. 1991. "Looking for My Penis: The Eroticized Asian in Gay Video Porn." In *How Do I Look? Queer Film & Video,* edited by Bad Object-Choices, 145–68. Seattle: Bay Press.

Gosine, Andil. 2007. "Brown to Blonde at Gay.com: Passing White in Queer Cyberspace." In *Queer Online: Media, Technology & Sexuality,* edited by Kate O'Riordan and David J. Philips, 139–53. New York: SUNY.

Green, Adam Isaiah. 2008a. "Erotic Habitus: Toward a Sociology of Desire." *Theory and Society* 37 (6): 597–626.

———. 2008b. "The Social Organization of Desire: The Sexual Fields Approach." *Sociological Theory* 26 (1): 25–50.

Han, Chong-suk. 2006. "Geisha of a Different Kind: Gay Asian Men and the Gendering of Sexual Identity." *Sexuality and Culture* 10 (3): 3–28.

———. 2007. "They Don't Want to Cruise Your Type: Gay Men of Color and the Racial Politics of Exclusion." *Social Identities* 13 (1): 51–67.

———. 2008. "No Fats, Femmes, or Asians: The Utility of Critical Race Theory in Examining the Role of Gay Stock Stories in the Marginalization of Gay Asian Men." *Contemporary Justice Review* 11 (1): 11–22.

Hook, Derek. 2012. *A Critical Psychology of the Postcolonial: The Mind of Apartheid.* East Sussex: Routledge.

Krishnan, Manisha. 2016. "So Many Gay Dudes Are Openly Racist on Dating Apps."
    Vice. Accessed February 1, 2017. https://www.vice.com/en_ca/article/so-many-gay-
    dudes-are-depressingly-racist-on-dating-apps.
McBride, Dwight. 2005. *Why I Hate Abercrombie & Fitch: Essays on Race and Sexuality*.
    New York: NYU Press.
McCaskell, Tim. 1998. "Towards a Sexual Economy of Rice Queenliness: Lust, Power
    and Racism." In *Rice: Explorations into Gay Asian Culture and Politics*, edited by Song
    Cho, 45–48. Toronto: Queer Press.
Nguyen, Tan Hoang. 2014. *A View from the Bottom: Asian American Masculinity and
    Sexual Representation*. Durham: Duke University Press.
Race, Kane. 2015. "Speculative Pragmatism and Intimate Arrangements: Online Hook-
    up Devices in Gay Life." *Culture, Health & Sexuality* 17 (4): 496–511.
Raj, Senthorun. 2011. "Grindring Bodies: Racial and Affective Economies of Online
    Queer Desire." *Critical Race and Whiteness Studies* 7 (2): 1–12.
Riggs, Damien W. 2013. "Anti-Asian Sentiment amongst a Sample of White Australian
    Men on Gaydar." *Sex Roles* 68 (11–12): 768–78.
Riggs, Damien W., and Martha Augoustinos. 2005. "The Psychic Life of Colonial Pow-
    er: Racialised Subjectivities, Bodies and Methods." *Journal of Community & Applied
    Social Psychology* 15 (6): 461–77.
Robinson, Brandon Andrew. 2015. "'Personal Preference' as the New Racism: Gay
    Desire and Racial Cleansing in Cyberspace." *Sociology of Race and Ethnicity* 1 (2):
    317–30.
Said, Edward. 1977. *Orientalism*. London: Penguin.
Sire, Zachary. 2011. "It Could End Up in a Date, but the Main Goal is Meeting New
    People." The Sword. Accessed February 6, 2017. http://www.thesword.com/it-
    could-end-up-in-a-date-but-the-main-goal-is-meeting-new-people.html.
Suler, John. 2004. "The Online Disinhibition Effect." *Cyberpsychology & Behavior* 7 (3):
    321–26.
Thorne, Adrian, and Justine Coupland. 1998. "Articulations of Same-Sex Desire: Les-
    bian and Gay Male Dating Advertisements." *Journal of Sociolinguistics* 2 (2): 233–57.
Vernon, Polly. 2010. "Grindr: A New Sexual Revolution." *The Observer*, Social Net-
    working. Accessed February 6, 2017. https://www.theguardian.com/media/2010/jul/
    04/grindr-the-new-sexual-revolution.
White, Jaclyn M., Sari L. Reisner, Emilia Dunham, and Matthew J. Mimiaga. 2014.
    "Race-based Sexual Preferences in a Sample of Online Profiles of Urban Men Seek-
    ing Sex with Men." *Journal of Urban Health* 91 (4): 768–75.

SIX

Coping with Racism and Racial Trauma

An Interpretative Phenomenological Analysis of How Gay Men from the African Diaspora Experience and Negotiate Racist Encounters

Sulaimon Giwa

Globally, Canada is reputed to be a welcoming country—a refuge for people fleeing repressive regimes of all kinds, including heterosexist social structures. Canadian multiculturalism and the language of diversity conspire to buttress an image of Canada as a cultural mosaic that includes all people, regardless of differences. For example, as a result of formal legal equality for same-sex-attracted people starting in the late 1960s, which culminated in the legalization of same-sex marriage in 2005 (Hurley 2005), differences based on sexual orientation have been assumed to be negligible. They are said to not negatively impact a person's ability to meet the ordinary demands of contemporary life.

The inclusion of same-sex-attracted people in the institution of marriage is taken to mean equality for both whites and non-whites. However, such thinking overlooks how inequality based on race and ethnicity shapes differential outcomes for white and gay men from the African and Caribbean diaspora (George et al. 2012; Wahab and Plaza 2009; Walcott 2016). The benefits of marriage widely celebrated by white gay men might be secondary or peripheral to the social struggle for racial justice among same-sex-attracted people in the African diaspora. (In this chapter, and consistent with current nomenclature, *African diaspora* refers to people of African heritage who now live outside of that continent's borders.)

While many factors shape a person's decision to leave his or her home country, for gay men of African descent living in Canada, the myth of Canadian diversity is an important consideration. In some African countries where same-sex attraction is criminalized, same-sex behavior can attract severe punishment, ranging from a term of fourteen years to life (Carroll 2016). In places like Mauritania and Sudan, moreover, an order to enforce the death penalty is codified in law (Lee and Ostergard 2017). These repressive practices rely on real or imagined threats that, in turn, create favorable conditions for emigration to Western countries such as Canada.

Once in Canada, gay men from the African diaspora are confronted with a new reality, namely racism (Brennan et al. 2013; Walcott 2016). The term *racism* describes a social process by which the dominant white racial group views itself as inherently superior to non-white racial groups, and then acts in ways that uphold that belief system (Fredrickson 2002), undermining the sense of worth and dignity of racially marginalized groups. In addition to the broader racism of Canadian society, and because gay men from the African diaspora occupy multiple marginalized groups, they are also subjected to racism in predominantly white gay men's communities (Norsah 2015).

In both contexts, but especially the latter, racism has its own psychic life, for racism is imbued with power differences that unfairly structure human relations. It works to privilege white gay men by allowing them to refuse to see and accept the negative social outcomes of whiteness on racially marginalized members. Whiteness can be conceived as a form of property ownership (Harris 1993), in which symbolic and material benefits accrue to white gay men and not to those pejoratively racialized. In addition, whiteness is invisible to those who are white. This is key to its normalization, which predictably helps to maintain an oppressive social order, since indiscernibility precludes the possibility for meaningful social action. Central to the power of invisibility, moreover, is the operation of whiteness as the standard against which racialized groups are measured (Giwa 2016). In this way, whiteness continues to evade scrutiny, while gay men from the African diaspora remain the object under surveillance. The constitutive relations of whiteness and racism, as inextricably linked phenomena, are thus fundamental to the production and preservation of the psychic life of racism in gay men's communities.

A general sense of apathy or indifference continues toward the racism enacted against gay men from the African diaspora (Majied and Moss-Knight 2012; Norsah 2015). In some ways, the word *racism* seems to have lost its social value. It has become absorbed into everyday lexicon, so as to lack the force it ought to have. Instead, it has been turned into a word that can be negotiated and thrashed out in open debate, often to placate white people and provide solace for them in their fragility and expectation for racial comfort (DiAngelo 2011). The danger, of course, is that the negative consequences of racism are rarely taken seriously; unspoken racism remains hidden beneath the surface, with the potential of wreaking havoc on a target's physical, emotional, spiritual, and psychological well-being (Ghabrial 2017; Giwa 2016). The needed attention that should be placed on the conditions created by racism are misdirected, focusing instead on white gay men's internalized sense of innocence.

A realignment of focus is needed, in which the experiences of non-white gay men are placed in the center. Here, the concept of *racial trauma* (Carter 2007) is useful, given its emphasis on how the stress of racism can become traumatic. Racial trauma describes a racism-related condition in which an emotionally and distressing experience can overwhelm an individual's ability to cope, and have potential negative health effects (Carter 2007). The racial microaggressions faced by gay men from the African diaspora are enduring and cumulative in nature; repeated acts of racism can pose a known risk to their health (Giwa 2016). At times, trauma has been defined in reference to extraordinary situations or events outside of everyday human experience, as illustrated by the example of a tsunami. Such a definition is reductionist, since it overlooks how daily, nonextraordinary, acts of racism can be traumatic. Trauma is not the absence of a major catastrophe or tragedy; rather, it relies on a subjective understanding of an objective traumatic experience regardless of the magnitude (Weinberg and Gil 2016). This is not to say that gay men from the African diaspora uniformly experience trauma. Such an idea would only simplify a subjectively complex process, one that is not necessarily homogeneous. But because the word *racism* is ubiquitous and used freely by white gay men to advance their sociopolitical and economic interests, as if to suggest that racism and discrimination based on sexual orientation are the same, racial trauma offers a language for explicating the consequences of racism on non-white gay men.

The above advantages notwithstanding, racial trauma can also give a false impression that gay men from the African diaspora lack strength and resolve in resisting their oppression. In other words, racial trauma can tread dangerously on deficit, and thus risk overlooking the dialectics of resistance to white racism. One form of resistance is coping—that is, cognitive and behavioral actions taken in response to a taxing situation or experience in one's life (Lazarus and Folkman 1984).

In the United States, where most of the research on coping with racism originates, findings suggest that gay men of color do not passively accept their experiences of racial discrimination. Insights from quantitative (Han et al. 2015) and qualitative (Choi et al. 2011) studies indicate that gay men of color adopt varying types of coping strategies in dealing with racism-based stress. These strategies can be crudely categorized as emotion- and problem-focused coping. In the former, an individual's effort is aimed at managing a negative emotional response to stress; in the latter, it is meant to remove or eliminate the source of stress (Lazarus and Folkman 1984). The effectiveness of a coping strategy depends on a person's appraisal and evaluation of his or her ability to deal with the racist event. Thus, emotion-focused coping, which some people might view as inferior, may be as valuable as problem-focused coping. No one style of coping is better than another.

Despite increasing acceptance of knowledge in this area, however, empirical research remains scant (Majied and Moss-Knight 2012). There is need for more research focused on the coping strategies used by black and other gay men from the African diaspora to deal with the social stressor of racism, most especially in Canada. This type of research is critical to advancing knowledge about individual, group, and community resilience, beyond deficit-oriented approaches that fail at a deeper understanding of people's lives.

This qualitative, exploratory chapter begins from the standpoint that gay men from the African diaspora exist within complex systems and structures. They must navigate their way through difficult social arrangements, which can affect their ability to live a life untethered from systems of oppression. In the face of adversity, how do they cope? Specifically, what strategies are employed to resist and speak back to a racial oppressive social order? This focus on coping is not meant to make these men responsible for their own oppression. Rather, this line of inquiry seeks to shift away from a deficit approach to a consideration of strength and resilience; that is, an individual's ability to respond to changing situational demands and bounce back from negative environmental risk experiences (Masten 2014; Rutter 1985). In this way, the study reported in this chapter aims to advance knowledge in this area, and create opportunities for new "truths" grounded in subaltern alternative accounts that contest the supremacy of white racism in gay men's communities.

The chapter is divided into five sections. Section 1 provides an overview of the available research on racism-related stress/trauma and coping. Section 2 offers a brief outline of the theoretical frameworks used in the implementation of the research study. Section 3 discusses the process of data collection and analysis. Section 4 presents the findings of the data analysis. Section 5 is a discussion of the findings in relation to previous research, and includes a consideration of the specific limitations of the study, followed by a conclusion.

MINING THE CANADIAN LITERATURE FOR RESEARCH ON COPING WITH RACISM AND RACIAL TRAUMA AMONG GAY MEN FROM THE AFRICAN DIASPORA

Despite incremental progress being made by Canadian researchers to explore the experience of racism among gay men of color, including those from the African diaspora, the bulk of available research remains focused on white gay men (Brennan et al. 2013; Ghabrial 2017; Norsah 2015). When non-white gay men are included in research, the general tendency has been to examine their lives from a deficit or pathological perspective (Akerlund and Cheung 2000; Giwa and Greensmith 2012). This focus has proven difficult to transcend, mainly because of the financial incentive provided by funding bodies for research that perpetuate a one-dimensional view of gay men who are not white. Such a funding scheme acts as a trap, luring researchers to accelerate the pace of HIV/AIDS research, so as to justify continuation of study support. In a problematic sense, HIV/AIDS has become the entry point for debate and analysis about social justice issues such as racism (Giwa 2016; Giwa and Greensmith 2012). Rather than occupy a primary focus of interest, racism is relegated to a subordinate status, where it becomes a footnote to the more profitable HIV/AIDS research. This limited focus has meant that studies involving non-white gay men have not progressed in the same way as those focused on white gay men.

Specifically, at the same time that racism is being recognized as a problem within gay men's communities in Canada, empirical investigations have not always delved beyond surface acknowledgment of this fact. Given the insidious nature of racism, however, a more comprehensive, deeper approach is required to understand the complexity of the lives of gay men from racially marginalized communities. This is of particular concern, since a limited but growing body of Canadian research suggests that racism can have an adverse impact on the health of black and African Canadians (James et al. 2010; Veenstra and Patterson 2016). Therefore, to reduce the negative effects of racism-related stress and trauma, it is important to understand how the targets of racism make sense of and cope with their experience. Currently, very little Canadian research examines the meaning-making, coping styles of gay men of color and, in particular, gay men from the African diaspora.

By contrast, an emerging body of American research has explored the coping responses of gay men of color to racism. One study examined the responses of Asian and Pacific Islander gay men ($N = 23$) to different types of social discrimination experiences, including racism, homophobia, and anti-immigrant discrimination (Wilson and Yoshikawa 2004). Among respondents, confrontational-type responses (i.e., putting down, insulting, and/or educating) were most common, at 18 percent; this was followed by self-attributed, external attribution, social-network-based and avoidance responses, at approximately 10 percent. In the case of the latter response style, evidence indicated that avoidance did not necessarily imply passivity. An important finding by the researchers was that some participants internalized the experience of racism, attributing its occurrence to themselves, rather than to the actual source of the discrimination. The researchers conjectured that these men might feel disempowered to negotiate risk-reduction strategies when confronted with the passive/submissive Asian stereotype.

Likewise, Bryant (2008) explored, among other factors, the strategies used by black men who have sex with men (MSM, N = 13) to cope with homophobia and racism. Consistent with Wilson and Yoshikawa's (2004) overall findings, Bryant's research showed that participants used confrontation (e.g., vocal disapproval of discriminatory interactions) and social-network coping responses when faced with multiple oppressions of homophobia and racism.

Choi et al. (2011) conducted the first study investigating the stigma strategies used by African American, Asian and Pacific Islander, and Latino MSM of color in the United States. It employed focus group discussions (n = 50) and in-depth interviews (n = 35) to explore how gay men of color managed their experiences of racism and homophobia. Of the five identified strategies, concealment of sexuality and disassociation from social settings were used to manage discrimination based on sexual orientation and racism, respectively. In contrast, direct confrontation, dismissing the stigmatization, and drawing strength and comfort from external sources were used concurrently to mitigate instances of racism and homophobia. Similar to Wilson and Yoshikawa (2004), Choi et al. found that not all stigmas and discriminations were created equal; each might require a different type of response.

Han et al. (2014) investigated how Asian gay men (N = 55) managed and negotiated the social stigma of race and racism within the larger gay community. Four racial stigma management strategies were identified, reflecting individual- and group-level processes. These were: passing, distancing and affiliating, promoting racial visibility, and increasing racial identification. According to the authors, some participants sought to manage their stigmatized identity by passing as non-Asians; however, this strategy had limited effectiveness outside of virtual reality, due to the visibility of racial markers such as skin color. Distancing and affiliating was somewhat successful; here, participants attempted to differentiate themselves from other Asian gay men, in order to associate more closely with white gay men, and to neutralize the perception of them as feminine and undesirable. One Asian gay man said: "I'm bigger than other Asian guys, so I think that white guys that don't normally go for Asian guys find me attractive. I also don't look like a bottom, so I usually don't get rice queens hitting on me, it's usually just ordinary white guys that hit on me" (Han, Proctor and Choi 2014, 227). Beyond increasing the self-esteem of such individuals, even if for a short period of time, these men might intentionally or unintentionally contribute to the stigmatization of their own group by reinforcing the same racial stereotypes that white gay men have perpetuated about them.

Unlike the first two strategies, which focus on the personal, promoting racial visibility as a strategy against the stigma of race/racism involved a set of actions meant to elevate the social status of the group as a whole. Becoming more visible in the gay community was thought to be important for recognition and to contest negative stereotypes held due to misinformation or ignorance by white gay men about Asian gay men.

Lastly, Asian gay men sometimes chose to identify more with their own racial group. This is consistent with the attitude or position of identity politics. Dating within the group and encouraging coalition among Asian gay men, as a political action, was also believed to improve the group's overall social status and protect or enhance their views of themselves; additionally, insisting on a social marketing portrayal of two Asian gay couples (as opposed to Asian-white gay couples) would help with how Asian gay men see themselves and how others see them.

More recently, Han et al. (2015) examined the coping strategies used by African American, Asian/Pacific Islander, and Latino men to determine the moderating effects of these strategies on race-related stress for sexual risk and unprotected anal intercourse. Their study comprised 403 African American, 393 Asian/Pacific Islander, and 400 Latino men, for a total sample of 1,196. Among the sampled population, 65 percent reported being stressed from the experience of racism; 19 percent reported that they experienced racism, but were not stressed by it; and only 16 percent said that they did not experience racism within the gay community.

There was a racial and ethnic difference in these findings. Compared to the African American and Latino groups, Asian/Pacific Islander men were more likely to report racism-related stress, at 73 percent. African American men reported stress from racism at 63 percent, followed by Latino men at 60 percent. Regarding the coping strategies used to deal with racism—avoidance, dismissal, social support, education, and confrontation—significant racial and ethnic difference was seen in the domain of education/confrontation. This strategy was most prevalent among the Asian/Pacific Islander men and less prevalent among African American and Latino men respectively. No significant racial and ethnic differences were reported for avoidance, dismissal, and social support strategies. Finally, analyses of bivariate and multivariate logistic regressions revealed that men who had experienced stress as a result of racism in the gay community had been more predisposed to engage in unprotected anal intercourse in the previous six months, with no reported differences in the prevalence and impact across racial and ethnic groups.

THEORETICAL FRAMEWORKS

The current study drew on several theoretical perspectives to enable a deeper understanding of the strategies used by gay men from the African diaspora to cope with racism and racial trauma. It was informed by critical social theories—in particular, critical race theory (CRT), queer critical theory (QCT), and Minority Stress Theory, which integrated insights from the transactional model of stress and coping. CRT challenges existing conceptions of race and racial power, by asserting the ordinariness of racism as a normal and integral feature of Canadian society (Aylward 1999; Razack and Jeffery 2002). Central to its critique is the notion of white supremacy and racial privilege, since these relate to the structural continuities of racism that help to maintain and reinforce white dominance. In its goal of eradicating racism, CRT seeks to unmask cultural patterns and practices that sustain racial inequality, using stories and counterstories to privilege the marginalized voices of non-white people (Han 2008; Solórzano and Yosso 2002).

QCT, an offshoot of CRT, extends CRT's analysis of race and ethnicity to include nonheteronormative discourse. It allows for a cogent analysis of race and racism within gay men's communities, emphasizing the interlocking nature of sexual orientation and racial/ethnic identity. A central premise of the theory is that an individual's experience of racism and sexual orientation can neither be compartmentalized nor theorized in isolation. These experiences are intertwined and must be conceptualized in their entirety, given the influence of one identity on the other. According to Misawa (2012), six themes guide this framework:

1. *the centrality of the intersection of race and racism with sexual orientation and homophobia*—describes how race and sexual orientation are interlocking, with the dynamics of racism and homophobia conspiring to affect the lives of gay men of color;
2. *a challenge to mainstream ideologies*—contests beliefs about racism, homophobia, and heterosexism that support the supremacy of the dominant group in power;
3. *a confrontation with ahistoricism*—calls attention to the dialectical relationship between the past and present, to underscore the importance of situating contemporary social justice issues in their historical contexts;
4. *the centrality of experiential knowledge*—draws on the lived experiences of gay men of color to inform understanding about the interlocking structures of race and sexual orientation;
5. *multidisciplinary aspects*—unify individual voices to create a collective narrative that will drive social change and social justice; and
6. *a social justice perspective*—acknowledges the simultaneity of oppression experienced by gay men of color and thus seeks to eradi-

cate all forms of oppression with the goal of an equitable and just society.

Minority Stress Theory emphasizes that difficult situations, like experiences of heterosexist (Meyer 1995, 2003) or racist events, can lead to deleterious mental and physical health for members of stigmatized groups, such as gay men from the African diaspora. It provides a way to understand people in their environment, and accounts for the salience of ameliorative effects of coping and social support on well-being. The latter—based on the transaction model of stress and coping developed by Lazarus and Folkman (1984)—suggests that successful coping with the challenges of minority stress may lessen its negative effects on health.

According to Riggs and Treharne (2017), some shortcomings to Minority Stress Theory are worth bearing in mind. Chief among them is the model's preoccupation with a subjective view of stress, in that the institutionalized effects of stress on well-being are overlooked, undermining the need for change in ideology and societal norms that lead to stress being experienced in the first place. My application of minority stress is consistent with the decompensation approach proposed by Riggs and Treharne, given its emphasis on social change and the resistance of gay men from the African diaspora to racism and racial trauma.

METHOD AND DATA ANALYSIS

The data for this project were derived from a small-scale study of thirteen participants. This study used a cross-sectional, qualitative research design, with respondent selection based on purposive homogenous and snowball sampling. The phenomenological study investigated the experiences of and coping responses to white racism among gay men of color who, according to the 2011 National Household Survey and the Ottawa Community Profile, comprise the top visible minority groups in the study area (Statistics Canada 2013). Included in these groups are blacks, East Asians (in particular, Chinese), South Asians, and Arabs or people of Middle Eastern descent. Among black participants—the focus of the current paper—the majority (three out of four) identified as African-born, with migration to Canada from Namibia and South Africa, Burundi, and Ghana. They ranged in age from 21 to 31 years, with a mean age of 27.3. Word of mouth, university and college student association listservs, and Facebook proved to be the most effective recruitment strategies. The small sample size was ideal, as it was necessary for the researcher to explore each participant's experience independently and within a group context. In determining the size of the group, I considered Smith et al.'s (2009) suggestion that a bigger sample size did not imply quality work, and followed Morgan's (1997) advice, who wrote: "Small groups are more useful when the researcher desires a clear sense of each participant's reaction to a topic simply because they give each participant more time to talk" (42). Later, he added, "I have conducted groups of 3 highly involved participants that would have been unmanageable at size 6, and I have led discussions in naturally occurring groups of 15 to 20" (43). An informed consent process was undertaken to safeguard the ethical involvement of participants in the study, which was approved by an ethics committee at York University.

The participants took part in an open-ended, two-hour focus group discussion moderated by the researcher—a Nigerian, thus specific to their ethnoracial group. Group discussion was held at Opinion Search (now Nielsen Opinion Quest), a research firm centrally located in downtown Ottawa, reachable by public transportation, and accessible to wheelchair users. The focus group was guided by a researcher-constructed interview protocol that included four specific sets of questions on coping; for example, "How have you coped with personal experiences of racism discussed in the group?" When appropriate, follow-up prompt questions were asked to get participants to think more deeply about the topic and to clarify vague comments or responses. The focus group was audiorecorded for transcription and coding, and in addition was videorecorded, to ensure participants' words were correctly matched to the right speaker. A $30 incentive was paid for participation in the study. Pseudonyms were assigned to all participants and identifying information was removed.

Findings were analyzed using interpretative phenomenological analysis (IPA), with data parsed twice, at the idiographic and group level (Smith et al. 2009). IPA aims to understand how people make sense of life experiences such as racism and racial trauma. Unlike thematic or grounded theory, in which the development and/or application of existing theories are privileged, IPA focuses on identifying and analyzing patterns in participants' narratives. It does not seek to propose theory and is not driven by one (Ghabrial 2017). Five steps comprise the data analysis process: reading and rereading of original data; initial noting or exploratory commentary; developing emergent themes; identifying connections across emergent themes; and looking for patterns across individual- and within-group-level themes (Smith et al. 2009).

FINDINGS

Analysis of idiographic and group-level data resulted in the following commonly discussed major themes: (a) avoiding noninclusive and nonaffirming gay spaces; (b) being vigilant against the social threats of racism and racial trauma; and (c) seeking social support from friends and other sources. These major themes reflect the forms of resistance and coping strategies employed by gay men from the African diaspora to deal with racism-based discrimination in the gay community of Ottawa.

Avoiding Noninclusive and Nonaffirming Gay Spaces

Participants were unanimous in the view that racism existed in the gay community of Ottawa; it was seen to manifest individually, institutionally, and culturally. They perceived the spatial context as both noninclusive and nonaffirming of them and others who were not white. The lack of inclusion and affirmation was linked to the cliquishness of white gay men, whose platonic and nonplatonic relationships were primarily with other white men. One exception was when they were being sexualized or exoticized by white gay men on the basis of their ethnoracial identity. On the one hand, this practice reinforced their tokenism and, on the other, contributed to their invisibility when not being tokenized. The resulting implication of this social exclusion was the experience of otherness and disconnection from the gay community that participants felt; all of them expressed a desire for inclusive and affirming spaces outside of the gay community. One participant suggested:

> I don't bother myself so much with wanting to feel validated in spaces that don't want to validate me. So even at school, in the GLBTQ community, I don't participate in many of the initiatives that are being put together. And you know, instead I want to focus my efforts on, you know, connecting with folks who share my experience and think the way I do, I guess. (Eddie, age 21, gay)

Another participant noted how the Ottawa gay community represented a painful site of un/belonging, such that he wanted to disassociate completely from the community and shunned the label *gay*, which he felt described the experience of white men in same-sex relationships. The trauma of racism was suggested to be an aggravating factor on his health, and underscored the possible link between traumatic racism and a gastrointestinal disorder. The combination of these factors reinforced his decision to avoid the predominantly white gay community, as a matter of physical and mental wellness crucial to one's overall health:

> I have a strong desire to create my own space, to find my own space. If there was like a viable black gay space, I would never go to a white gay community. It's unfortunate we don't have the numbers here . . . we'd have our own space. I don't have anything against white people . . . it's difficult to love someone who doesn't love you. I'm still looking for a different . . . label to describe myself instead of gay. [Racism] definitely has . . . affected the way I define myself . . . I don't define myself as gay . . . I don't want to be put in that same category as [white gay men] . . . I don't have anything in common with them. I don't feel part of that community . . . I feel uncomfortable being identified with that community. I don't feel comfortable going there because you're going

to repeat the same treatment . . . the same uncomfortable experience . . .
I have irritable bowel syndrome . . . I won't go there because the treatment [is] traumatic. (Kwame, age 31, same-gender-loving/homosexual)

The far-reaching effect of traumatic racism, as another participant remarked, can be seen in its dehumanization and erasure of black and other
gay men of the African diaspora from the gay community. The participant expressed how rare it was for him to see men who look like him
patronizing gay spaces, suggesting that their absence or marginality may
be related to an individual or collective need to reduce the stress of racial
discrimination. Importantly, his comment points to the self-sanitizing effects of racism, such that black and other gay men of the African diaspora
are forced to remove themselves from spaces where the effects of racist
behaviors are omnipresent. Those brave enough to enter this space, as he
and his friends do, feel stripped of their humanity. Divested of human
and personal subjectivity, they are treated as objects and commodities for
white consumption.

> Respondent: Like I go out with my friends and it's really rare to see
> other black men out. And [ ] sometimes [in the gay clubs] they just see
> young black men dancing on the dance floor, like when you're going
> out, it's like the exotic they like, not the human being.
>
> Interviewer: And how does that make you feel when you go out, to see
> and experience stuff like that?
>
> Respondent: I feel insulted. [ ] Like Oprah said, you have to be respon-
> sible of the energy you bring into a room. And then you go there [to the
> gay club] as a human being, I'm a human being, and then they don't
> even see the human being. It's like they just see the object. And some-
> times, like especially older guys, sometimes they really look at you and
> you feel naked, yet you're dressed. (Philippe, age 30, gay)

Being Vigilant against the Social Threats of Racism and Racial Trauma

Participants expressed a conscious awareness of existing in a social
context where their skin color negatively differentiated them from their
white gay counterparts. This racialized reality, they believed, required
them to be vigilant or attentive to the threat of racism both imagined and
real. Often, this took the form of excessive thinking or rumination and
tempering expectations of their acceptance by white gay men. In this
way, they would be prepared to address the racist behaviors directed at
them, either by confronting the racist perpetrator or reframing the meaning of the traumatic racist behavior, so that they are less stinging. One
participant remarked:

> I guess [ ] I'm not allowing myself to be desensitized to things. Like I
> try not to find myself in a position where I think it's normal to be
> treated a certain way, right. I need to be very critical about everything,

so I try to sort of have my critical thinking cap on always. When I see something [ ] I deconstruct it and I think about [ ] who is framing that picture, who's framing the narrative, who's framing the conversation. That's one thing I do. (Eddie, age 21, gay)

As another participant suggested, expecting white gay men to accept him and other black men as they are is unrealistic at worst and wishful thinking at best. Coming to terms with always being seen as the other means freedom from hoping for acceptance where none is likely to come. It also means being clear-eyed or pragmatic about the burden of responsibility being on white gay men to deal with the internal discomfort that leads to the practices of racism. Such pragmatism can reduce the likelihood that racism will go uncontested or escape the attention of its targets.

> For me, personally, to believe that I will be accepted on the same level as other white gay men, is a little bit unrealistic. I have given up on the hope that they will accept me the way I want them to. [ ] I don't want to say it's not true, but at some level I believe that I'm always going to be perceived as an other, not in a good way. I believe that there is that internal discomfort of me being recognized, of me being accepted as an equal. And that kind of recognition is normally limited to the white gay community. (Kwame, age 31, same-gender-loving/homosexual)

Vigilance, while necessary, should not be so intruding as to consume one's entire existence. Hypervigilance can, according to the participant quoted below, come at the expense of perspective-taking. A target might develop tunnel vision, in which he becomes fixated on identifying racism and wrongdoers, without attempting to understand the perspectives of individuals on the opposite side (i.e., alleged racist perpetrators). The words *don't always*, as used by the participant, signal his awareness of racism-related vigilance in managing the social threat of traumatic racism. However, for this participant, vigilance and perspective-taking are complementary and not mutually exclusive phenomena. The former, when overdone, can deepen division between races, overriding our sense of shared humanity.

> I don't always think about it. And, but the difference, like I said earlier, I'm interested in people, not in their color. [ ] There are some people who, any small thing they see racism in it. Like it's as if they're looking for that, you know, that racist comment, all the time. I'm not like that. I'm just, I don't want to think about it. (Philippe, age 30, gay)

The idea of perspective-taking notwithstanding, there is a danger in not being vigilant against the social threats of traumatic racism and oppression, as the participant's quote below illustrates. Targets might wrongly and conceivably shoulder responsibility for racist acts perpetrated against them; they might begin to doubt and question themselves about their negative experiences. Such situations are made worse by racist perpetrators who refuse to take responsibility, holding their own targets blameworthy:

> Respondent: So whenever I talk about my experiences, it's denied; it doesn't exist and it's only [ ] in my imagination.
>
> Interviewer: Denied by whom?
>
> Respondent: By mostly white gay men. My account of what happened, for example, in the bar, you know, when I go to the bar people just withdraw. Like there is this unspoken, I don't want to say, should I say aversion, it's just kind of people just move away from you, like there's a problem.
>
> Interviewer: So these white individuals, what kind of things would they say to you?
>
> Respondent: They say it's not true. They try to minimize it; they try to dismiss it, that it's not true. People wouldn't do that. I know someone with a black boyfriend, you know, that is what they say. (Kwame, age 31, same-gender-loving/homosexual)

Seeking Social Support from Friends and Other Sources

Participants commonly expressed the importance of social support for coping with the stress of traumatic racism. In particular, support from queer and gay men from the African diaspora seemed preferable to formal social support. This type of support was seen to promote camaraderie, which facilitated a safe space for disclosure of shared lived experience with social marginalization. In many ways, informal support of friends afforded connection with like-minded people, minimizing feelings of social isolation. That is, participants did not feel alone in their experience when their realities were validated by others in the group. One participant suggested:

> Another thing I do, some of my fabulous, radical, queer friends of mine, we have black family evenings and stuff. And so we go out and we have martinis and we just get together and talk about stuff that we can't really speak about [in other contexts]. There was an incident [where this individual] was clearly being racist and we can come together and really vent and speak about that and get that off our chest, right. We party together. (Eddie, age 21, gay)

The benefit of social support, as the participant quoted below suggests, extends beyond conversation or debriefing about each other's experiences. It can also be used for protecting oneself against the possible occurrence of racial trauma in places like gay nightclubs. In this instance, having the support of friends afforded the participant the ability to go out and dance, while being in a social group might have acted as a deterrent for external threats of racism or discrimination on other grounds.

But I've got a way of, like protecting myself. As [Kwame] was saying, you go somewhere and then people just, like disappear. What I, we do, I rarely, rarely, and like I love going out and dancing, and I rarely go alone. I can never go alone. I'm always with my friends. [ ] When I go out [I don't like] how people look [at me]: I'm not white, don't have six packs, black gay man, and fat. So maybe it's a way of protecting myself so that I don't see that [racism]. (Philippe, age 30, gay)

Social support can also be broadly conceptualized to include information-seeking from key figures and scholars from one's ethnoracial group. This type of support is most helpful in the absence of formal support, and where an individual lacks informal systems of support, such as friends. In this case, these figures and scholars are seen as invaluable sources of knowledge and wisdom for learning about and making sense of one's oppression:

> I listen to a lot of progressive people within that area. I listen to Melissa Harris-Perry. She's also an African American woman. So I listen to these people and they give me a sense of meaning, they try to explain it to me. They try to make meaning out of something difficult. I think that really trying to make meaning of it, trying to break it apart and trying to understand it, really helps. (Kwame, age 31, same-gender-loving/ homosexual)

This same participant underscored the significance of one's social bond to friends and other sources of support, saying that it was about survival—a sentiment that was echoed by others. For this participant, having the ability to draw on the strength and resilience of other black and/or gay men from the African diaspora was critical to avoiding the pathological trap of racism. In this way, he was able to maintain his mental health and sanity:

> It's a coping strategy. Without it I don't think I would be sane. I [would] really be on edge, you know. It's very crucial for me [to have those connections]. Words cannot describe how important that connection is, you know. And at the same time, words cannot describe how it feels when that connection is broken. (Kwame, age 31, same-gender-loving/homosexual)

DISCUSSION

This study was undertaken with the goal of understanding how Canadian gay men from the African diaspora in Ottawa experience and cope with racism and racial trauma. It offers a critical intervention in our knowledge about the performativity of white racism and, most importantly, emphasizes participants' "transformational resistance" (Solórzano and Bernal 2001, 324) to racial oppression. As a study focused on the enactment of white racism against racialized others, the notion of transformational resistance is an important one. For too long, the literature about racism in gay men's communities privileged a one-dimensional narrative, with the unintentional result of recentering whiteness and the power of white gay men as key actors (Giwa 2016; Han 2007, 2008). This kind of myopia explains, in part, how the real and productive work of resistance being performed by non-whites has been effaced. In the first instance, whiteness is taken to be synonymous with purpose, intentionality, and agency. By contrast, non-whiteness is equated with being passive, unresisting, and lacking agency. This false binary has saturated our thinking about the operation of racism in gay men's communities, foreclosing opportunities for counterstories at the heart of the racial problem (Han 2008). In overlooking the counterstories of resistance, power to frame the discussion about racism—in terms of whose voices get heard and why—remains largely in the hands of white gay men.

This double standard reflects a structural system of racial hierarchy in society at large, where whiteness becomes the conceptual lens through which non-white experiences of marginalization are supposedly knowable. Thus, as a system of racial oppression, whiteness assumes an unassailable character, with the power to define the reality of the oppressed. The lack of attention to the danger inherent in white people speaking for the oppressed reifies a colonial power/knowledge structure from which the latter are denied a voice in making narratives about their lived realities knowable. The current project attempted at subverting this white racial structure of domination by centering the voices of gay men from the African diaspora, highlighting multiple resistances or coping strategies used in dealing with the stress of racism and racial trauma.

Three coping strategies emerged from the study about how gay men from the African diaspora coped with racism and racial trauma: (a) avoiding noninclusive and nonaffirming gay spaces; (b) being vigilant against the social threats of racism and racial trauma; and (c) seeking social support from friends and other sources. Despite participants' unique characteristics and the distinct exploratory themes generated, all regarded these three coping strategies as effective for mitigating their exposure to perceived and/or real threats of racism and racial trauma.

Avoidance

Participants experienced the gay community of Ottawa as not welcoming of them and other gay men of color. They generally found that white gay men kept to themselves and behaved like a clique, except when sexually exoticizing them for the sole purpose of sexual intercourse. This practice reinforced their precarious status, such that they existed at the margins of the gay community, where they were treated as if they were less than their white counterparts. The exposure to repeated acts of racial exclusion and marginalization led them to reconsider their relationship to the gay community: they either felt it was in their best interest to avoid certain areas of the community (e.g., nightclubs) that were unwelcoming to them or to remove themselves from the community altogether. By taking these actions, participants sought to minimize their exposure to racism-related stressors and its associated negative health impacts.

Thus, racism acted as a push factor from certain areas of the community or the community at large. Research by Nakamura, Chan, and Fischer (2013) on the experiences of community integration among first- and second-generation Asian MSM in Canada supports the above finding. The authors found that, although some Asian MSM held a more positive impression of the gay community than their ethnoracial community, others found it racist, a place where it was difficult to make friends and meet people; the sense of the gay community as being "cliquey" and "hard to crack" were highlighted as contributing factors in this experience. Similarly, some African American participants in the study by Choi et al. (2011) intentionally avoided social situations and settings where they expected to be subjected to racism. Others, however, chose to avoid certain individuals rather than distance themselves completely from these settings. Finally, when it comes to negotiating online sexual racism, the participants in Callander, Holt, and Newman's (2015) study reported that, to reduce their exposure to racism, they disconnected from seeking partners online.

Vigilance

In the second instance, participants expressed the importance of vigilance as a coping strategy for dealing with racism and racial trauma, at the same time noting its potential drawbacks (see Himmelstein et al. 2015 and LaVeist et al. 2014 for discussions on the negative aspects of vigilance). Beyond overt, heightened vigilance, in which participants did not allow themselves to be caught off guard by racist attacks, subtle vigilance functioned as a reality check. Specifically, participants held lower expectations for improved treatment and acceptance by white gay men. In so doing, they took control of negative situations, thereby limiting the ability of white gay men to dictate their social worth. In overt, heightened vigilance, the expectation of being confronted with racism and racial trauma can lead the targets of racism to be hypervigilant (Mays, Cochran, and Barnes 2007). Conversely, subtle vigilance offered a sense of control, as it brought into sharp focus the futility of waiting for white validation and acceptance. This is noteworthy, as earlier expectations of acceptance might have eliminated the need for racism-related vigilance.

Accepting that white gay men may be indisposed to treat them as equals means freedom from the shackles and reliance on white ideas about their inferiority. It also means freedom to call out racism at the individual, institutional, and cultural levels, without regard for political correctness or concern about appearing too angry. This latter point is important, in preventing the transference of responsibility for racism to the target, since, as the findings suggested, the tactic of denial used by white gay men blames the targets for their own negative experience. In both cases, racism-related vigilance was perceived to stave off threats of racial discrimination. This finding corroborates, to some degree, the research by Meyer et al. (2011) in which participants expressed vigilance in dealing with the minority stress of homophobia, racism, or sexism. In an ideal world, free from stigma and social inequality, these participants believed continuous vigilance would be unnecessary.

Seeking Social Support

Finally, in seeking social support from friends and other sources, participants underscored the significance of connecting with people who have similar, shared experiences. This typically involved support from others with similar racial backgrounds, since the common denominator in their oppression was the color of their skin. In this setting, participants felt free to vent their emotions and feelings, which was denied to them in the broader social context. More often than not, social support tended to be informal (e.g., *Black Fam*, a term used by participants to refer to the black racial composition of the social support group they were part of), being flexible to cater to the specific needs and interests of group members. Although participants were not completely opposed to formal support from mainstream organizations and service providers, for example, they held informal support in higher regard. Two insights from the current study explain this finding.

First, participants with past negative experiences with a mainstream organization or a service provider were less likely to view these as safe spaces or resources for support. In this way, previous negative experiences served as deterrents to future service utilization and unwillingness to seek support from professionals. Second, participants generally felt that service providers and other professionals lacked knowledge about the challenges they faced as individuals with multiply stigmatized identities. For one participant, moreover, the intersection of his physical disability with his race and sexual orientation also meant that he experienced oppression in a specific and unique way. The complexities of participants' lives were also often perceived to be reduced to the problem of HIV/AIDS, without regard for their present and future aspirations. This narrow focus, they argued, overlooked their desire for positive mentorship, among other goals.

As the data suggest, social support was not confined to a physical space; it extended to support received in the context of social outings—simply being in a group of friends could act as a preventive measure against racism and racial trauma. Participants found strength in numbers. The ability to draw on the confidence and emotional asset of the group helped them to feel empowered when facing discrimination from white gay men. Likewise, in contexts where support from black and/or gay men from the African diaspora was beyond reach, the scholarship, teachings, and life lessons of black scholars and intellectuals in the area of racism offered participants a way to make sense of their oppression. However, if this was an exercise pursued in solitude, it is possible that the inability to process these teachings and insights with others was a disadvantage.

Previous studies have linked social support with positive outcomes (Noh and Kaspar 2003; Yoshikawa et al. 2004). For example, Choi et al. (2011) found that African American MSM in their study relied on the strength of role models from their ethnoracial community to cope with racism. Their finding corroborates the research by Bryant (2008) and Yoshikawa et al. (2004). In their study, Yoshikawa et al. showed that family and friendship networks were effective in coping with racism, homophobia, and anti-immigration discrimination. Such support was also associated with lower levels of unprotected anal intercourse with a primary partner. Yet, as Han et al. (2015) recently found, the positive effects of social support had no influence on sexual risk for HIV among African American, Asian/Pacific Islander, and Latino MSM. The fact that Han et al. measured social support seeking and not the type of support received might explain the difference in findings.

Overall, the findings of the current study demonstrate that participants used emotion- and problem-focused coping strategies to deal with racism and racial trauma. Although the latter strategy would appear optimal, given the expectation that it could eliminate the source of stress, the findings underscored the utility of both approaches for responding to racial discrimination. Regardless of coping style, the important point was that participants found the approach useful in helping them to cope with racism-related situations. For example, although the emotional coping strategy of social support did not eliminate threats of racism or racial trauma, the fellowship of in-group members provided a reprieve from the toxic environment of white racism. This comradeship, as the data suggested, was important in counteracting feelings of social isolation that targets of racism often experience (Harrell 2000). For health and social service providers, the implication of this finding is that they need to consider the benefits of a particular coping strategy for an individual, without assuming that his choice of coping strategy is wrong or inadequate to achieve mental health and emotional well-being during times of adversity.

CONCLUSION

Certain limitations exist with this study that must be borne in mind when interpreting the findings. As phenomenological research, the sampling strategy was motivated by a concern for in-depth knowledge about how gay men from the African diaspora coped with racism and racial trauma. Thus, the sample was restricted to a small number of people, allowing each participant to speak in detail about his individual experiences in a focus-group setting. In this way, the sample was not intended to be representative; however, research findings might be transferable to gay men from the African diaspora in other, comparable cities. Since the study relied on self-reported information, response bias may have resulted in some participants under- or over-reporting incidents of racism or racial trauma, including coping mechanisms used to attenuate the stress of racial discrimination.

These limitations notwithstanding, it should be noted that the selection of Ottawa as the study site was a unique departure from other research that explored the experiences of these men and other gay men of color in Canada. In most cases, and not surprisingly, these studies were concentrated primarily in the city of Toronto, despite the increasingly growing ethnic and racial diversity of Canadian cities generally. It is necessary for academic research to move beyond the nucleus of Toronto and similar leading cities (e.g., Montreal and Vancouver) in order to increase national discussion of issues faced by this population. Finally, in light of the finding that formal support was prioritized less than informal support networks, future research should explore factors that might facilitate the effective use of formal support as a means of coping with racism and racial trauma.

In conclusion, and contrary to the long-standing view of non-white gay men as passive recipients of discrimination, this study revealed three coping strategies used by gay men from the African diaspora in coping with racism and racial trauma. Regardless of the category of coping style—emotion- or problem-focused—participants found all three strategies useful in mitigating the impact of racism-related stress. Important to the study is the concept of racial trauma, given its concern for the cumulative negative impact of racism. Whereas the term *racism* focuses on abusive behavior directed at members of an oppressed racial group, racial trauma calls attention to the effects of these abusive behaviors, underlining the dialectics of oppression. In the former, white gay men are positioned as dominant, free to act upon the racialized other without acts of resistance. However, the personal and social coping strategies used by gay men from the African diaspora in the study contrasted sharply with this narrative and notion of passivity.

This finding highlights the need for more asset-based rather than deficit-based research. A continued focus on deficit, in which the social realities of racism are defined by a unidirectional flow, risks undermining the strengths and resilience that promote the group's ability to cope with stress and adversity. If racism is to be addressed in gay men's communities, there is a need to go beyond the superficial discussion of diversity that masks and denies the real effects of racial trauma. Going forward, it will be critical that dialogues about racism begin to consider the relationship between oppression and resistance, with a view to understanding individual and collective opposition to the system of white hegemony.

REFERENCES

Akerlund, Mark, and Monit Cheung. 2000. "Teaching Beyond the Deficit Model: Gay and Lesbian Issues among African Americans, Latinos, and Asian Americans." *Journal of Social Work Education* 36 (2): 279–92.

Aylward, Carol A. 1999. *Canadian Critical Race Theory: Racism and the Law*. Halifax: Fernwood.

Brennan, David J., Kenta Asakura, Clemon George, Paul A. Newman, Sulaimon Giwa, Trevor A. Hart, Rusty Souleymanov, and Gerardo Betancourt. 2013. "Never Reflected Anywhere: Body Image among Ethnoracialized Gay and Bisexual Men." *Body Image* 10 (3): 389–98.

Bryant, Lawrence Oliver. 2008. "How Black Men Who Have Sex with Men Learn to Cope with Homophobia and Racism." PhD diss., University of Georgia.

Callander, Denton, Martin Holt, and Christy E. Newman. 2015. "Not Everyone's Gonna Like Me: Accounting for Race and Racism in Sex and Dating Web Services for Gay and Bisexual Men." *Ethnicities* 16 (1): 3–21.

Carroll, Aengus. 2016. *State-Sponsored Homophobia: A World Survey of Sexual Orientation Laws—Criminalisation, Protection and Recognition*. 11th ed. Accessed March 6, 2017. http://ilga.org/downloads/02_ILGA_State_Sponsored_Homophobia_2016_ENG_WEB_150516.pdf.

Carter, Robert T. 2007. "Racism and Psychological and Emotional Injury: Recognizing and Assessing Race-Based Traumatic Stress." *The Counseling Psychologist* 35 (1): 13–105.

Choi, Kyung-Hee, Chong-suk Han, Jay Paul, and George Ayala. 2011. "Strategies for Managing Racism and Homophobia among U. S. Ethnic and Racial Minority Men Who Have Sex with Men." *AIDS Education and Prevention* 23 (2): 145–58.

DiAngelo, Robin. 2011. "White Fragility." *International Journal of Critical Pedagogy* 3 (3): 54–70.

Fredrickson, George M. 2002. *Racism: A Short History*. Princeton: Princeton University Press.

George, Clemon, Barry D. Adam, Stanley E. Read, Winston C. Husbands, Robert S. Remis, Lydia Makoroka, and Sean B. Rourke. 2012. "The MaBwana Black Men's Study: Community and Belonging in the Lives of African, Caribbean and Other Black Gay Men in Toronto." *Culture, Health & Sexuality* 14 (5): 549–62.

Ghabrial, Monica A. 2017. "Trying to Figure Out Where We Belong: Narratives of Racialized Sexual Minorities on Community, Identity, Discrimination, and Health." *Sexuality Research and Social Policy* 14 (1): 42–55.

Giwa, Sulaimon. 2016. "Surviving Racist Culture: Strategies of Managing Racism Among Gay Men of Colour—An Interpretative Phenomenological Analysis." PhD diss., York University.

Giwa, Sulaimon, and Cameron Greensmith. 2012. "Race Relations and Racism in the LGBTQ Community of Toronto: Perceptions of Gay and Queer Social Service Providers of Color." *Journal of Homosexuality* 59 (2): 149–85.

Han, Chong-suk. 2007. "They Don't Want to Cruise Your Type: Gay Men of Color and the Racial Politics of Exclusion." *Social Identities* 13 (1): 51–67.

———. 2008. "No Fats, Femmes, or Asians: The Utility of Critical Race Theory in Examining the Role of Gay Stock Stories in the Marginalization of Gay Asian Men." *Contemporary Justice Review* 11 (1): 11–22.

Han, Chong-suk, George Ayala, Jay P. Paul, Ross Boylan, Steven E. Gregorich, and Kyung-Hee Choi. 2015. "Stress and Coping with Racism and Their Role in Sexual Risk for HIV Among African American, Asian/Pacific Islander, and Latino Men Who Have Sex with Men." *Archives of Sexual Behavior* 44 (2): 411–20.

Han, Chong-suk, Kristopher Proctor, and Kyung-Hee Choi. 2014. "I Know a Lot of Gay Asian Men Who Are Actually Tops: Managing and Negotiating Gay Racial Stigma." *Sexuality & Culture* 18 (2): 219–34.

Harrell, Shelly P. 2000. "A Multidimensional Conceptualization of Racism-Related Stress: Implications for the Well-Being of People of Color." *American Journal of Orthopsychiatry* 70 (1): 42–57.

Harris, Cheryl I. 1993. "Whiteness as Property." *Harvard Law Review* 106 (8): 1710–91.

Himmelstein, Mary S., Danielle M. Young, Diana T. Sanchez, and James S. Jackson. 2015. "Vigilance in the Discrimination-Stress Model for Black Americans." *Psychology & Health* 30 (3): 253–67.

Hurley, Mary C. 2005. "Bill C-38: The Civil Marriage Act." Accessed March 6, 2017. http://www.lop.parl.gc.ca/About/Parliament/LegislativeSummaries/bills_ls.asp?ls=c38&Parl=38&Ses=1.

James, Carl, Wanda Thomas Bernard, David Este, Akua Benjamin, Bethan Lloyd, and Tana Turner. 2010. *Race and Well-Being: The Lives, Hopes, and Activism of African Canadians.* Halifax: Fernwood.

LaVeist, Thomas A., Roland J. Thorpe Jr., Geraldine Pierre, GiShawn A. Mance, and David R. Williams. 2014. "The Relationships Among Vigilant Coping Style, Race, and Depression." *Journal of Social Issues* 70 (2): 241–55.

Lazarus, Richard S., and Susan Folkman. 1984. *Stress, Appraisal, and Coping.* New York: Springer.

Lee, Chelsea, and Robert L. Ostergard, Jr. 2017. "Measuring Discrimination against LGBTQ People: A Cross-National Analysis." *Human Rights Quarterly* 39 (1): 37–72.

Majied, Kamilah, and Tamarah Moss-Knight. 2012. "Social Work Research Considerations with Sexual Minorities in the African Diaspora." *Journal of Social Work Values and Ethics* 9 (2): 56–67.

Masten, Ann S. 2014. *Ordinary Magic: Resilience in Development.* New York: Guilford.

Mays, Vickie M., Susan D. Cochran, and Namdi W. Barnes. 2007. "Race, Race-Based Discrimination, and Health Outcomes Among African Americans." *Annual Review of Psychology* 58: 201–25.

Meyer, Ilan H. 1995. "Minority Stress and Mental Health in Gay Men." *Journal of Health and Social Behavior* 36 (1): 38–56.

———. 2003. "Prejudice, Social Stress, and Mental Health in Lesbian, Gay, and Bisexual Populations: Conceptual Issues and Research Evidence." *Psychological Bulletin* 129 (5): 674–97.

Meyer, Ilan H., Suzanne C. Ouellette, Rahwa Haile, and Tracy A. McFarlane. 2011. "We'd Be Free: Narratives of Life without Homophobia, Racism, or Sexism." *Sexuality Research and Social Policy* 8 (3): 204–14.

Misawa, Mitsunori. 2012. "Social Justice Narrative Inquiry: A Queer Crit Perspective." In *Proceedings of the 53rd Annual Adult Education Research Conference, Saratoga Springs*, 239–46. Manhattan: New Prairie Press.

Morgan, David L. 1997. *Focus Groups as Qualitative Research.* 2nd ed. Thousand Oaks: Sage.

Nakamura, Nadine, Elic Chan, and Benedikt Fischer. 2013. "'Hard to Crack': Experiences of Community Integration among First- and Second-Generation Asian MSM in Canada." *Cultural Diversity & Ethnic Minority Psychology* 19 (3): 248–56.

Noh, Samuel, and Violet Kaspar. 2003. "Perceived Discrimination and Depression: Moderating Effects of Coping, Acculturation, and Ethnic Support." *American Journal of Public Health* 93 (2): 232–38.

Norsah, Kofi. 2015. "How You Doin'? Social Discrimination and its Impact on Health among Black Men Who Have Sex with Men in Montreal." Master's diss., McGill University.

Razack, Narda, and Donna Jeffery. 2002. "Critical Race Discourse and Tenets for Social Work." *Canadian Social Work Review* 19 (2): 257–71.

Riggs, Damien W., and Gareth J. Treharne. 2017. "Decompensation: A Novel Approach to Accounting for Stress Arising from the Effects of Ideology and Social Norms." *Journal of Homosexuality* 64 (5): 592–605.

Rutter, Michael. 1985. "Resilience in the Face of Adversity: Protective Factors and Resistance to Psychiatric Disorder." *The British Journal of Psychiatry* 147 (6): 598–611.

Smith, Jonathan A., Paul Flowers, and Michael Larkin. 2009. *Interpretative Phenomenological Analysis: Theory, Method and Research.* London: Sage.

Solórzano, Daniel G., and Dolores Delgado Bernal. 2001. "Examining Transformation Resistance through a Critical Race and LatCrit Theory Framework: Chicana and Chicano Students in an Urban Context." *Urban Education* 36 (3): 308–42.

Solórzano, Daniel G., and Tara J. Yosso. 2002. "Critical Race Methodology: Counter-Storytelling as an Analytical Framework for Education Research." *Qualitative Inquiry* 8 (1): 23–44.

Statistics Canada. 2013. "Ottawa, CDR, Ontario (Code 3506) (table). National Household Survey (NHS) Profile, 2011" (Statistics Canada Catalogue no. 99–004-XWE). http://www12.statcan.gc.ca/nhs-enm/2011/dp-pd/prof/details/Page.cfm?Lang=E&Geo1=CD&Code1=3506&Data=Count&SearchText=Ottawa&SearchType=Begins&SearchPR=01&A1=All&B1=All&GeoLevel=PR&GeoCode=10.

Veenstra, Gerry, and Andrew C. Patterson. 2016. "Black-White Health Inequalities in Canada." *Journal of Immigrant and Minority Health* 18 (1): 51–57.

Wahab, Amar, and Dwaine Plaza. 2009. "Queerness in the Transnational Caribbean-Canadian Diaspora." *Caribbean Review of Gender Studies* 3: 1–34.

Walcott, Rinaldo. 2016. *Queer Returns: Essays on Multiculturalism, Diaspora, and Black Studies.* London: Insomniac Press.

Weinberg, Michael, and Sharon Gil. 2016. "Trauma as an Objective or Subjective Experience: The Association Between Types of Traumatic Events, Personality Traits, Subjective Experience of the Event, and Posttraumatic Symptoms." *Journal of Loss and Trauma* 21 (2): 137–46.

Wilson, Patrick A.-D., and Hirokazu Yoshikawa. 2004. "Experiences of and Responses to Social Discrimination among Asian and Pacific Islander Gay Men: Their Relationship to HIV Risk." *AIDS Education and Prevention* 16 (1): 68–83.

Yoshikawa, Hirokazu, Patrick A.-D. Wilson, David H. Chae, and Jih-Fei Cheng. 2004. "Do Family and Friendship Networks Protect against the Influence of Discrimination on Mental Health and HIV Risk Among Asian and Pacific Islander Gay Men?" *AIDS Education and Prevention* 16 (1): 84–100.

SEVEN

"It Can't Possibly Be Racism!"

*The White Racial Frame and
Resistance to Sexual Racism*

Jesus Gregorio Smith

On October 29, 2015, the Daily Beast, an American news and opinion website,[1] published an article on its public Facebook page titled, "'No Blacks' Is Not a Sexual Preference. It's Racism." The story, written by Samantha Allen, engaged the controversial idea of sexual racism, or racial discrimination in a sexual context (Plummer 2008), in the gay community. Often seen on dating apps in the form of "No Blacks," or "White Only," the topic has been discussed at large in popular[2] and academic press (Callander, Holt, and Newman 2012; Han 2008; Robinson 2015). The Daily Beast story focused largely on the research conducted by sexuality scholars Denton Callander, Christy Newman, and Martin Holt and their article "Is Sexual Racism *Really* Racism?" (2015). Samantha Allen interviewed Denton Callander about racial preferences. In the interview Callander stated, "I am not interested in condemning or criticizing people's desire." This was to make the discussion less about calling people racist, and more about what Callander suggests is our need to "recognize prejudice within ourselves" to "challenge and confront it." Still, the discussion about sexual racism remains to be a divisive one, with white people often defensively arguing that racial preferences are natural, innocent, and not racist.

Sexual racism remains to be an imperative topic of evaluation. There has previously been research regarding the development of a framework for investigating sexual racism (Plummer 2008). Also, studies examining the interpretation of and reaction to sexual racism from people of color (Callander, Holt, and Newman 2016), the impacts on partner selection due to sexual racism (Ro et al. 2013), and its role in the spread of HIV/AIDS (Han et al. 2014). While much work on sexual racism has focused on racialized language and personal preference (Callander, Holt, and Newman 2012; Riggs 2013; Robinson 2015), far less has examined the mechanisms of and avoidance to discussions of sexual racism by white people in general, and white gay men in particular (Riggs and Due 2010). This is especially true regarding white interpretations, narratives, and emotions towards the topic (Cabrera 2014; Goodman and Rowe 2014). Often, white women and gay men are marginalized social groups, based on gender and orientation. Thus, how they participate in discussions about racism may reveal that despite their own marginalization, they still engage in subtle forms of racism.

The aim of this chapter is to analyze the comments from users of the Daily Beast's Facebook page in reaction to Samantha Allen's article. Doing this will help make sense of how white users approach and respond to sexual racism. Often times white people tend to be uncomfortable with discussions about racism, developing strategies of avoidance and deflection so that they appear color-blind instead (Bonilla-Silva 2010; McCoy, Winkle-Wagner, and Luedke 2015; Solomon et al. 2005). By analyzing online conversations instead of face-to-face interviews, the comments are less restrained by social norms, thanks in part to the anonymity of the internet. In what follows, literature regarding the theoretical framing of this study will first be assessed, followed by the elucidation of the data and methods, and concluded with a presentation of findings. In discussing the topic, it will become clearer how white people, regardless of gender or orientation, rhetorically perpetuate claims to supremacy.

THE WHITE RACIAL FRAME AND
FOLK THEORY OF RACISM

The White Racial Frame (WRF) is the dominant collective racialized worldview held by white people, containing a "broad and persisting set of racial stereotypes, prejudices, ideologies, images, interpretations and narratives, emotions . . . as well as racialized inclinations to discriminate" (Feagin 2013, p. 3). In fact, the strength in using the term WRF is that it captures how white people think and feel about race (Cabrera 2014). The frame is an embedded perspective for all white individuals, encompassing shared histories which are used in processing everyday circumstances and interactions (Feagin 2013). Among these facets is the negative portrayal and imaging of Black people and other people of color. Aided with these implicit biases, white people operate out of the WRF, assuming white people possess inherently good qualities while Black people have fundamentally bad characteristics. Of note is the fact that most white people are unaware of this framing (Feagin 2013), resulting in the perpetuation of the folk theory of racism (Hill 2008).

Folk theory is comprised of two parts: the biological construction of race (race as a biological category can be assigned for each human and is a result of the evolution of distinct biological populations), and the concept that racism operates exclusively on an individual level in terms of beliefs, actions, and intents (Hill 2008). Application of folk theory functions as follows: people who hold racist views and/or white supremacists are those that believe people of color are biologically inferior, racism is limited to the actions and words of these people, and these people are ignorant or relics of the past that can be convalesced into mainstream society through education (Hill 2008). Per folk theory, to be explicitly racist is to be bad; therefore, color-blind approaches are utilized when talking about race.

Bonilla-Silva (2002) styled color-blind racism's ideology with "slipperiness, apparent nonracialism, and ambivalence" (41). White people specifically circumvent engaging in direct racial language, use "semantic moves" in order to voice racial views, project, and utilize diminutive language, and many have difficulty speaking coherently on the matter when prompted (Bonilla-Silva 2002). This coincides with the idea of "social alexithymia," or white Americans' absence of compassion for the outlooks of people of color (Feagin 2013). Folk theory is used to define racism, so that if one perceives another's actions or words as racist, it is concluded that the one who perceived the action is insulted and oversensitive. This interpretation gives the individual in question sole authority with what their words or actions are conveying. For this chapter, the WRF was used to frame the comments of the white users and counterframe the words of people of color. The folk theory of racism aided in clarifying the reasoning behind the comments, whether they believed the statement was racist or not, and color-blind racism aided in determining the semantic moves white people use to appear color-blind.

DATA

This chapter utilized user comments from an article on the Facebook page of the Daily Beast. The article was posted on October 29, 2015, and had 128 individual responses and 203 total comments beginning at 9:44 pm and ending on October 30, 2015, at 2:19 am. All the comments were read and re-read for explicit themes regarding White Racial Framing and the folk theory of racism, as well as any semantic moves that commenters engaged in to resist discussing sexual racism. This article was selected for two reasons. First, the article title was controversial enough to provoke a wide range of responses from a variety of people. Second, the article went into a lengthy and in-depth discussion of the study "Is Sexual Racism *Really* Racism?" This raised the standard of the article from being a simple think piece on sexual racism to more of an actual intellectual discussion on empirical research that tested the assumption "are sexual preferences racist?" Access to this article and the comments are publicly available and can be achieved via a Google search of "The Daily Beast Sexual Racism Facebook." Many of the users openly revealed their race and sexuality within their comments. Despite the public availability of the article and comments, pseudonyms are utilized in the analysis below to protect the identity of the commenters.

METHODS OF ANALYSIS

First, grounded theory guided the development of codes that were reflective of the data (Robinson 2015). Next, an inductive process was employed to identify themes from the coded data. To assist with this process, Critical Discourse Analysis (CDA) was utilized. Critical Discourse Analysis (van Leeuwen 1993) aims to highlight "the power embedded in texts and images by the discursive choices that are made by the writer" (Han 2008, p. 14). CDA guided the analytic process by means of focusing on how the text is "framed," what information is foregrounded, what insinuations are made, what is topicalized, what is omitted, and how visual aids are used to support the narrator's arguments. With the aid of CDA in the analysis of the narratives, counter-frames were identified. Last, a deductive approach considered the relationship between the themes and prominent theories of white racism, lending themselves more accurately to the White Racial Frame (Feagin 2013), the folk theory of racism (Hill 2008), and the linguistic strategies of color-blind racists (Bonilla-Silva 2002).

WHITE DENIALS OF SEXUAL RACISM

Working out of the White Racial Frame (WRF), white users and their apologists employed varying methods of deflection and reaction. The online comments centered on the utilization of predominantly four linguistic methods that deflected and distorted the actual arguments in the article, reinforcing aspects of the WRF and reviving folk theories of racism. These four methods included: *defining racism* and not seeing racial preferences in a partner as racist, claiming that the discussions on sexual racism were no more than *political correctness, falsely equating* sexual orientation with sexual preference, and using arguments based on *biological essentialism* to suggest that sexual racial desires were motivated by some sort of biological impulse and not racist personal desire. Despite these methods by some white people, people of color counter-framed with a more inclusive definition of racism, addressing the complexity of desire and seeing people of color as diverse and not a monolithic group. The four methods of deflection and reaction as well as the counter-framing by people of color are explored in detail below.

DEFINING RACISM

The ability to define what racism is and isn't is paramount for white people to avoid difficult discussions about systemic racism. By defining racism, white people maintain power and control over the discussion, allowing themselves to perpetuate racial inequality while maintaining the illusion of being perceived as "not racist" (Riggs and Due 2010). In the following comments, many of the users used white narratives and interpretations of racism to explain that "racial preferences" are not *real* racism. The goal in this line of thinking is to shift the focus from how racial preferences can be racist to how desire can't be racist. A white female user, Hillary, stated: "It is entirely possible to respect and admire people without wanting to pork them." Hillary began her comment with affirming language, like respect and admire, to minimize the racism (Bonilla-Silva 2010). In suggesting that one can "respect and admire" people without "wanting to pork them," Hillary made the two mutually exclusive. Really, one could respect and admire people and still be sexually racist, just like one could "wanna pork" people of color and still be racist. By starting off her comment with that point, Hillary associates racism with disrespect, and since Hillary can respect and admire someone, by this logic, her preference is not racist. Using these semantic moves, Hillary only defines extreme versions of racism as *real* racism, perpetuating the folk theory of racism (Hill 2008). For those who seek to control the narrative around what constitutes real racism and what doesn't, this method hides racist preferences behind the smiling face of discrimination (Bonilla-Silva 2006) in order to soften the blow of outright racial rejection. Another white female user echoed the same sentiment. Cassie stated:

> Not being attracted to someone based on what they look like is not racism. I am white and am not in any way attracted to white men with red hair. Does this make me racist against white people? Obviously not. If you're not sexually attracted to someone, how are you going to be in a relationship with them? I wouldn't want to be in a relationship with someone who I could connect to on every level but who wasn't attracted to me. That makes zero sense. . . . There is a big difference in "I don't date black people because I hate black people" and "I don't date black people because they are not physically attracting to me."

Here Cassie, like Hillary, suggested racism was something different than preference. Yet Cassie used an interesting logical twist to her reasoning. First, stating that "not being attracted to someone based on what they looked like" is a straw argument or misrepresentation of the original points of the article. The original argument is about racial preferences being *possibly* rooted in racist beliefs, not just looks. By beginning her response in this way, Cassie argued on her terms, based on a definition of racism she agreed with. She then stated, "I am white and am not in any way attracted to white men with red hair. Does this make me racist against white people? Obviously not." Cassie goes on to mention that she herself is white, but instead of saying she is not attracted to white people in general, she specifies that she is not attracted to white people with "red hair." This pivot to specifying what sort of white men she is attracted to allowed Cassie to maintain the diversity and complexity of white people while suggesting non-white people all have the same "look."

Cassie then, without providing evidence, asked a question and answered her own question by suggesting that it is obvious that white people who are not attracted to certain white people couldn't possibly be racist against white people. Importantly, however, what Cassie argued to be obvious should be held up to scrutiny, because the reasoning for why someone might not be attracted to people of a certain racial or ethnic group could very much be based on racist stereotypes and beliefs. Cassie then indicated that one could not be in a relationship with someone they are not sexually attracted to. Yet Cassie and many other users relied on the idea that sexual attraction is immediate and not something that can grow organically through time, once you get past the first "look." Finally, Cassie stated, "There is a big difference in "I don't date black people because I hate black people" and "I don't date black people because they are not physically attracting to me." Cassie, like Hillary, suggested that unless it is "hate," then it isn't racism. This again plays into the folk idea that many white people have of racism, often invoking the KKK as the prime example of what racism is, and then suggesting that anything else is simply not racism (Hill 2008). Still, Cassie wasn't the only one who used this line of reasoning to justify her argument. Duffy, a woman of color, also said something similar. Duffy stated: "It's absurd to call someone racist because they aren't attracted to other races. So all those that date within their race are racist? . . . So, if my personal preference is to not date outside my race or if I choose not to date Latinos, I am a racist?"

Utilizing the rhetorical-question strategy, Duffy made sure to add a statement on personal preference to her question. By doing this, she was trying to invalidate the Daily Beast article without ever engaging with the complicated arguments in it. That is because by making it about personal choice, it removed the discussion from the realm of white influences on her desires to personal choices of what she wanted in a partner. People of color operating out of the White Racial Frame (Feagin 2013) is not unusual. In fact, white people have exploited people of color who regurgitate the same racist reasoning as them as proof that they are not racist. In doing so, Duffy herself employed a racist essentializing of Latinos to make her point. Latinos are varied racially, representing all racial groups. So when Duffy stated, "If I choose not to date Latinos am I racist?" she never even explained what she meant by this. If she prefers to date within her race, whatever that may be, that may or may not include Latinos. If her point was that culturally she prefers to date people that are similar, then she would not be making a preference based only on race. It is these complex ideas that are purposefully left out of discussions about race and desire by white people and their apologists in order to maintain the status quo.

PC BACKLASH

A second strategy employed by many of the users was to frame the Daily Beast article as nothing more than political correctness (PC). By complaining about PC, white users engaged social alexithymia to dismiss the arguments put forth in the article, and signal to other sexual racists that the "PC police" were trying to politicize sexuality and force white people to have sex with people of color. For example, white user Marco stated:

> Saying I'm not physically attracted to a black guy has nothing to do with superiority. I'm not un-attracted to him because I think I'm superior as a white person. I'm simply just not physically attracted to him. That's not racism. I'm certainly open to a relationship with a black guy, of course, but generally speaking they don't really turn me on and I'm sure there are plenty of black guys who feel the same about me—and that's ok. Stop trying to politicize sexual relations. It's none of your business.

Like those who attempted to define racism on their own terms, Marco proposed that racism occurs only when someone sees themselves as superior to another. In a contradictory fashion, he still talked about being open to a relationship with a Black man but then stated Black men don't turn him on. He then advocated that there might be "plenty of black guys who feel the same" about him. Marco, working out of the emotions of the WRF, defended his feelings by incorporating mythical Black men he assumed would feel just like him. He finished his statement in an aggressive manner saying, "Stop trying to politicize sexual relations. It's none of your business." The demand, reeking of defensiveness, speaks to the emotional discomfort many whites have engaging in racial conversations. Marco demanded that sexual relations not be politicized, harkening back to the general dislike white people have of what they term is PC culture. By arguing that discussions about racism in our sex lives are "political," Marco ended the opportunity to talk about how racism is maintained in our private lives and beyond.

Still, complaints of political correctness were often and varied. From one user saying, "Give me a fucking break. PC culture is completely out of hand. Am I homophobic because I won't date a guy?" to another saying, "That's the next step in politically correct (d)evolution." Both comments, by white men, spoke to the feeling of exasperation that came from many of the comments regarding sexual racism, once again reinforcing the emotional aspects of the WRF. In fact, Donovan, a white male, bellowed, "This is stupid. Everything has to be politically correct nowadays to a point where no matter what is said someone will find a way to make it offensive. I mean they are saying that you can't choose a particular for your own penis or vagina? That's ludicrous." Donovan, working from the white narrative and interpretation of the WRF, was defensive regarding the discussion of sexual racism as well. Using the language of political correctness, Donovan steered the conversation away from the arguments of the article, and instead suggested that "they are saying that you can't choose a particular for your own penis or vagina." No one made that argument in the article, a point that renders Donovan's comment quite "ludicrous" indeed. Judd, another white male, stated:

> I won't let someone tell me who I should let fuck me. If am only attracted to white & Latino & middle eastern men, then that's what I like. I am not going to sleep with a black man just so I won't be called a racist. Makes no sense at all. My preference is to get fucked in the ass only. I can fuck guys too but I prefer not too because I enjoy getting fucked more. Does that make me a racist because I won't fuck other guys even though I can? No it does not. It's all a matter of attraction, not blackmailing someone into sleeping with you so they won't be called racist.

For Judd, the Daily Beast article is akin to "blackmailing someone into sleeping with you so they won't be called racist." By using the word "blackmail," Judd linked PC culture's discussion of sexual racism to sexual extortion, where white people are forced into sex with people of color or are labeled racist. Like Donovan, Judd wouldn't let someone dictate to him whom he "should let fuck" him. In fact for him, racial preferences are like preferring sexual positions and even though he could "fuck other guys," it's not what he enjoys, preferring to be the receptive partner during sex.

Finally, those who did engage the content of the story nonetheless dismissed it. As demonstrated by Israel who stated:

> This is a tired old argument that needs to go away. And all these "studies" never come up with a definitive answer, it's always; "it's possible." "It's likely," "there's a good chance" . . . all appear to approach the question from "we think its racist, let's see if we can prove that." . . . Different people have sexual attraction to different things. The argument that a white guy who isn't sexually attracted to a black man is a racist is insulting to thinking people. . . . The whole "suppressed racism" because you list it in your profile is bullshit and political correctness run amok. . . . I think most guys would rather be told

upfront that someone is not interested because of some physical characteristic than have that awkward conversation.

Israel seemed to have at least read the article to some extent but dismissed it as "political correctness run amok." For Israel, the argument was old and "insulting to thinking people." Israel's tactic was to attack not only what he saw as the PC of the article, but also the scientific validity of the study in the article. By questioning how studies are careful to state their findings by saying "it's possible," "it's likely," and "there is a good chance," Israel was dismissive of the findings, even thinking that they work from the presumption of racism. In fact, Israel thought that profiles that stated "no Blacks" or "no Asians" were not the result of "suppressed racism" but doing people of color a favor because they would "rather be told upfront that someone is not interested" than have an "awkward" conversation about it after. Still, there are a few things of note in his response. Israel never talked about the actual findings of the study but just how they were phrased. He also oddly put "suppressed racism" in quotation marks as if it is not a real thing. Finally, he assumed that the statements on people's profiles, such as "no Blacks," were for the benefit of people of color and not just so white people would not have to be confronted about their racism. For all his attacks on assumptions in the Daily Beast article and study, Israel seemed to be assuming a lot himself.

FALSE EQUIVALENCY

One of the most common strategies for rejecting discussions about sexual racism centered on the ability of users to utilize comparisons in order to attack the logic of the article. This comparison, called false equivalence, assumed two things were logically similar when in fact they were not. Oftentimes the users compared racism to sexism, and racism to homophobia. The goal always seemed to be to demonstrate that sexual preferences could not possibly be impacted by sexual racism. As Andy, a white male, specified: "I prefer dogs to cats. I must be cruel to animals." As can be seen from Andy's comment, he compares someone who prefers dogs to cats with someone who prefers not to date or have sex with people of color. This comparison takes humans and compares them to animals. This is ironic because Black people have been historically treated like animals because of racism. Andy's flippant comparison demonstrated his lack of historical perspective. Also, his suggestion that he "must be cruel to animals" once again speaks to the folk theory of racism that only extreme versions of racism, such as cruelty, are racist. Human relationships with other humans are very different from human relationships with animals and comparing the two fails to take into account the differences. White male Jonathan detailed his argument:

> If I say on a dating site that I don't prefer women does that make me misogynistic? No. It means I prefer men. All people have a basic attraction to a certain type or look of a person. Some like blondes, some like brunettes, some like short, and some like tall. Just because you're not interested in dating/having sex with black people or any other race or ethnicity, including whites, does not in any way make you a racist.

Like many of the other users, Jonathan rejected the idea that stating your racial preferences on a dating site was racist. For Jonathan who operated out of the visual component of the WRF, "people have a basic attraction to a certain type." These types can include blondes, brunettes, short people, and tall people, but Jonathan seemed to forget that people of color can have and be these things as well. Thus, the comparison of attributes we like on partners versus the racial and ethnic makeup of potential partners was false.

While Andy compared racial preferences to preferring pets and Jonathan compared them to body types, Lowell, a part-Polynesian-and-white male, on the other hand compared racial preferences to sexual orientation. He expressed:

> This is sort of article that shows just how fucked up the American obsession with identity politics has become. If you take this stupid argument about a person not being sexually attracted to people of particular races and applied it to other things people are sexually attracted to, you could argue that all gays are misogynists because they are sexually attracted to men or all lesbians are men-haters because they are sexually attracted to women. We know that neither is the case. I'm not sexually attracted to blonds. It doesn't mean I hate Scandinavians. I'm not sexually attracted to Polynesians but it doesn't mean I hate Polynesians. In fact, it would be hard to do so as I am (part) Polynesian!

Lowell's statement harkened back to the PC arguments made by others regarding what they saw as the stupidity of politics impacting sexual desire, assuming sex is devoid of politics. Yet Lowell applied the argument to a different area for comparison, such as gay men not being into women and lesbian women not being into men. The problem with Lowell's comment is that it conflated sexual orientation with sexual preference, two concepts that seem similar on the surface but are actually different. For those who believe sexual orientation is fixed, they would argue that sexuality cannot be changed and is inherent to their identity, thus an orientation. Certainly, the recent Supreme Court victories for marriage equality in the United States seem to suggest there is a legitimacy to this argument. Those that would argue that sexuality is a preference, on the other hand, suggest it can be changed. Thus within the very definition of preference and orientation lies the difference between the two. Also, while sexism against women and misandry towards men can both result in oppression, they are not the moral equivalent to racism.

White racism has a different and very particular history attached to skin color (Feagin 2013). Being ahistorical regarding that history resulted in Lowell making a false comparison between them.

Lowell went on to suggest that since he isn't into blonds, that doesn't mean he hates Scandinavians. This comparison is also problematic because it assumed all and only Scandinavian people are blond, and compared hair color to geographic location. Then to complicate things even more, Lowell discussed not being sexually into Polynesians although he is Polynesian himself. He then stated that this does not mean he hates Polynesians, a reference again to the folk theory of racism that defines racism as only hate. The goal again is to use what would seem to be a logically equivalent comparison to drive home the point that sexual racism is not in fact racism. Instead, the users demonstrated that their logic was faulty and incoherent (Bonilla-Silva 2002).

BIOLOGICAL DETERMINISM

Comments operating from the racial stereotypes component of the WRF often used biologically based reasoning to suggest that racial desires were in fact not racist. This line of reasoning, often in connection with false equivalency, was intended to argue that those who were not interested in people of color for sex or dating were not because their desires were out of their control and more of a mechanism of something innate. Race is very much a biological fiction and not a genetic reality, despite the real-life consequences of racism (Smedley and Smedley 2005). Unfortunately, the myth about race as biology has persisted in the public sphere, as reflected in many users' responses. This fictional narrative allowed many of the users to suggest that racial preferences were nothing more than the natural result of biological difference between racial groups and impulses that could not be controlled or changed. For example, Sally, a white woman, stated, "More like focusing on what I'm attracted to. I am attracted to jews and blacks mostly. I don't control who my pussy gets wet for. It's not a choice. Are gay men sexist because they aren't attracted to women? Nope." Sally mentioned how she was attracted "mostly" to "jews and blacks," explaining that like sexual orientation, her racial preferences were "not a choice" but a reaction to what her "pussy gets wet for." Here, biological determination rendered Sally's desires out of her control. In essence, Sally's argument rested not just on biological determinism alone, but it working in tandem with false equivalency by comparing racism with sexism. Also, Sally aimed to define racism to her liking by rejecting sexual racism with a simple "nope." One is left to contemplate how Sally's "pussy" magically identified Jews, being that they are as racially diverse as Black people. The ludicrousness of her argument seemed never to register with her. Sally was not the only person to use biological determination to suggest that racial preferences were fixed. Martin, a white man, argued in a similar vein, in stating:

> Dating/mate selection is a naturally discriminatory selection process. The process is discriminatory when it comes to both physical and mental attributes. It is a personal choice based on one's self-interest and individual desires. It is naturally influenced by both biological and social factors. Nature shows us many examples of this. Some animals even mate based on a hierarchy system.

Martin, unlike Sally, argued that dating and mate selection were "naturally discriminatory selection" processes when it comes "to both physical and mental attributes." For Martin, racial preferences were "naturally influenced by both biological and social factors." For proof, Martin pointed to how "nature shows us many examples of this," comparing once again the mating habits of animals to those of humans, minus the complex racist history of slavery and colonization, of course. Martin repeated the word "nature" and its variation "natural" several times, in order to drive home the idea that racial preferences were deeply a part of human nature. While Martin at the very least considered social factors, he described the two almost like a balancing act where both drive desire and not one more so than the other. The problem is, race *is* a social construct and not a biological fact, meaning that the social does have a larger role in desire than the vaguely referenced biological.

Finally, in addition to mentions of fixed desire, there were also biological arguments about what was physically possible to do during interracial sex and what was physically desirable. As white male Bobby affirmed: "Blacks have extremely large penises and some white[s] cannot accommodate them." Bobby played on the racist stereotype created by white people of Black men, as he insisted that they all have large penises. Bobby resisted sex with Black men because he believed some white people were physically unable to sexually take large Black penises. With this line of logic, Bobby assumed that all Black men had large penises, and that all Black men want to be the anally insertive or top partners during sex. This of course is not true of all Black men. Yet it became another line of defense against accusations of racism since if one can't possibly handle an "extremely large penis," then it is out of their control. The generalizing of Black men down to their penis size was not uncommon. Peter, a white male, also justified his "racial preferences" based on the mythical Black penis. When asked by another user what all Black men had in common, Peter stated: "Black cocks! Ugly fucking things. How's that for a universal element in this context?" Peter did not mince words when it came to his essentializing of and disdain for Black men. Peter's emotional expression, as epitomized with his exclamation point, reflected his frustration with the discussion surrounding sexual racism. Despite the diversity in Black men, Peter used the stereotypical Black penis to suggest that it was the biological element that was universal with all Black men. If Black men cannot change this physically, and most certainly cannot, then it becomes impossible for Peter to change his preference, thus justifying his rigid racial desires.

FORMS OF RESISTANCE

While many white users and fewer people of color operated out of the White Racial Frame to perpetuate the folk theory of racism, the reverse was true for most people of color and the few white people that used counter-framing (Feagin 2013) to resist the white logic and methods that were used to justify sexual racism. For example, Carly, a woman of color, expressed clearly what racism was to her. She said:

> If you announce that you aren't attracted to any black people, it's racist. It assumes that you know what all black people are like. That there is no black person in the world that you could find attractive or have things in common with. All black people/ Asians/ Hispanics/ white people do not look the same. It's a racist place to even think that. . . . Not being attracted to black men is a wildly broad statement. What do millions of black men ALL have in common? They're light, dark, tall, short, thin, fat, straight haired, kinky haired, brown eyed, blue eyed, green and grey eyed? What one feature makes them unattractive that they all have in common?

Carly did not hesitate to express her thoughts on racism. Unlike the definitions of white users and their apologists, Carly suggested racism was assuming "that you know what all black people are like." By this definition, Carly is countering the racist logic of Cassie in regard to looks. For Carly, all "black people/ Asians/ Hispanics/ white people do not look the same. It's a racist place to even think that." Carly's definition of racism is more about essentializing people down to their skin color (Omi and Winant 1994) and making racial preferences into racial absolutes (Holland 2012). In fact, Carly resisted the idea of racial preferences by emphasizing that there is not one factor that all Black men have in common and that Black people are in fact as varied and diverse as any other racial group. This definition seemed to be more in line with treating all people as individuals and not as representatives of entire racial or ethnic groups. Similarly, Jake, a white man, also defined racism along the same lines when he said:

> Don't want to date black people? Why? You would NEVER consider it? Even if it was someone who shared your desires and dreams? Thinks you're hot and funny and smart? Categorically rejecting someone based entirely on their race IS ACTUAL RACISM. It's the definition of the word. The point here is that you should judge people individually, not on the color of their skin. How hard is that?

While a majority of the comments defending sexual racism came from white people, a few white people did argue that racial preferences were by definition racist. Jake was one of those people. Jake, in the same vein as Carly, found that racial absolutes, highlighted in his comment with all capital letters in "NEVER," epitomized "ACTUAL RACISM," as he again stressed. In fact, Jake goes into detail about how our attractions to people can and often do go beyond just physical appearance and incorporate sharing "dreams and desires." He stressed that we should "judge people individually, not on the color of their skin," incorporating the lines made famous by Martin Luther King Jr.

Finally, Devon, a gay Black man, also expressed how racist it was to objectify a person on the basis of views about his or her race. Devon argued:

> I don't see how it isn't. If you say you have a preference ok fine but how can you say you prefer one race over another when you are seeking love and companionship? Please explain as I thought love sees no boundaries when it comes to race. I like white and Latino guys but I be damn if I turn down a black guy if he fits the bill. . . . I used to tell myself I was only attracted to white men until I started to realize such about our community. Honestly as I get older I do find my own race of guys more and more attractive as I appreciate my worth as well as the next guy. I just say keep your heart open and let it find your soul mate.

While many of the white users simplified racial desire as nothing more than preference not unlike preferring blondes and thinness, Devon instead engaged in the complicated reality of desire and preference when it came to a partner. To begin, Devon admitted having a preference is "ok," but questioned why someone would prefer one race over another for "love and companionship" because he thought "love sees no boundaries" when it comes to race. For Devon, love and companionship take precedence over skin color when it comes to a partner. This meant that he liked "White and Latino guys" but wouldn't turn down a Black man if "he fit the bill." Devon's openness to different racial partners was in contrast to the absolute rigidness of many of the white users. Compared to Duffy who was a Black woman who preferred her own race, Devon demonstrated that one could have a preference for his own race and still be open to other races as well.

Perhaps one of the most telling parts of Devon's commentary was how he described how his preferences in a partner have grown through time. As Devon stated, he used to tell himself that he was "only attracted to white men," but as he got older and started appreciating his own self-worth, Devon began to see more Black men as attractive. This is important for a number of reasons. For one, Devon's definition of racism spoke to the way that racism constructs particular bodies as less than others. This racism is less about individuals being blatantly racist to each other and more about the way society says whiteness is more attractive than Blackness. This definition makes it less about individuals and more about white supremacy in society. Second, Devon counters the perspective of many of the white users that racial preferences are absolutes and fixed and instead he showed how desire very much changes through time. Third, Devon spoke to how internalized racism might have made him dislike other Black men but he was able to grow out of this racism and value himself and others like him, countering the narrative of people of color being less than whites.

CONCLUSION: MAINTAINING THE STATUS QUO

For many of the white users and their apologists, deflecting from and distraction to conversations about sexual racism allow their claims to white supremacy to remain unchallenged. This resulted in the users engaging in four main methods of deflection and reaction regarding sexual racism: defining racism to control the narrative around it; dismissing it as nothing more than political correctness to distract from conversation about it; using false equivalency arguments in reaction to it; and finally, dismissing is as biologically determined so as not to change it. People of color resisted these attempts by defining racism themselves, complicating the narrative around desire and being open to racial diversity.

Defining racism was the most common reaction of whites regarding sexual racism. By defining racism in a narrow fashion, they could absolve themselves from being seen as racist, perpetuate the folk theory of racism, and linguistically maneuver around the valid points presented in the Daily Beast article via "semantic moves." These moves, similar to what Bonilla-Silva calls color-blind racism (Bonilla-Silva 2010), suggested only extreme versions of "disrespect" were racist like Hillary's, and they used their own dislike of their white race to demonstrate that if white people do it, it couldn't possibly be racist, as Cassie did. Often people of color view desire through the lens of the White Racial Frame (Feagin 2013). This allowed Duffy to essentialize all Latinos. The white users simplified partner preferences and desires even though the topic is often very complicated.

For many of the users who commented on the Daily Beast article, they viewed it as nothing more than a politically correct assault on their individual choice, as Marco did, and one meant to force them to sleep with people, as Donovan felt. Some used legalistic codes for the severity of the implication that they might be racist, such as suggesting that they were being forced or blackmailed into sex with people of color or else would be called racist, as Judd felt. For others it was an insult to their intelligence and politicizing of intimate matters. While most didn't engage in the actual argument, others that did dismissed it outright for being politically correct pseudoscience that assumed preferences were racist but could not give definitive answers, as Israel suggested. As such, many of the users simply dismissed the arguments as PC in an effort to shut down and redirect conversations about sexual racism.

The utilization of the false equivalency argument served to demonstrate that sexual racism was not racism by comparing it to other seemingly similar things that were actually logically dissimilar, resulting again in the perpetuation of the folk theory of racism where only extreme versions of racism are racist. Some compared humans to animals, like Andy, or height and hair color to skin color, like Jonathan. Others, like Lowell, crafted incoherent comparisons like geographic location to hair color or sexual orientation to sexual preference. While they seemed like intelligent comparisons, they often fell apart under scrutiny.

For those who used the argument that racial preferences were biologically determined, it meant that desire was unchangeable. Sally pointed to her body's reaction to men she desired, such as her "pussy getting wet," as an indicator that these things were rooted in biology, despite the biological fiction surrounding race. For Martin racial preferences were a natural process of selection found in nature. Biological arguments were not only about what was controllable and what wasn't but also about physicality. Regurgitating the white-framed stereotype about hung Black men, Bobby argued some white men could not physically handle sex with Black men and that influenced their sexually racist desire. Peter, on the other hand, argued the Black penis was the consistent attribute across all Black men that physically represented what he was not sexually into and since Black men could not change this, it was impossible to change.

Unlike most white users who commented on the article, most people of color and a small number of white people resisted the white logic and methods of distraction and deflection regarding sexual racism. Instead, people of color and a few white people counter-framed sexual racism by suggesting that all people should be judged individually, defined racial absolutes as racist, and highlighted societal influence on racial desire. They also complicated desire by suggesting that people's yearnings can change through time and openness, as Carly, Jake and Devon did. Unlike many white respondents, it appeared as though the counter-framing by mostly people of color was based on actually reading the article and not outright dismissing it.

Most of the white users, women and men, gay and straight, operated out of the White Racial Frame (Feagin 2013). This meant they believed in racial stereotypes about people of color's sexuality, maintained racist narratives and interpretations justifying racial preferences in partners, and used racial images for white standards of beauty and emotional reactions to discussions regarding sexual racism. These thoughts and feelings all went into their inclination to discriminate during sex and relationships. Many times, the folk theory of racism was used as reasoning for why racial preferences could not be racist since the white users claimed they did not "hate" people of color. While most discussions about racism are disguised with color blindness, discussions of sexual racism are typically blatant, since many white people do not see racial preferences as racist. Despite this, they still engage in rhetorical strategies of avoidance and deflection regarding sexual racism, possibly revealing their true racist intent.

ACKNOWLEDGMENTS

Jesus would like to express his gratitude to Michael Shae Reed, Gabe Miller, and Melissa Ochoa for their contributions to this chapter.

NOTES

1. The Daily Beast describes itself in this fashion.
2. The Huffington Post discussed the *Daily Show*'s own video on the subject.

REFERENCES

Allen, Samantha. 2015. "'No Blacks' Is Not a Sexual Preference. It's Racism." *The Daily Beast.* Accessed January 5, 2017. http://www.thedailybeast.com/articles/2015/09/09/no-blacks-is-not-a-sexual-preference-it-s-racism.html.

Bonilla-Silva, Eduardo. 2002. "The Linguistics of Colorblind Racism: How to Talk Nasty about Blacks without Sounding Racist." *Critical Sociology* 28 (1): 41–64.

———. 2010. *Racism without Racists: Color-Blind Racism and the Persistence of Racial Inequality in the United States*. Lanham: Rowman & Littlefield.

Cabrera, Nolan L. 2014. "'But I'm Oppressed Too': White Male College Students Framing Racial Emotions as Facts and Recreating Racism." *International Journal of Qualitative Studies in Education* 27 (6): 768–84.

Callander, Denton, Martin Holt, and Christy E. Newman. 2012. "Just a Preference: Racialised Language in the Sex-Seeking Profiles of Gay and Bisexual Men." *Culture, Health & Sexuality* 14 (9): 1049–63.

———. 2016. "'Not Everyone's Gonna Like Me': Accounting for Race and Racism in Sex and Dating Web Services for Gay and Bisexual Men." *Ethnicities* 16 (1): 3–21.

Callander, Denton, Christy E. Newman, and Martin Holt. 2015. "Is Sexual Racism *Really* Racism? Distinguishing Attitudes Toward Sexual Racism and Generic Racism Among Gay and Bisexual Men." *Archives of Sexual Behavior* 44 (7): 1991–2000.

Feagin, Joe R. 2013. *The White Racial Frame: Centuries of Racial Framing and Counter-framing*. 2nd ed. New York: Routledge

Goodman, Simon, and Lottie Rowe. 2014. "'Maybe It Is Prejudice . . . but It Is NOT Racism': Negotiating Racism in Discussion Forums about Gypsies." *Discourse & Society* 25 (1): 32–46.

Han, Chong-suk. 2008. "No Fats, Femmes, or Asians: The Utility of Critical Race Theory in Examining the Role of Gay Stock Stories in the Marginalization of Gay Asian Men." *Contemporary Justice Review* 11 (1): 11–22.

Han, Chong-suk, George Ayala, Jay P. Paul, Ross Boylan, Steven E. Gregorich, and Kyung-Hee Choi. 2014. "Stress and Coping with Racism and Their Role in Sexual Risk for HIV Among African American, Asian/Pacific Islander, and Latino Men Who Have Sex with Men." *Archives of Sexual Behavior* 44 (2): 411–20.

Hill, Jane. 2008. *The Everyday Language of White Racism*. Hoboken: Wiley-Blackwell.

Holland, Sharon Patricia. 2012. *The Erotic Life of Racism*. Durham: Duke University Press.

McCoy, Dorian L., Rachelle Winkle-Wagner, and Courtney L. Luedke. 2015. "Color-blind Mentoring? Exploring White Faculty Mentoring of Students of Color." *Journal of Diversity in Higher Education* 8 (4): 225–42.

Omi, Michael, and Howard Winant. 1994. *Racial Formation in the United States: From the 1960s to the 1990s*. 2nd ed. New York: Routledge.

Plummer, Mary Dianne. 2008. "Sexual Racism in Gay Communities: Negotiating the Ethnosexual Marketplace." Dissertation Abstracts International: Section B: The Sciences and Engineering. http://ovidsp.ovid.com/ovidweb.cgi?T=JS&PAGE=reference&D=psyc6&NEWS=N&AN=2008-99040-087.

Riggs, Damien W. 2013. "Anti-Asian Sentiment Amongst a Sample of White Australian Men on Gaydar." *Sex Roles* 68 (11–12): 768–78.

Riggs, Damien W., and Clemence Due. 2010. "The Management of Accusations of Racism in Celebrity Big Brother." *Discourse & Society* 21 (3): 257–71.

Ro, Annie, George Ayala, Jay Paul, and Kyung-Hee Choi. 2013. "Dimensions of Racism and Their Impact on Partner Selection among Men of Colour Who Have Sex with Men: Understanding Pathways to Sexual Risk." *Culture, Health & Sexuality* 15 (7): 836–50.

Robinson, Brandon Andrew. 2016. "'Personal Preference' as the New Racism: Gay Desire and Racial Cleansing in Cyberspace." *Sociology of Race and Ethnicity* 1 (2): 317–30.

Smedley, Audrey, and Brian D. Smedley. 2005. "Race as Biology Is Fiction, Racism as a Social Problem Is Real: Anthropological and Historical Perspectives on the Social Construction of Race." *American Psychologist* 60 (1): 16–26.

Solomon, R. Patrick, John P. Portelli, Beverly-Jean Daniel, and Arlene Campbell. 2005. "The Discourse of Denial: How White Teacher Candidates Construct Race, Racism and 'White Privilege.'" *Race Ethnicity and Education* 8 (2): 147–69.

van Leeuwen, Theo. 1993. "Genre and Field in Critical Discourse Analysis: A Synopsis." *Discourse & Society* 4 (2): 193–223.

EIGHT

Recentering Asianness in the Discourse on Homonationalism

Alexandra Marie Rivera
and Dale Dagar Maglalang

For ethnic minority gay men, sexual identity is more than the perception of one's own sexuality and expression—it is also fundamentally political and pertains to national identity (Chan 1995). Jasbir K. Puar's seminal work, *Terrorist Assemblages: Homonationalism in Queer Times* (2007), simultaneously highlights and problematizes the ways in which sexuality has become a crucial formation in the United States, much like race, class, gender, and nationalism. In aligning with the United States' nationalist homonormative rhetoric—that is, the United States as a progressive, gay-friendly country—the country's social strata inherently welcome and sanction the rights of certain groups while excluding others (Puar 2013). As such, homonationalism is a racialized construct which may deny the ability of non-white, non-middle/upper-class, non-able-bodied gay men to access citizenship, inclusion, and acceptance. In other words, homonationalism is racially hierarchized so that white gay men are ascendant.

We all resist or comply with the homonationalist agenda as part of our identification as a United States resident or citizen (Puar 2013). Being complicit necessitates a certain understanding of this racial hierarchy. Puar (2007) writes that we can note, for example, that liberal notions of "diversity" offer false inclusion. While they may appear to welcome people of color into the upper social echelons, they do so through exclusion and only when "the ethnic is . . . straight, usually has access to material and cultural capital . . . and is in fact often male" (243). To achieve true inclusion, the American dream, a gay man of color must learn to love the nation which stigmatizes him (Ahmed 2005).

This chapter intends to recenter Asian American voices in the conversation about homonationalism and queer communities in the United States. We propose that, due to racial triangulation and the Model Minority Myth, many Asian American gay men—here we also include transgender and gender non-conforming (TGNC) men who identify as gay—feel pressured to align with homonationalism in efforts to be legitimized as "true Americans." At the same time, these same men may experience greater racism and discrimination due to homonationalism, particularly as enacted by white gay men. For these reasons, many choose to actively challenge homonationalism. This chapter delineates these issues and discusses them from the perspectives of two queer Asian American authors.

ASIAN AMERICA AND NATIONALISM

Asian Americans in the United States have been used as an apparatus to shape, form, and continually reconstruct nationalism, and by extension, homonationalism. While literature on homonationalism in Asian American gay men is relatively sparse, we can make inferences about its origins by examining the sociopolitical and imperialist histories of Asians in America over the last two centuries. As we consider Asian Americans as potential subjects of salvation and terror for the sake of fostering patriotism and empire formation, we can then ask where gay Asian American men fall within these iterations of racialization and sexualization, and in which ways they act as vessels for homonationalism.

Asian Americans have oscillated from symbols to adversaries of nationalism and patriotism in the United States, historically and currently. The large migration of Asian Americans to the United States began with the Chinese in the late 1800s, who were recruited as cheap laborers to build railroads, for mining, and as launderers and farmers (Takaki 1989). Chinese Americans were initially welcomed, but as migrants, not citizens. They were thus viewed as "non-threatening" to the resources and labor opportunities available to the citizenry. However, with the shortage of job opportunities in the latter half of the ninteenth century, the Chinese Exclusion Act of 1882 was passed, prohibiting the migration of Chinese to the United States (Calavita 2000). Similar subsequent laws were passed to prevent other Asian groups from migrating, such as the Gentlemen's Agreement of 1907 for Japanese immigrants (Calavita 2007) and the Tydings-McDuffie Act of 1934 for Filipinos (San Buenaventura 1996). In excluding Asian immigrants, United States nationalism racialized and defined what it meant to be an American—a person of white and European descent.

Asian Americans have contested the hegemony of Americanness by appealing to claims of their whiteness through litigation. In the case of *Ozawa v. United States* in 1922, for instance, plaintiff Takao Ozawa applied for United States citizenship, citing his whiter skin as his main defense, but was denied because the Japanese were deemed to be an "unassimilable race" (Lee and Bean 2007). In *United States v. Thind* in 1923, Bhagat Singh Thind argued that Indians were part of the Caucasian race due to shared ancestry (Tehranian 2000), but his appeal was denied as well. The court ruling of Roldan v. Los Angeles County and the State of California 1933 determined that interracial Asian-white couples could not obtain a marriage license due to anti-miscegenation laws (Baldoz 2004). The ruling re-categorized and racialized Filipinos as "Malays," deeming them ineligible to marry Caucasians. These cases constructed and reaffirmed racial and national boundaries of Americanness, making it clear that it was not skin color, nor DNA, nor a lack of desire to acculturate that made Asians un-American, but rather national widespread, systemic, legalized racism.

Asian American gay men were no doubt also historically subjugated, and perhaps more so, although literature on their reactions to national oppression is obscured by white- and straight-dominated academia. However, we can presume that, through this evolution of legalized racial forging and reproduction, the United States created an archetype of the homonational American that Asian American gay men strove to embody. The futility of this feat compelled them to embrace, though not without resistance, characteristics and positionalities that were viewed as non-threatening and beneficial to the needs of white citizens. This adaptiveness ensured that Asianness survived despite the implicit pro-white rhetoric of homonationalism in the United States. To understand the racial hierarchy of homonationalism means peering deeper into the dichotomy that informs the behavior of both those who hold power in the gay community—gay white men—and one group who are made subject to it, namely gay Asian American men.

IMPERIALISM, WAR, AND
ASIAN AMERICAN NATIONAL IDENTITY

Imperialism is not a thing of the past, but continues to colonize the psyches of Asian American gay men as they form identities and contend with homonationalism. The tools of imperialism employed by the United States—education, public health, and war—groom Asian American gay men towards assimilation in order to facilitate their contribution to the homonational agenda as laborers and sexual commodities. In promoting the United States as a gay-friendly nation, it might be suggested, Asian American gay men are complicit in their own colonization. They are taught to embrace effeminate and submissive traits so that they may be acknowledged as "good gays," and have a sense of social capital and mobility within the gay community. While superficially this may look like acceptance, it in fact reinforces the white-dominated hierarchy.

United States imperialism designed and imposed tools and institutions on Asia and Asian America under the guise of patriotism. The conquest of the Philippines after the Philippine-American War (1898–1902), for instance, led to the enforcement of Benevolent Assimilation, which mandated American education be administered to its newly designated United States nationals living in the Philippines (Miller 1982). By forcing Filipinos to use the English language, American teachers, and tools like the *Filipino Teacher's Manual,* served to produce "cosmopolitan learners." These educational systems were central to the spread of U.S. imperialism and developed "present-day colonialism, white supremacy, neoliberal globalization, and settler colonialism" (Alidio 2016, 121).

The United States also established Western public health in the Philippines, which was positioned as cultivating "healthy and hygienic manners," though not necessarily designed to improve the health of Filipinos for their own well-being. Rather, the aim was to protect the bodies of useful, productive American subjects (Anderson 2006). On the mainland, similar biopolitical policies and approaches were imposed on Chinese Americans living in San Francisco. Chinese Americans were depicted as filthy, diseased, and a threat to the health of the American public. Thus the Board of Health officials in San Francisco imposed "routine sanitary surveillance, vaccination campaigns, and fumigation of dwellings in Chinatown" (Shah 2001, 37). By participating in these national systems, the Asian national subject was able to validate their patriotism and allegiance to the nation-state.

Asian Americans have been exploited as emblems of United States democracy and empire formations, particularly in times of war. During the Cold War, the United States intervened in Korea and the Southeast Asian nations of Vietnam, Laos, and Cambodia under the façade of eliminating Communist threats in the name of democracy. American soldiers participated in these wars with the belief that they were defending the nation-state, an act of heroism. These countries and their people became tokens of American exceptionalism through the foundation of thousands of transnational Asian adoption agencies, particularly Korean, to facilitate the creation of nuclear white American families (Pate 2014) and the relocation of Asians to the United States as a consolation of American defeat from a Communist regime (Le Espiritu 2014).

THE MODEL MINORITY MYTH

The "Model Minority Myth" is central to the Asian American gay experience of homonationalism, perpetuating the notion that Asianness is a shining beacon which inherently propels them toward universal and unparalleled academic and occupational success, success which reaches a status almost, but not quite equal to, white straight men (Kabayoshi 1999). This rhetoric is highly problematic—it suggests that somehow this success will render Asianness and gayness invisible and completely acceptable to white middle/upper-class America if only these men try "hard enough." Homonationalism benefits greatly from Asian gay men buying into this rhetoric; it projects the illusion to the world that the United States is indeed not only gay-friendly, but diversely, happily gay. But is this the case?

A large body of scholarship has critiqued the racial and political motivations forming the construction of Asian Americans as model minorities, asserting that the myth upholds a false narrative—namely, that anyone, even those subjected to oppression and systemic racism, can attain the American Dream. This rhetoric serves to discount the challenges of Asian gay men, masks serious inequities within this heterogeneous population, and, in doing this, serves to suppress important political, health, and other discussions, which remain focused on white narratives of gayness (Lee 2015). Many studies have pointed to the fact that model minority status ignores the struggles of non-East Asian gays; American gay men and Pakistani gay men, for instance, have vastly different experiences and perceptions in the United States compared to Chinese or Japanese gay men (Lowe 1991).

Qualitative studies on the use of the Model Minority Myth in the gay community have revealed that Asian gay men have a difficult time balancing the rhetoric of this myth (e.g., Asians being "smart," highly mathematical, or obedient) with the racism or microaggressions that accompany the false inclusion of homonationalism. These two seemingly contradictory reactions to Asianness are often perceived as difficult to reconcile, as Terrell L. Strayhorn suggests:

> Contrary to what people think, there's a lot of racism within the gay community, I'd say. I've met gay people through Lambda who ask me to attend their events on campus, to march in their parades, to wear their t-shirts for Pride Day, even help them with their homework because "all Asians are good at math" . . . but they won't even try saying my name right . . . or make racist jokes about my eyes, oh yea, or speak very loud [sic] to me like I can't speak English-which I can . . . I'm not [expletive] deaf, I'm Asian, you know. It's so frustrating. (2014, 591)

U.S. nationalism benefits from the model minority narrative, then, as it leads Asian Americans to believe that they have access to the same opportunities as white Americans, if only they obscure their Asianness. Many Asian American gay men may choose to subscribe to the Model Minority Myth in hopes that they will benefit from the American Dream, a dream perpetually out of reach for ethnic minorities. As Edward Said asserts in his work *Orientalism Reconsidered* (1985), nationalism functions best when the dominant social group can sustain its rule with the "cooperation" of those who are ruled. In believing that they will be legitimized, as pseudo-white U.S. citizens, Asian American gay men who subscribe to the myth maintain the very cycle which oppresses them.

RACIAL TRIANGULATION THEORY

Racial Triangulation Theory elucidates the ways in which white supremacy employs Asian Americans against Blacks as a form of "relative valorization" to subject both racial groups as well as "civically ostracize" Asian Americans through the promulgation of the perpetual foreigner image (Kim 1999). As a result, communities of color may feel compelled to comply with stereotypical racialized tropes to demonstrate citizenship and patriotism in order to navigate and maneuver access to limited resources and capital to survive. These images have manifested in caricatured forms for Asian American men.

Historically, Asian American men were depicted as the "Yellow Peril," hypersexualized and beguiling threats to innocent white women who were personified as vessels of United States democracy and morality (Shek 2007). But as Asian Americans became citizens, mainstream media began portraying Asian American men as rudimentary, effeminate, and nonthreatening figures, which directly contrasted with images of Black men as violent, hypersexualized, and abusive (Collins 2004). Through the preservation of these caricatures, white supremacy controls and dictates the mobility of Asian American men and undermines their capacity to challenge hegemonic racial, gender, and sexual hierarchies.

Kumashiro (1999) describes Asian American gay men as "doubly oppressed," experiencing intersecting oppressions of heteronormative masculinity and gendered racism. That is, Asian American gay men are simultaneously coerced to perform straight masculine behaviors, like dating women and policing their bodies, *and* expected to be feminine, "bottom" sexually, and submissive (Phua 2007). Research suggests that white gay men often hold these views of Asian American gay men, and Asian American gay men who aspire to fit into homonationalist schemas of gay equality may put themselves at risk for contracting sexually transmitted infections (STIs), due to the preferences and demands of white male partners. These preferences might include going bareback or choosing not to use condoms during sexual intercourse (Han 2008). While Asian American gay men fulfill the fantasies of white men to dominate, it is the inverse for Black men. The hypermasculinization of Black men satisfies the lusting of white gay men to be dominated (Han 2007). Thus, racial triangulation permits white gay males to commodify and objectify gay men of color and control the type of imagery they will accomplish based on their fantasies.

Several Asian American gay male porn actors have emerged to challenge the hegemony of dominant top white gay men in the U.S. porn industry, undermining the white homonationalism narrative. For instance, the rise of Brandon Lee in the gay porn industry in the late 1990s as a verbal, "gifted," and masculine top has altered the racialized sexual coding of Asian American gay porn actors (Nguyen 2014). More recently, porn actor Peter Le launched the gay porn series "Peter Fever," featuring Asian American gay male porn actors as tops. While there is still a paucity of Asian American gay porn actors after Brandon Lee's debut and prominence, his presence and recognition in a non-diverse industry nonetheless complicates the imagery and possibilities for the Asian American gay male narrative.

Recent portrayals of Asian American men have evolved to include complex and diversified representations with the help of prominent individuals who subvert emasculation and underrepresentation in the public sphere. Examples of this include sports figures like Jeremy Lin (Park 2015), male television leads with romantic interests, such as Steven Yeun in *The Walking Dead* and Daniel Dae Kim in *Hawaii Five-0* (Ho 2016), and gay Asian American characters like Mateo played by Nico Santos in *Superstore,* Sebastian Chen played by David Lim in *Quantico,* and Oliver Hampton played by Conrad Ricamora in *How to Get Away with Murder.* Despite such changing narratives, which now include gay and heterosexual Asian American men in the media, these renderings are still problematic as they are primarily confined to cisheterosexual male images.

Within the context of homonationalism, racial triangulation theory allows white gay males to position Asian American gay males and Black gay males as inferiors and superiors and insiders and foreigners as dictated by their fantasies. Indeed, gay men of color succumb to these desires to feel visible despite the prospect that it may place them at risk sexually. Although there has been increasing presence of complex Asian American gay characters in mainstream media and gay porn, their characters are generally reproductions of the white gay male fantasies.

RECENTERING RACE IN QUEER POLITICS: SEXUAL RACISM

Within the gay community, white supremacy persists, often according to white gay men the ability to control and dictate sexual positions and practices. Asian American gay men may succumb to these pressures for many reasons: to feel a sense of belonging, to exemplify the "model citizen," to prevent exclusion, or to fit the preferences of white gay men as sexual partners. Sexual choice holds power, both in the acceptance and denial of a sexual partner, which can reinforce individual self-esteem and identity, and historical patterns of race and sex, as well as future choices beyond any one encounter (Ruez 2017). Sexual encounters can certainly produce spaces in which prejudices can be challenged and difference celebrated, but research has shown that these moments can also be rife with racialized exclusion, microaggressions, and overt acts of discrimination—what has commonly been conceptualized as "sexual racism." Sexual racism occurs when racialized sexual preferences devalue an individual and limit their options sexually or intimately (Callander, Holt, and Newman 2012). There remains a need to better understand dating and sex as significant moments of encounter across racialized difference in the context of urban diversity and migrant settlement.

Queer spaces, in particular, can act as hotbeds for a variety of emotional responses, and these are made even more complex by racialized identity and immigration. For instance, literature has suggested that sensations experienced within queer spaces often "produce embodied emotions of attraction, disgust, arousal, identity, (dis)connectivity and belonging" (Taylor and Falconer 2015, 45). Recent literature has also reported on the mixed experiences of stress and sensuousness associated with migrant settlement and bodies, which may directly impact perceptions of Asian American gay men, many of whom are immigrants (Lobe 2014). Migrant bodies hold hurt, anger, intergenerational trauma, and loss, all of which can cause bodily stress. This stress may be perceived as difference and thus racialized, especially in Western environments where white bodies are privileged (Ahmed 2007). However, migrant bodies can also be sensualized, seen as exotic and new. In these ways, Asian American gay men may be projected upon as both "good" and "bad" racial Others, depending on the space and person or group projecting.

Research on specific accounts of sexual racism for Asian American gay men has noted that some men encounter racist language on hook-up apps (e.g., Grindr), as well as micro- and macro-aggressions on dates, when approaching individuals in a bar, and when seeking a partner in a sex-on-premises venue. Moreover, men have frequently described these events as important to their sense of self, their location, and their subjective feeling of belonging. Specifically, they describe these experiences as obstacles to their desired sexual outcome, an affront to their "self-image," and as a barrier to inclusion within queer spaces (Ruez 2017). Many Asian American men report feeling "targeted," and comment that they rarely feel targeted outside of these types of queer spaces, making the experience especially appalling for them. One Asian gay man provides the following account of sexual racism in online dating:

Gay people always talk about being careful or sensitive for people but they give more racism to me than any other people do. You'd think that they would be better since people discriminate against them too, but I would say gays can be very racist to Asian men. Whenever I read on a [dating] ad online saying "no Asians," it's usually a White guy. Or if I meet somebody and say, "Hey, I'm Korean," then he will say, "Oh . . . so I know you're very smart." It sounds like a nice thing, but it's not really and it makes me very mad. (Strayhorn 2014, 590)

ASIAN AMERICAN RESISTANCE

Gay Asian Americans often choose to become active agents in challenging, resisting, and subverting homonationalism. Those who resist include artists, scholars, and often "ordinary" individuals using everyday lived experiences to contest and dismantle hegemonic ideals and institutions that continue to oppress and marginalize particular factions of society. Homonationalism has been a medium of fictitious acceptance and survival for the gay community in the United States. Puar (2007) demonstrates how life post–9/11 shifted the stigma from (nominally white) gay men to Arabs, Sikhs, and Muslims. In many respects, white gay men embraced this libertarian logic by participating in homonationalist acts. That is, they displayed outward patriotism (e.g., blatant display of the American flag in gay bars) while perpetuating the rhetoric that the United States is a more gay friendly and feminist country compared to Middle Eastern countries who subjugate their women and queer people (Puar 2007). This sudden form of "progressive" acceptance serves to bolster the nation-state, as well as solidify the loyalty and allegiance of a formerly ostracized group. Yet as can be seen from the arguments presented above, claims to the United States being "gay friendly" are arguably limited to *white* gay men.

Instances of Asian American resistance to homonationalism can be seen in the Filipino American queer community. Martin Manalansan IV (2003) proposes that the Filipino *bakla* culture—roughly translated as "homosexuality, hermaphroditism, cross-dressing, and effimanancy" (ix) in the Filipino community—does not necessarily assimilate into mainstream U.S. society, but instead creates its own sense of belonging. The bakla culture defies white notions of gayness by crafting its own queerness by actively negotiating identity through a hybrid of Filipino tradition and newfound culture. In doing this, it thwarts colonial impositions of white ownership over gay culture in the United States. In another instance, the Mail Order Brides (M.O.B.) collective, comprised of three Filipina American artists from San Francisco, created a video installation entitled *Always a Bridesmaid, Never a Bride,* critiquing the institution of same-sex marriage as a homonationalist endeavor with its continual disregard of the "affective labor provided by Filipino/as performing forms of feminized labor (whether female-assigned or not)" (Velasco 2013, 351).

It is important to note, however, that resistance to homonationalism can also reify and maintain other forms of oppression. Morgensen (2010) warns of the perils of non-Native queers who engage in challenging homonationalism in ensuring that they are not consuming the powers of the settler and re-enforcing settler colonialism through such arguments of having the inherent rights of belonging in Native land because of their identities. Instead, non-Native queers can commit to forging a "national community that exceed[s] the heteropatriarchal nation-state form" (123), learning the histories of indigenous nations, and acknowledging and working alongside Native Americans in dismantling the proliferation of the empire.

Simply put, disobedience, through the production of competing identities, spaces, and artistic and scholarly material, engenders critical examination and the re-imagination of the roles of Asian American gay men within the nation-state. These actions can undo daily experiences of intra/inter-personal and institutional discrimination. However, one must resist with social consciousness and with acknowledgement of the systems of power to which they are contributing, such as settler colonialism.

CONCLUSION

Homonationalism has become increasingly salient during the era of the Trump presidency. This is an era which reinforces social pressures to conform, prove, and affirm a gay person's allegiance to the nation-state. This chapter calls attention to the need to examine an Asian person's place within the homonationalist hierarchy, rather than blanketly accepting the notion that the United States is "friendly," and equally so, to all who identify as part of the gay community. We argue that, by making such a claim, racial disparities are marginalized, as well as those disparities experienced by gay-identified men who also identify as transgender or gender non-conforming.

Undoubtedly, Asian American queers may choose to identify with homonationalism as it aligns with ingrained racial narratives in the United States, such as the Model Minority Myth and racial triangulation theory, which suggest that Asians, through a strong work ethic and superior academic abilities, may somehow rise to meet a pseudo-white level of success to the detriment of others, like Black and Latinx Americans. While these narratives have persisted for several decades, they mask the very real inequality that Asian queers face in the gay community. There are those, however, who choose to challenge homonationalism, through art, scholarly pursuits, and simply *living* in a way which resists prescribed and "acceptable" notions of gayness by forging new paths which are explicitly non-white, and often non-cisgender and anti-colonialism. These stories may not be observed in mainstream media, but are nevertheless important to uncover. Recentering Asianness forces us to acknowledge the complexities of gay identity, yes, but importantly, it also forces us to acknowledge the oppressive forces which have shaped and continue to affect diverse gay communities today. Recentering Asian voices requires us to expose the white-dominated narrative of gayness in the United States. For these reasons, it is imperative that research seek to highlight the voices of Asian American gay male Muslims, Sikhs, Arabs, and others who are being targeted by the current administration as threats to the nation-state. Deviating from the portrayal of the U.S. as "gay friendly" compared to Asian nations, as well as the conscious effort of Asian Americans to recognize the lived experiences of Asian American Muslims, South Asians, and other Asians hailing from West Asia, will be crucial in opposing the maintenance of homonationalism as a hierarchical construct.

REFERENCES

Adachi, Jeff. 2006. *The Slanted Screen*. San Francisco: AAMM Productions.
Ahmed, Sara. 2005. *The Cultural Politics of Emotion*. London: Routledge.
Alidio, Kimberly. 2016. "A Wondrous World of Small Places: Childhood Education, US Colonial Biopolitics, and the Global Filipino." In *Filipino Studies: Palimpsests of Nation and Diaspora*, edited by Martin F. Manalansan IV and Augusto F. Espiritu, 106–27. New York: New York University Press.
Anderson, Warwick. 2006. *Colonial Pathologies: American Tropical Medicine, Race, and Hygiene in the Philippines*. Durham: Duke University Press.
Baldoz, Rick. 2004. "Valorizing Racial Boundaries: Hegemony and Conflict in the Racialization of Filipino Migrant Labour in the United States." *Ethnic and Racial Studies* 27(6): 969–86.
Balsam, Kimberly F., Yamile Molina, Blair Beadnell, Jane Simoni, and Karina Walters. 2011. "Measuring Multiple Minority Stress: The LGBT People of Color Microaggressions Scale." *Cultural Diversity and Ethnic Minority Psychology* 17(2): 163–74.
Bell, David. 1995. "Pleasure and Danger: The Paradoxical Spaces of Sexual Citizenship." *Political Geography* 14(2): 139–53.
Calavita, Kitty. 2000. "The Paradoxes of Race, Class, Identity, and 'Passing': Enforcing the Chinese Exclusion Acts, 1882–1910." *Law & Social Inquiry* 25(1): 1–40.
———. 2007. "Immigration Law, Race, and Identity." *Annual Review of Law and Social Science* 3: 1–20.
Callander, Denton, Martin Holt, and Christy E. Newman. 2012. "Just a Preference: Racialised Language in the Sex-Seeking Profiles of Gay and Bisexual Men." *Culture, Health and Sexuality* 14(9): 1049–63.
Chan, Connie S. 1995. "Issues of Sexual Identity in an Ethnic Minority: The Case of Chinese American Lesbians, Gay Men, and Bisexual People." In *Lesbian, Gay, and Bisexual Identities Across the Lifespan: Psychological Perspectives*, edited by Anthony R. D'Augelli and Charlotte J. Patterson, 87–101. New York: Oxford University Press.
Chua, Peter, and Dune C. Fujino. 1999. "Negotiating New Asian-American Masculinities: Attitudes and Gender Expectations." *The Journal of Men's Studies* 7(3): 391–413.
Collins, Patricia H. 2004. *Black Sexual Politics: African Americans, Gender, and the New Racism*. New York: Routledge.

Gupta, Aparna, Dawn M. Szymanski, and Frederick T.L. Leong. 2011. "The 'Model Minority Myth': Internalized Racialism of Positive Stereotypes as Correlates of Psychological Distress, and Attitudes Toward Help-Seeking." *Asian American Journal of Psychology* 2(2):101–14.

Han, Chong-Suk. 2007. "They Don't Want to Cruise Your Type: Gay Men of Color and the Racial Politics of Exclusion." *Social Identities* 13(1): 51–67.

———. "A Qualitative Exploration of the Relationship between Racism and Unsafe Sex Among Asian Pacific Islander Gay Men." *Archives of Sexual Behavior* 37(5): 827–37.

Ho, Helen K. 2016. "The Model Minority in the Zombie Apocalypse: Asian-American Manhood on AMC's The Walking Dead." *The Journal of Popular Culture* 49(1): 57–76.

Kim, Claire J. 1999. "The Racial Triangulation of Asian Americans." *Politics and Society* 27(1): 105–38.

Kobayashi, Futoshi. 1999. *Model Minority Stereotype Reconsidered*. Washington, DC: ERIC Clearinghouse.

Kumashiro, Kevin K. 1999. "Supplementing Normalcy and Otherness: Queer Asian American Men Reflect on Stereotypes, Identity, and Oppression." *International Journal of Qualitative Studies in Education* 12(5): 491–508.

Le Espiritu, Yen. 2014. *Body Counts: The Vietnam War and Militarized Refugees*. Oakland: University of California Press.

Lee, Jennifer, and Frank D. Bean. 2007. "Reinventing the Color Line: Immigration and America's New Racial/Ethnic Divide." *Social Forces* 86(2): 561–86.

Lee, Stacey J. 2005. *Unraveling the "Model Minority" Stereotype: Listening to Asian American Youth*. New York: Teachers College Press.

Lobo, Michele. 2014. "Everyday Multiculturalism: Catching the Bus in Darwin, Australia." *Social and Cultural Geography* 15(7): 714–729.

Lowe, L. 1991. "Heterogeneity, Hybridity, Multiplicity: Marking Asian American Differences." *Diaspora: A Journal of Transnational Studies* 1(1), 24–44.

Maira, Sunaina M. 2009. *Missing: Youth, Citizenship, and Empire After 9/11*. Durham: Duke University Press.

Manalansan IV, Martin F. 2003. *Global Divas: Filipino Gay Men in the Diaspora*. Durham: Duke University Press.

Miller, Stuart C. 1982. *Benevolent Assimilation: The American Conquest of the Philippines, 1899–1903*. New Haven: Yale University Press.

Morgensen, Scott L. 2010. "Settler Homonationalism: Theorizing Settler Colonialism within Queer Modernities." *GLQ: A Journal of Lesbian and Gay Studies* 16(1–2): 105–31.

Nakanishi, Don T. 1993. "Surviving Democracy's 'Mistake': Japanese Americans and the Enduring Legacy of Executive Order 9066." *Amerasia Journal* 19(1): 7–35.

Nguyen, Tan H. 2014. *A View from the Bottom: Asian American Masculinity and Sexual Representation*. Durham: Duke University Press.

Park, Michael K. 2015. "Race, Hegemonic Masculinity, and the 'Linpossible!' An Analysis of Media Representations of Jeremy Lin." *Communication and Sport* 3(4): 367–89.

Pate, SooJin. 2014. *From Orphan to Adoptee: US Empire and Genealogies of Korean Adoption*. Minneapolis: University of Minnesota Press.

Phua, Voon C. 2007. "Contesting and Maintaining Hegemonic Masculinities: Gay Asian American Men in Mate Selection." *Sex Roles* 57(11): 909–18.

Puar, Jasbir K. 2007. *Terrorist Assemblages: Homonationalism in Queer Times*. Durham: Duke University Press.

———. 2013. "Homonationalism As Assemblage: Viral Travels, Affective Sexualities." *Jindal Global Law Review* 4(2): 23–43.

Ruez, Derek. 2017. "'I Never Felt Targeted as an Asian . . . Until I Went to a Gay Pub': Sexual Racism and the Aesthetic Geographies of the Bad Encounter." *Environment and Planning* 49(4): 893–910.

Sabsay, Leticia. 2012. "The Emergence of the Other Sexual Citizen: Orientalism and the Modernisation of Sexuality." *Citizenship Studies* 16(5–6): 605–23.

Said, Edward W. 1985. "Orientalism Reconsidered." *Race & Class* 27(2): 1–15.

San Buenaventura, Steffi. 1996. "Hawaii's '1946 Sakada.'" *Social Process in Hawaii* 37: 74–90.

Shah, Nayan. 2001. *Contagious Divides: Epidemics and Race in San Francisco's Chinatown* (Vol. 7). Oakland: University of California Press.

Shek, Yen L. 2007. "Asian American Masculinity: A Review of the Literature." *The Journal of Men's Studies* 14(3): 379–91.

Strayhorn, Terrell L. 2014. "Beyond the Model Minority Myth: Interrogating the Lived Experiences of Korean American Gay Men." *Journal of College Student Development* 55(6): 586–94.

Szymanski, Dawn M., and Mi R. Sung. 2010. "Minority Stress and Psychological Distress Among Asian American Sexual Minority Persons." *The Counseling Psychologist* 38(6): 848–72.

Takaki, Ronald. 1989. *Strangers from a Different Shore: A History of Asian Americans.* New York: Penguin Books.

Tehranian, John. 2000. "Performing Whiteness: Naturalization Litigation and the Construction of Racial Identity in America." *The Yale Law Journal* 109(4): 817–48.

Velasco, Gina. 2013. "Performing the Filipina 'Mail-Order Bride': Queer Neoliberalism, Affective Labor, and Homonationalism." *Women and Performance: A Journal of Feminist Theory* 23(3): 350–72.

Conclusion

Gaps, Questions, and Resistance

Damien W. Riggs

As the chapters in this book so clearly demonstrate, there are a diversity of racisms enacted within the context of gay men's communities. Arguably, this plurality of racisms is united under the broader context of nationalisms, colonization, and the hegemony of white Western understandings of homosexuality, just as the plurality of racisms identified in this book are united by a reliance upon stereotypes and binaries of privilege and disadvantage, as is true for racism more broadly. Yet the initial typology of racisms explored in this book would also seem to suggest that racism within gay men's communities takes specific forms, perhaps most notably with regard to the psychic life that it displays, one centered upon the visual, and one that seeks to deny diversity in favor of an understanding of sexuality that centers the values of white middle-class men.

In this final chapter of the book we turn to consider what has been left outside the frame of the book, namely groups of gay men whose experiences of racism require further attention; questions of the ontological status of gender and sexuality and their relationship to racism; the role of new media forms in perpetuating old forms of racism in new guises; and the need to acknowledge and support forms of resistance against racism in gay men's communities. It is these topics that this final chapter now explores, each in turn.

GAPS AND ABSENCES

As with any edited collection, there are topics that are not addressed. Despite concerted attempts at including an even more diverse range of topics, it is notable that in terms of religion and racism, only Islamophobia is addressed in the book (see chapter by Abraham). Missing are discussions of, for example, racism in gay men's communities that speak to the experiences of Jewish or Hindu men. Given long and ongoing histories of anti-Semitism and anti-Hinduism within the Western world, we should not be surprised to find that such histories play out in specific ways within the context of gay men's communities. Most notable with regard to anti-Semitism is the growing body of research on white gay men involved in neo-Nazi collectives (e.g., Borgeson and Valeri 2015), and white gay men who engage in Nazi fetishes (e.g., Beusch 2008). Understanding how such groups of white men enact forms of racism within gay communities requires ongoing consideration.

Another gap in this book is a focus on what might alternately be termed queer settler nationalism or queer colonialism. Such a focus, as has been explored in other edited collections (e.g., Driskill, Finley, Gilley, and Morgensen 2014; Hodge 2015), requires a focus on how First Nations people experience racism within gay communities, and how non-indigenous gay men potentially enact forms of racism against First Nations men in ways that are specific to histories of colonization. Gay Indigenous men, for example, have spoken publically about the racist stereotypes often employed by non-indigenous gay men on dating apps such as Grindr, stereotypes specific to colonizing understandings of Indigenous people (e.g., Dustin Mangatjay McGregor in Verass 2016). More work is still to be done, however, to further understand how specific forms of racism that exist in contexts of colonization play out in gay men's communities.

While a number of chapters in this book include transgender gay men in their remit (e.g., see chapter by Rivera and Maglalang), none of the chapters provide a substantive focus on experiences of racism amongst transgender men. Given previous research indicating the intersections of racism and cisgenderism in the lives of transgender people of color (e.g., Singh 2013), it is important that researchers continue to explore how this plays out specifically in the lives of gay transgender men of color and gay First Nations men, and as enacted by white gay cisgender men. Missing from this list, however, are white gay transgender men, who are no more outside of racism than are any other group of gay men. Exploring their engagements with racism within gay communities (alongside potential experiences of cisgenderism) is thus another important avenue for future research.

Finally, and perhaps most notably of all, what are missing from this book are the voices of white gay men who enact racism towards other gay men. It is perhaps unsurprising that researchers have struggled to identify such men willing to speak about their actions, given taboos surrounding racist talk, but also because racism within gay men's communities is so often framed as "just a preference," and hence is often not seen as racism (Callander, Holt, and Newman 2012). One example of a white gay man speaking about "sexual racism" appeared in an Australian first-person media piece, in which the author (Matheson 2012) proudly claimed, "I'm a sexual racist . . . although I am not a racist." The author uses a false analogy to justify his stance: he isn't attracted to women and that doesn't make him a misogynist, so not being attracted to men who are not white does not make him racist. The author has since retracted his article and apologized for the sentiment expressed, though this may perhaps say more about prohibitions on talking about racism than necessarily indicating a shift from viewing racialized desire as "just a preference" to viewing it as a form of racism. Whether this is true of the author and other men like him remains a topic requiring empirical investigation.

THE QUESTION OF ONTOLOGY

In considering the question of the psychic life of racism in gay men's communities, the chapters in this book, each in their own way, consider questions of ontology. Specifically, the chapters in this book take up a point made by Thomas (2007) in his Pan-African account of gender and sexuality, namely that "there are never, ever merely girls and boys, men and women, without race and class. Analytically speaking, there are instead a legion of genders and sexualities, so to speak; and they cannot be reduced to the anatomy of any one white elite" (68). A similar point is made by Smith (2014) in the context of First Nations genders and sexualities:

> The central anxiety with which the western subject struggles is that it is, in fact, not self-determining. The western subject differentiates itself from conditions of "affectability" by separating from affectable others–this separation being fundamentally a racial one. The western subject is universal; the racialized subject is particular but aspires to be universal. (44)

Both Thomas and Smith, and many others writing against the hegemony of whiteness in terms of gender and sexuality, draw our attention to the fact that white ontologies do not capture diverse ways of understanding gender and sexuality, even if, as Smith notes, the white Western subject claims a place within the universal. In other words, there is a vast difference between claiming to occupy a universal subject position, and the fact that such a subject position is a fantasy premised upon the disavowal of "affectable others." As the chapters in this book have so deftly demonstrated, the white subject too is an affectable other, and indeed it is precisely this capacity to be affected that this book has argued shapes the forms of racism that circulate within gay men's communities. To consider oneself marginalized on the basis of sexuality—and hence as an affected other—propels some white gay men to reclaim a place within the universal by constructing other gay men as the more properly affected other.

Drawing on writings about Indigenous ontologies (e.g., Moreton-Robinson 2003), then, we can suggest that despite the positioning of racism as all-encompassing (in terms of encompassing all there is to know about people who are positioned as racial others), white Western ontologies repeatedly fail to capture their object. Diverse ontologies precede and exceed white Western ontologies, positing radically different understandings of bodies, identities, and relationships to the world around us, including understandings of what in the English-speaking world we refer to as genders and sexualities. As the editors of the collection *Queer Indigenous Studies* suggest (Driskill, Finley, Gilley, and Morgensen 2014), First Nations accounts of gender and sexuality don't simply "add on" additional genders to the binary gender model as understood within the West. Rather, First Nations accounts offer radically different ways of understanding bodies and identities. In their own ways too, the chapters in this book, albeit written about diverse groups of gay men living in the West, posit alternate ways of understanding gender and sexuality, claiming sites of resistance that refuse the terms currently on offer within typically white-dominated gay communities.

NEW TECHNOLOGIES, OLD RACISMS?

As mentioned in chapters in this book by Daroya, and by Rivera and Maglalang, a key site where racism plays out in gay men's communities is in dating apps designed for smartphones, or on dating websites. As Callander, Newman, and Holt note, examining

> the prominence of online sex and dating practices is significant because the way we behave online may be different from other social contexts. The perception that the online domain is anonymous, aphysical, and depersonalized may lead some to demonstrate . . . [an] online disinhibition effect. Such disinhibition may promote freer sharing of attitudes or perceptions with respect to race and partner-seeking. The nature of online interactions, which are predominantly text-based and archival, also makes it easier than in offline settings to identify and examine the mechanisms of racial interactions. While people rarely proclaim in a public space that they are, for example, not attracted to Asian men, they may be more comfortable about doing so via online sex and dating profiles. (Callander, Newman, and Holt 2015, 1992)

In addition to these points, there may be other ways in which dating apps and websites facilitate expressions of racism. Given the way in which profiles are exhibited on dating apps (in grids, with images of faces and/or bodies), there is a sense in which dating apps facilitate the viewing of profiles as "there for the choosing," which brings with it the possibility that certain profiles will not be chosen. This type of logic, echoing the argument made in the introduction to this book (i.e., that gay liberation is centrally understood as relating to sexual freedom), establishes intimate partner profiling as a logical and justifiable behavior. Yet we may conjecture that in a way the racialized I/eye of the white gay dating app user engages in surveillance and screening practices that are akin to racial profiling: such practices distill the lives of individual men to a series of stereotyped assumptions based primarily on skin color. As such, it could be argued, the grids that organize dating apps are predisposed to mark certain bodies as undesirable *in the context of other bodies on the grid.*

In addition to the racial profiling that may occur on dating apps and websites, there is also the potential for white gay users to enact forms of racism in their own profiles. As Daroya and Rivera and Maglalang note in their chapters in this book, racial epithets are used to discourage certain groups of men from even making contact with the white users who include such epithets on their own profiles. Racial epithets, however, are not "just a preference" as many such men argue. Rather, they distill broader racist logics into a series of what Butler (1997) has termed "excitable speech." Importantly, Butler's focus on speech was on speech made under duress, so we must ask what duress are white gay users of dating apps and websites under when they utilize racial epithets? It could be argued, as has been done throughout this book, that the duress is of the fantasy of whiteness as hegemonic: that there are no gaps in the power of whiteness to regulate those positioned as racial others. Given that there are always gaps and resistances, as we see in the following section and in the previous section with regard to ontology, white gay men's use of racial epithets go far beyond simply "stating a preference." Indeed, if anything, the preference they state is a desire to deny that whiteness is a fantasy, by making a claim to whiteness as universal through the localizing and marginalizing of certain profiles, hence leaving the white user as racially unmarked yet universally white. Certainly, racial epithets as they appear on the profiles of white users have affects: they marginalize their targets. But they also render visible the affective nature of whiteness: its fears and insecurities, and the constant repetition it requires to maintains its tenuous claim to hegemony (Ahmed 2004; Hook 2005).

POINTS OF RESISTANCE

Continuing on with the points above with regard to whiteness and gay men's communities, it is important to ask why it is that such communities—which have at certain points engaged in critical conversations about race, class, and sexuality—now so readily on the whole appear to embrace a neoliberal account of gay sexuality, one that strives for what Duggan (2012) has termed "homonormativity." Writing about the history of gay movements in the United States, Morgensen (2011) suggests that at least some early gay organizations centrally focused on the intersections of race and sexuality, specifically with regard to interventions related to HIV transmission. Increasingly, however, such an intersectional approach was seen as antithetical to achieving the agendas of (primarily white) gay men, who instead advocated for an approach to political organizing that emphasized heterogeneity within gay communities. Certainly, critical examinations of race within gay men's communities do continue to occur amongst some white gay men, and perhaps justifiably these occur in conversation with gay men who are not white.

The question remains, though, of what it would look like for white gay men to organize politically around race alongside sexuality. What would it look like, for example, if instead of marriage equality or the right to serve in the armed forces being key points of focus, attention was paid to the over-incarceration of Black and Indigenous men, or the differential rates of HIV transmission amongst Black and Indigenous men as compared to white gay men? Certainly, some white gay men have engaged in such a shift of focus (e.g., Barnard 2003), but such accounts by and large constitute a minority position. This type of shift in focus in order to identify possible points of resistance would require white gay men to more widely engage with the dominance of neoliberalism and whiteness in much of gay political organizing, and to consider the needs of a much more diverse population of gay men.

Shifting the focus away from white gay men, in reading for this chapter I was struck, particularly with regard to two key anthologies of queer Black writing (Johnson 2016; Johnson and Henderson 2005), by the relative lack of attention to racism within gay communities (though see McBride 2005). Yet in reflecting on this further, I wondered whether a refusal to speak yet again about such racism constitutes a form of resistance in and of itself. In other words, the writing and theorizing of Black gay men offers much more than simply an account of racism in gay communities; it offers radical resistance by thinking through Black gay subjectivities in a range of contexts and as situated in a range of histories. Necessarily different to the points of resistance available to white gay men—which as suggested above require an explicit orientation *towards* racism—it is entirely possible that the resistances mounted by Black gay men may entail a turning *away from* racism. This is not to suggest that Black gay men do not face racism in their everyday lives and respond to and resist it. Rather, it is to suggest that Black gay men may combat racism within gay communities via a myriad of strategies, some of which may include disengagement (a point made in the chapter in this collection by Giwa).

Turning to consider Asian gay men's experiences of racism, projects such as Sexual Racism Sux have similarly aimed not simply to focus on racism within gay men's communities, but have also aimed to challenge racism by shifting public representations of gay men away from white gay men, and towards the diverse experiences of Asian gay men (Mansfield and Quan n.d.). Gay Muslim organizations in the UK too have sought to shift beyond a sole focus on Islamophobia, and to also promote positive representations of queer people and Islam within the media (Haritaworn, Tauqir, and Erdem 2008).

Another key point of resistance, as outlined previously in this chapter, arises from First Nations people, and the fundamental fact of their sovereign ontological relationship to their country. Certainly, colonization has made a significant impact upon how First Nations genders and sexualities are experienced and lived. But this does not mean that long-standing understandings of bodies and identities rooted in tradition and culture do not continue, and do not offer key sites of resistance to the imposition of colonizing understandings of First Nations peoples' genders and sexualities (Morgensen 2011). The very fact of First Nations peoples' sovereignty functions as a point of resistance to whiteness in gay men's communities, and such resistance is furthered by the claiming and reclaiming of First Nation understandings of what it means to be gay, understandings that resist Western anthropological accounts.

CONCLUSION

In conclusion, it is important for us to reflect on what has been gained by the initial typology of racisms within gay men's communities as mapped out in this book. To engage in such reflection, we might ask why the differentiation of racisms is so important, especially given their connections to racism more broadly, and as seemingly unified under a particular psychic life. What the chapters in this book each demonstrate is that beneath these seeming connections and unities, sit very specific differences: different stereotypes are employed, different histories shape these stereotypes, and each form of racism has different implications, both in the ways they privilege white gay men and in how they marginalize diverse groups of gay men.

Certainly, each form of racism documented in this book serves to prop up a white hegemony. Yet at the same time, such props are differentially enacted, whether that involves fetishizing certain groups or men, or depicting other groups of men as inherently undesirable. Further, the props are differentially enacted dependent on whether they offer a certain form of normalizing inclusion to some groups of men, while depicting other groups of men as forever excluded under the guise of, for example, the "war on terror." Acknowledging and exploring these differences is thus important, as to treat racism as a homogenous entity within gay communities would only serve to repeat neoliberal claims to homogeneity within gay communities more broadly. Certainly, acknowledging racism at all is a step beyond such a homogenizing account of gay men's communities, but challenging and resisting racism within such communities then requires an unpacking of the diverse ways in which racism plays out.

As a contribution, then, the typologies addressed in this book add to the many key points of resistance to racism that already exist within gay men's communities. As noted above, additional cartographies are required to further diversify the accounts provided in this book. By offering an account of the psychic life of racism in gay men's communities, the chapters in this book call attention to how racialization and racism are formative of gay lives in the Western world, and that rather than seeing both as marginal issues, it is important that gay community organizing pays close attention to the types of psychic lives currently rendered intelligible, as well as opening up possibilities for alternate ways of thinking about intimacy and relatedness amongst gay men.

REFERENCES

Ahmed, Sara. 2004. *The Cultural Politics of Emotion*. New York: Routledge.
Barnard, Ian. 2003. *Queer Race: Cultural Interventions in the Racial Politics of Queer Theory*. New York: Peter Lang.
Beusch, Danny. 2008. "'It's Not a Political Thing for Me–Just Sexual': Gay Men and Nazi Fetishism." In *Bound and Unbound: Interdisciplinary Approaches to Genders and Sexualities*, edited by Zowie Davy, Julia Downes, and Lena Eckert, 164–80. Newcastle: Cambridge Scholars Publishing.
Borgeson, Kevin, and Robin Valeri. 2015."Gay Skinheads: Negotiating a Gay Identity in a Culture of Traditional Masculinity." *The Journal of Men's Studies* 23 (1): 44–62.
Butler, Judith. 1997. *Excitable Speech: A Politics of the Performative*. New York: Routledge.
Callander, Denton, Martin Holt, and Christy E. Newman. 2012. "Just a Preference: Racialised Language in the Sex-Seeking Profiles of Gay and Bisexual Men." *Culture, Health and Sexuality* 14 (9): 1049–63.
Callander, Denton, Christy E. Newman, and Martin Holt. 2015. "Is Sexual Racism Really Racism?: Distinguishing Attitudes Toward Sexual Racism and Generic Racism Among Gay and Bisexual Men." *Archives of Sexual Behavior* 44 (7): 1991–2000.
Driskill, Qwo-Li, Chris Finley, Brian Joseph Gilley and Scott Lauria Morgensen. 2014. *Queer Indigenous Studies: Critical Interventions in Theory, Politics, and Literature*. Tucson: The University of Arizona Press.
Duggan, Lisa. 2012. *The Twilight of Equality?: Neoliberalism, Cultural Politics, and the Attack on Democracy*. Boston: Beacon Press.
Hodge, Dino, ed. 2015. *Colouring the Rainbow: Blak Queer and Trans Perspectives*. Adelaide: Wakefield Press.
Haritaworn, Jin, Tamsila Tauqir, and Esra Erdem. 2008. "Gay Imperialism: Gender and Sexuality Discourse in the 'War on Terror.'" In *Out of Place: Interrogating Silences in Queerness/Raciality*, edited by Adi Kuntsman and Esperanza Miyake, 71–95. York: Raw Nerve Books.
Hook, Derek. 2005. "Affecting Whiteness: Racism as Technology of Affect." *International Journal of Critical Psychology* 16: 74–99.
Johnson, E. Patrick, ed. 2016. *No Tea, No Shade: New Writings in Black Queer Studies*. Durham: Duke University Press.
Johnson, E. Patrick, and Mae. G. Henderson, eds. 2005. *Black Queer Studies: A Critical Anthology*. Durham: Duke University Press.
Mansfield, Tim, and Andy Quan. n.d. *Sexual Racism Sux*. Accessed July 31, 2017. https://sexualracismsux.com.
Matheson, Jesse. 2012. "I'm a Sexual Racist." *Star Observer*. Accessed July 31, 2017. https://web.archive.org/web/20150220031624/http://www.starobserver.com.au/opinion/soapbox-opinion/im-a-sexual-racist/91678.
McBride, Dwight A. 2005. *Why I Hate Abercrombie & Fitch: Essays on Race and Sexuality*. New York: New York University Press.

Moreton-Robinson, Aileen. 2003. "I Still Call Australia Home: Indigenous Belonging and Place in a White Postcolonizing Society." In *Uprootings/Regroundings: Questions of Home and Migration*, edited by Sara Ahmed, Claudia Castada, Anne-Marie Fortier, and Mimi Sheller, 23–40. New York: Bloomsbury Publishing.

Morgensen, Scott Lauria. 2011. *Spaces Between Us*. Minneapolis: University of Minnesota Press.

Singh, Anneliese A. 2013. "Transgender Youth of Color and Resilience: Negotiating Oppression and Finding Support." *Sex Roles* 68 (11–12): 690–702.

Smith, Andrea. 2014. "Queer Theory and Native Studies: The Heteronormativity of Colonialism." In *Queer Indigenous Studies: Critical Interventions in Theory, Politics, and Literature*, edited by Qwo-Li Driskill, Chris Finley, Brian Joseph Gilley, and Scott Lauria Morgensen, 43–65. Tucson: The University of Arizona Press.

Thomas, Greg. 2007. *The Sexual Demon of Colonial Power: Pan-African Embodiment and Erotic Schemes of Empire*. Bloomington: Indiana University Press.

Verass, Sophie. 2016. "Racism on Grindr: Indigenous Gay Man Screenshots Racial Abuse Online." Accessed July 31, 2017. http://www.sbs.com.au/nitv/sexuality/article/2016/04/14/man-shares-experiences-of-racism-on-grinder.

Index

About the Contributors

Ibrahim Abraham is a postdoctoral research fellow in the discipline of Social and Cultural Anthropology at the University of Helsinki, Finland. A graduate of Monash University and the University of Bristol, he has published on various aspects of the relationship between contemporary religion and sex, finance, and rock 'n' roll.

Denton Callander is a research scientist studying sex, sexualities, and sexual health. His work focuses on sex workers, gay and bisexual men, people who use drugs, and technology.

Jacks Cheng is a PhD Student and Associate Instructor in the Department of Counseling and Educational Psychology, Indiana University Bloomington.

Emerich Daroya is a PhD Candidate at the Australian Research Centre in Sex, Health & Society, La Trobe University. His current research focuses on barebacking among gay men. His scholarly interests also include issues on racialized desires. He has completed his MA in Sociology from Carleton University.

Sonny Dhoot is a PhD Candidate at the University of Toronto's Women and Gender Studies Institute. His research engages *queer of color critique* to explore how queers of color's partner preferences and erotic desires are inflected by class and racial logics.

Sulaimon Giwa is an Assistant Professor in the Faculty of Social Work at Memorial University of Newfoundland. His applied research program and professional activities centralize critical race transformative pedagogies and theories as frameworks and analytic tools for social justice and equity. His research interests are in the areas of race and sexuality; critical social work pedagogy; antiracism/oppression; and the criminal justice system.

Martin Holt is an Associate Professor at the Centre for Social Research in Health, UNSW Sydney, Australia. He conducts HIV prevention research, primarily with gay and bisexual men, drawing on contemporary social science research to improve public health outcomes.

Dale Dagar Maglalang, MA, is a graduate student in the MSW/PhD program at Boston College School of Social Work. His research interests include social determinants of health and racial health justice. Dale earned his BS and BA at the University of California, Davis, and MA at San Francisco State University.

Christy Newman is an Associate Professor of health, sexuality, and relationships. At the Centre for Social Research in Health, UNSW Sydney, she investigates social aspects of sexual health, infectious disease, and chronic illness across diverse contexts and communities, particularly through critical, sociological, and qualitative methodologies.

Damien W. Riggs is an Associate Professor in social work at Flinders University and an Australian Research Council Future Fellow. He is the author of over 200 publications in the fields of gender and sexuality studies, family studies, and critical race and whiteness studies, including (with Clemence Due) *A Critical Approach to Surrogacy: Reproductive Desires and Demands* (Routledge, 2017).

Alexandra Marie Rivera, PsyD, is a Psychologist at the Native American Health Center and Research Consultant with the Asian American Women's Health Initiative Project. She specializes on the intersections of multiculturalism, trauma, and community health and has written numerous articles and book chapters on Asian American and LGBTQ mental health. Dr. Rivera received her doctorate in Clinical Psychology at the PGSP-Stanford PsyD Consortium.

Jesus Gregorio Smith received his PhD from Texas A&M University in 2017. His expertise centers on the intersections of race, gender, and sexuality online and how they impact condom use for gay men. He currently serves as an Assistant Professor at Lawrence University in Appleton, Wisconsin, within the program for Ethnic Studies.